"In *Victimology of a Wrongful Conviction: Innocent Inmates and I*
son, Kathryn M. Campbell and Margaret Pate powerfully po
who are wrongly convicted as 'victims' of a criminal legal syst
The authors take their analysis one-step further, and extend
the other victims of wrongful convictions - the families of t
ginal survivors of actual crimes, and society at large. Grounded in qualitative research and in
victim theories, this book is a welcome and compelling addition to the wrongful conviction
literature."

**Jessica S. Henry**, *author of* Smoke but No Fire: Convicting the
Innocent of Crimes that Never Happened.

"The subject matter of the *Victimology of a Wrongful Conviction: Innocent Inmates and Indirect
Victims* – is an important contribution to the study of wrongful convictions. Professors Jackson, Campbell, and Pate have undertaken a tremendous task – to situate the experiences of
the wrongly convicted as victims, and their families as secondary victims of a state crime –
and they have succeeded. They have also forced readers to confront the realities that exonerees and their families experience – enduring great emotional, psychological and financial
hardships, similar to other crime victims. This comprehensive, academic analysis of the victimology of a wrongful conviction, is a must-read for innocence scholars and victimologists."

**Mark Godsey**, *author of* Blind Injustice: A Former Prosecutor Exposes the
Psychology and Politics of Wrongful Convictions.

# THE VICTIMOLOGY OF A WRONGFUL CONVICTION

This book exposes the myriad of victims of wrongful conviction by going beyond the innocent person who has been wrongfully incarcerated to include the numerous indirect victims who suffer collaterally. In no way overlooking the egregious effects on the wrongfully convicted, this book widens the net to also examine consequences for family, friends, co-workers, witnesses, the initial victims of the crime, and society in general – all indirect victims who are often forgotten in treatments of wrongful conviction.

Through interviews of exonerees and indirect victims, the authors capture the tangible and intangible costs of victimization across the board. The prison experience is examined through the lens of an innocent person, and the psychological impact of incarceration for the exoneree is explored. Special attention is given to the often-ignored experience of female exonerees and to the impact of race as a compounding factor in a vast number of miscarriages of justice. The book concludes with an overview of the victimization experiences that follow exonerees upon release.

Unique to this book is its interdisciplinary approach to the troubling subject of wrongful conviction, combining perspectives from a number of fields, including criminal justice, criminology, victimology, psychology, sociology, social justice, history, political science, and law. Undergraduate and graduate students in these disciplines will find this book helpful in their respective areas of study, and professionals in the legal system will benefit from appreciation of the far-reaching costs of wrongful convictions.

**Nicky Ali Jackson** is Professor and Coordinator of Criminal Justice in the Department of Behavioral Sciences at Purdue University Northwest (PNW). Dr. Jackson is the Executive Director of the Center for Justice and Post-Exoneration Assistance at PNW. She also serves as President of the Willie T. Donald Exoneration Advisory Coalition. Dr. Jackson is a 2021 recipient of the prestigious Sagamore of the Wabash Award, the highest civilian honor, bestowed by Indiana Governor Eric Holcomb for her humanity and service to the citizens of Indiana.

**Kathryn M. Campbell** is a Professor in the Department of Criminology at the University of Ottawa, Canada, and has published extensively in the area of miscarriages of justice. Dr. Campbell is the faculty director of Innocence Ottawa, a pro bono, student-run innocence project aimed at helping the wrongly convicted who are seeking exoneration apply for conviction review to the Minister of Justice.

**Margaret Pate** is an Associate Professor in the Department of Criminal Justice at Radford University. Dr. Pate is also the Associate Director in the Office of Undergraduate Research & Scholarship at Radford.

# THE VICTIMOLOGY OF A WRONGFUL CONVICTION

## Innocent Inmates and Indirect Victims

*Nicky Ali Jackson, Kathryn M. Campbell and Margaret Pate*

Routledge
Taylor & Francis Group

NEW YORK AND LONDON

Cover image: Pitiphothivichit

First published 2023
by Routledge
605 Third Avenue, New York, NY 10158

and by Routledge
4 Park Square, Milton Park, Abingdon, Oxon OX14 4RN

*Routledge is an imprint of the Taylor & Francis Group, an informa business*

*Library of Congress Cataloging-in-Publication Data*
A catalog record for this title has been requested

ISBN: 978-0-367-63904-4 (hbk)
ISBN: 978-0-367-63719-4 (pbk)
ISBN: 978-1-003-12125-1 (ebk)

DOI: 10.4324/9781003121251

Typeset in Bembo
by Taylor & Francis Books

# CONTENTS

| | |
|---|---|
| *List of illustrations* | ix |
| *Foreword* | x |
| Lenore E. Walker | |
| *Preface* | xii |
| Jeffrey Mark Deskovic | |
| *Acknowledgements* | xvi |

**PART 1**
**Victimology: The Wrongly Convicted as Victims**    **1**

1 Introduction: Definitions, Methodology, and Demographics    3
  *Nicky Ali Jackson*

2 Victimology: Theoretical Perspectives and their Applications to the
  Wrongly Convicted    11
  *Nicky Ali Jackson*

3 The Nature and Extent of Wrongful Convictions    23
  *Kathryn M. Campbell*

4 Victimizing the Innocent: Racism, Wrongful Convictions, and
  Exonerations of Black Men in the Criminal Legal System    35
  *Angela Hattery and Earl Smith*

**PART 2**
**The Many Victims of a Wrongful Conviction**    **55**

5 The Exoneree as Victim    57
  *Nicky Ali Jackson*

 6  Female Victims of a Wrongful Conviction: Continual Marginalization          71
    *Kathryn M. Campbell*

 7  Families as Victims of a Wrongful Conviction                                87
    *Margaret Pate*

 8  Revictimization of the Original Victim                                      103
    *Margaret Pate*

 9  Society as a Victim of a Wrongful Conviction                                115
    *Kathryn M. Campbell*

10  Post-Release Victimization: "Freedom Is Never Free"                         124
    *Nicky Ali Jackson*

11  Final Thoughts and Future Considerations                                    138
    *Kathryn M. Campbell and Nicky Ali Jackson*


*Appendix*                                                                      *143*
*References and Further Reading*                                                *145*
*Index*                                                                         *162*

# ILLUSTRATIONS

## Figures

| | | |
|---|---|---|
| 1.1 | Gender of Exonerees | 7 |
| 1.2 | Race of Exonerees | 7 |
| 1.3 | Age at False Arrest | 7 |
| 1.4 | Time Spent Falsely Imprisoned | 8 |
| 1.5 | Charges for Wrongful Convictions | 8 |
| 1.6 | Familial Relationship to Exoneree | 8 |
| 4.1 | Median Net Worth by Household Income and Race. Courtesy Hamilton Project (2020), Brookings Institution. | 46 |
| 4.2 | Exonerations by Race and Crime. Courtesy of the Innocence Project (2021). | 48 |
| 4.3 | Exonerations in Relation to Crimes Committed | 49 |
| 6.1 | Female Exonerees' Charged Crimes | 75 |
| 6.2 | Female Exonerees' Sentence Lengths | 76 |
| 6.3 | Female Exonerees' Time Served | 76 |
| 10.1 | Male Exonerees' Employment Status | 126 |
| 10.2 | Female Exonerees' Employment Status | 126 |

## Tables

| | | |
|---|---|---|
| 5.1 | Physical and Psychological Consequences Shared by Wrongly Convicted and Prisoners of War | 69 |
| 5.2 | Physical and Psychological Consequences Shared Among the Wrongly Convicted and Battered Women | 70 |

# FOREWORD

*Lenore E. Walker*

The idea that people once branded as criminals can be rebranded as victims is new and, some may think, radical. In this book, *The Victimology of a Wrongful Conviction: Innocent Inmates and Indirect Victims*, authors Jackson, Campbell, and Pate provide the convincing arguments. You might ask, "Why is this important?" The answer is simple. The only way those wrongfully convicted can possibly heal from such outrageous injustice is to follow the information we have learned about helping other victims heal from other forms of victimization. This means labeling them as victims, accepting that they have experienced unwanted trauma from the criminal justice system as well as from society or other individuals, and then offering some reparations to them and their wrongly victimized families. Providing trauma-specific treatment is only one of many ways to try to make right these unspeakable injustices.

Jackson and her colleagues have organized this book in a clear step-by-step way to prove to even skeptics that wrongfully convicted people and their families have been victimized by what has been done to them. They begin by defining what is a wrongful conviction. Not only is it being accused of a crime the individual didn't commit, even if they gave a false confession, but it is also being convicted for a crime that did not exist. We now have almost irrefutable scientific evidence such as DNA that proves this (or the real perpetrator confesses), and we also know that it happens more often than we as a society want to believe.

The authors then go on to give an excellent summary of the victimology research where we first learn about personal and institutional victimization and then posit how the experiences of wrongfully convicted and their families fit into the victimology literature. A following chapter gives examples of different types of contributing factors to wrongful convictions and some challenges in substantiation. A visit to any prison in the United States today will make obvious the racist nature of who serves time for crimes: Black men and women. Experts in the victimization of people of color contribute a chapter focusing on the racist abuses in the criminal justice system that lead to wrongful convictions. They shine a light on the problem's seriousness and emphasize the need to reform the entire criminal justice system beginning with police interrogations that put the mentally ill or deficient at risk of a false confession, to overzealous prosecutors, unprepared defense attorneys, inadequate or absent psychological experts, and overworked or lazy judges.

A number of chapters that follow specify the role that criminal justice system actors may play in contributing to the victimization of the wrongly convicted; in particular, the role of police, prosecutors, and judges is underscored as in their zeal to close cases, errors can occur. Reviewing the specific exoneree cases gives a poignant viewpoint into how victimization occurred, with some actors unintentionally and some deliberately framing suspects. While most people who have been exonerated are men, the wrongful convictions of women make it clear that they, too, may be victimized multiple times because of gender, race, and the type of alleged crime. Some women victims have been abused by their intimate partners and their children are harmed, and sometimes killed, by these partners. Nonetheless, the women may be charged with the same or even more serious crime than the actual perpetrator. In some cases they receive longer sentences than the person who committed the actual harm to the child. Some may falsely confess, naively believing that the police will save them from their abusive partner. Thus, they become victims of the system as well as their batterers.

A unique part of this book is the authors' ability to convince us that not only are those who are wrongfully convicted victims themselves but so too are their families. Think about the children who go through life without being raised by their loving fathers or mothers. Or the added burden families endure in supporting (or not) their loved ones who maintain their innocence. Think of the many trips to lawyers and visits to prison that families undertake when they could have been spending their money and time on other life-affirming things.

Be prepared to have your sympathetic emotions evoked throughout this book. Nowhere will your heart break more than when reading the last two chapters documenting the challenges that continue to be faced by those released on post-conviction exoneration. We know that victims can heal with trauma-specific treatment – this has been determined by decades of research and study. Perhaps now that those falsely convicted are designated as victims, they will be eligible for such treatment both while incarcerated and upon release. This is just the beginning; society must find a way to make reparations for what has been done to them. However, the stark reality is that they can never be given back the time they have lost to live their lives in their own way.

Fortunately, the authors close by giving us hope in their recommendations to reduce the victimization of innocent persons by the criminal justice system. While they acknowledge that some important research contributions have been made in this regard in recent decades, what they also advocate for is an acknowledgment of the wrongly convicted as victims and the concomitant assistance it would require. We all need to take part in demanding such reforms, starting right now. It could be you or your loved ones next if we do nothing.

Lenore E. Walker, EdD
Professor Emerita
Nova Southeastern University
College of Psychology
Fort Lauderdale, Florida
12–10-2021

# PREFACE

*Jeffrey Mark Deskovic*

I spent 16 years in prison, from age 17 to 32, for a murder and rape I did not commit. I was 16 when I was arrested and turned 17 just before the trial started. Despite a pretrial negative DNA test result that demonstrated that semen found on the victim did not match mine, I was convicted. My wrongful conviction was based on many of the factors discussed in chapter 3 of this book: I was a victim of tunnel vision on the part of detectives who coerced a false confession from me and lied about it in court. The prosecution rushed to indict me one day before officially receiving the negative DNA test results, and then at the trial he invented an explanation for why the DNA test results didn't match me – painting the victim as promiscuous – without providing a shred of evidence. The medical examiner, who fabricated findings to help the prosecutor advance the "promiscuous victim" explanation of the DNA, had received complaints from authorities in neighboring counties for untruthful testimony, yet none of these written complaints were turned over by the prosecutor to my lawyer. My own lawyer had a conflict of interest in my case and incompetently defended me by failing to: call my alibi witness, cross-examine the medical examiner, and utilize the DNA in arguing that the confession was coerced and false. In my fight for exoneration, I lost seven appeals and was later turned down for parole based on the nature of the crime and in part because I chose not to express remorse for a crime I did not commit. Ultimately, I was exonerated by further DNA testing, via the DNA Databank, which identified the actual perpetrator, who subsequently confessed. His DNA was in the databank because, left free while I was serving time for his crime, he killed a second victim just 3½ years after killing the victim in my case.

My mission in life is to fight wrongful conviction while also pursuing broader criminal justice reform. Upon exoneration, I earned a master's degree and then became an attorney. I have become a strong advocate for the wrongly convicted and for legislative reform to prevent future miscarriages of justice. Using some of the compensation that I received, I established the Jeffrey Deskovic Foundation for Justice, which has thus far freed 13 wrongfully convicted people and helped pass three laws aimed at preventing wrongful convictions. As an advisory board member of the It Could Happen to You coalition, of which the Foundation is part, I regularly meet with elected officials in three states – New York, Pennsylvania, and California – building support for criminal justice reform.

Thus, my views about wrongful conviction and about this book, which examines wrongful conviction from a victimology perspective, are shaped not only by my own unique, personal experiences as a victim of the criminal justice system but by my expertise in this field.

I believe this book is a valuable and unique addition to the considerable body of work on wrongful conviction; that in and of itself is an accomplishment. As I read about the topics covered, I reflected on my own case, my reintegration back into the community, and other books and scholarly literature I previously read. This book, however, has a number of distinctive features. For one, the overall premise of the book – that the wrongly convicted are victims – is unique; there is no other literature that discusses wrongful convictions from that perspective. The authors make a convincing case for that premise. We are like other victims of crime – we have suffered many losses as a result of our wrongful conviction, and more victims were created – our families and society suffered, too. Another important aspect is that the majority of the book is based on interviews with the wrongly convicted themselves. Most criminological and legal writing about the wrongly convicted does not bother to get our opinion about things – most of what is written *about* us is certainly not *from* our perspective. When I was reading these chapters, I saw many experiences that mirrored my own. An additional unique feature of this book is the inclusion of women; the authors interviewed eight female exonerees and included a chapter specifically addressing the wrongful conviction of women. This is particularly important as female exonerees are often ignored in the scholarly literature for various reasons, due in part to their smaller numbers, and due to the fact that most innocence organizations in the field only take on cases that involve DNA, which is usually found in cases of murder and rape – crimes typically perpetrated by men.

As I read the many chapters in this book that convey how the wrongfully convicted are also victims themselves, it brought back painful memories for me. The exonerees interviewed shared many of the difficulties they experienced upon release, nearly all of which I experienced, too. When I was released, I had never lived on my own, gone shopping, had a driver's license, written a check, or balanced a budget. I was released with nothing, and given that it took 5 years before I was compensated, my difficulties were amplified. I was always passed over for gainful employment because would-be employers wanted someone with experience who could hit the ground running. Because of that, I lacked stable housing. It was only through the kindness of strangers that I survived; otherwise, I would have been homeless. By not receiving government assistance on reintegrating back into society, I was revictimized.

In my view, the state should have assisted me – as well as all other exonerees – with housing, cost of living money, mental health services, medical and dental care, access to public transportation, classes on technology, and job training and placement. I had been convicted at 17, and when I was released 16 years later, I had no job experience. Technology had passed me by: while I was wrongfully imprisoned, cell phones, the Internet, and GPS were created. The culture was different, and cities looked different. It left me feeling like I was in a parallel world where I did not belong.

The private sector did not provide much assistance to me, either. I was locked out of many jobs due to my lack of experience and the stigma associated with my conviction. That stigma frustrated me in my personal life as well. I had been *wrongfully* imprisoned for 16 years, *yes*, but I had also been *imprisoned* for 16 years. How much of that rubbed off on me? Was it safe to "be alone" somewhere with me? That stigma hurt me when it came to rebuilding my life and personal relationships. Lastly, on the friendship level, few people extended themselves to me in fellowship; the skills I used in prison to connect with others did not translate to the free world.

As the authors discuss in chapter 5, I suffered as all exonerees do from psychological after-effects but was not provided with any mental health services by the government. I had post-traumatic stress disorder (PTSD), panic attacks, anxiety, a feeling of processing things at a slower speed, fear on seeing law enforcement, and a feeling like I had been frozen in time. I was released at 32, but felt like I was 17 years old, as that was how old I was when I was last free. I was one of the lucky ones, as I found a series of mental health professionals to help me. I went to counseling four times a week for 6 years. One treated me out of mercy, while another was willing to work on a lien against my compensation efforts – if I was not successful at being compensated, he would receive nothing. The reality is that few are willing to work on that basis, nor should they have to; the government should provide exonerees with mental health services as well as the other services mentioned above.

As covered in chapters 7, 8, and 9, a wrongful conviction creates other victims. Essentially, the general public was victimized by what happened to me as well. The "real" killer of the victim in my case was Steven Cunningham. Free in the community while I was serving time for his crime, Cunningham killed the sister of his girlfriend, a schoolteacher named Patricia Morrison, who had two children. Had the police and prosecutor done their jobs properly, I would not have been falsely accused and wrongfully convicted, Steven would have been convicted, and Patricia would still be alive. Over the years, I met with several members of her family, and the authorities never explained anything to them, nor did they offer them any services. They were left in the dark. The family of Angela Correa, the victim in the case I was wrongly convicted for, was also victimized. I met Angela's mother outside of the courtroom when Cunningham was sentenced for her murder. I later spent a couple of weekends at their house. I learned that while Angela's sister thought that there was something funny with the case and I was probably innocent, her mother thought that I was guilty. She spent 16 years believing that I was guilty and hating me.

My family was victimized by my wrongful conviction, too. During the trial, my mother and aunt Janet, who accompanied me to court, felt the strain of the uncertain outcome. My case was a high-profile one, with virtually all the media coverage biased toward a guilt-oriented perspective – my name and my family's name were dragged through the mud. Even the management company of the apartment complex where my family lived attempted to evict them, based on the publicity. Once I was wrongfully convicted, it only made things worse. I was ripped from my family and we were robbed of the time that we could have spent with each other. My mother often said that the most difficult part of my being wrongfully imprisoned was that at the end of visits, she could not bring me home with her. She was also fearful that something would happen to me in prison. My wrongful imprisonment cost her financially – visiting me was an expensive 4½-hour trip for her; she would purchase food items for me to eat from the vending machines in the visiting room; she would leave money for commissary; and she spent money buying food packages for me. My grandmother passed away while I was wrongfully imprisoned and thus she missed me not being part of her waning years. My brother was affected by my wrongful imprisonment as well: the kids at school used to tell him that his brother was a rapist and try to hit him and stab him with pencils. That affected him greatly and he eventually dropped out of school, never to return. Additionally, he later turned to drugs and alcohol to deal with the pain. He eventually cleaned himself up, but the mannerisms and language he learned while addicted carry through to this day. Thus, my wrongful conviction continues to impact him. My former friends and classmates were victimized as well by me being taken from them.

It makes no sense – the wrongly convicted are all victims of the system's errors, but very few of us get any acknowledgement or compensation. While I was able to pursue and ultimately obtain financial compensation from New York State while also successfully bringing a 1983 civil rights lawsuit against all of the entities that the wrongdoers in my case worked for, it took me 5 years until I got anything and a total of 10 years before the entire case was finished. I wanted an apology from the City of Peekskill when I settled my lawsuit against them, but they refused. Similarly, none of the people originally involved in my wrongful conviction ever apologized. I was fortunate in that I did receive a "symbolic" apology from the district attorney in office when I was exonerated, as well as from the prosecutor in the courtroom at that time and the judge on the bench who had presided over those proceedings. But they were not their counterparts who had originally been involved in my wrongful conviction. Most exonerees do not even receive formal apologies from the police, prosecutors, or judges in the original case.

As discussed in chapter 9, society was victimized by my wrongful conviction as well – mainly in financial ways. In the lawsuits I had to file for compensation for my ordeal, the municipalities and counties involved had to spend a lot of money in legal fees for representation. On top of that, because I was successful, the defendants collectively paid out more than $21,800,000 in compensation to me – of which my attorneys received one-third, while I also had to pay the litigation expenses. While I was entitled to what I received for the 16 years of hell I spent in prison as a victim, all of that money could have been saved had the wrongful conviction not happened in the first place.

This book reflects the true experiences of 24 wrongfully convicted men and women. I know they are speaking the truth about their victimization because I experienced the same things. I was lucky in some ways, but those experiences will always remain and affect the person I am. I hope that others can read this book and have a better idea of what it is like to be a victim of a wrongful conviction and the multifaceted impact it can have: on your family, your health, and your future. At the end of the day, even in the best system with all of the reforms and best practices passed into law and followed by police and prosecutors in good faith, the system is still run by people, and people make mistakes. Too often, though, these mistakes are avoidable, good faith is not applied, and best practices are not implemented. I hope that this book can be a catalyst for enhancing a greater understanding about how wrongful convictions happen, the best practices for avoiding them, and the long-term effects they can have on the victims they create. May it also ultimately help in avoiding similar errors in the future, while enhancing efforts to assist exonerees once exonerated.

# ACKNOWLEDGEMENTS

## Nicky Ali Jackson

I want to thank my husband, Ralph, and children, Rhys and Bryn, for their understanding and patience as I spent countless hours sitting at my desk working on this project. They sacrificed a lot for me to work on this project. Thank you for believing in me. I love you all so much! I must also recognize my parents and my siblings for their love and support of my work. I am one lucky daughter and sister! I would also like to thank Kathryn Campbell for her welcome guidance, expertise, and hard work on this book. Thank you for editing our manuscript. That was a major undertaking. Most important, thank you for your friendship and guidance. We are cut from the same cloth! I must also thank Maggie Pate for her help with all things computer related. I learned so many computer skills that I did not know existed! I conducted all of the interviews for this book, and I want to extend my deepest appreciation to all of the exonerees who took the time to speak with me. As promised, your voices are echoed throughout the pages of this book. Thank you for trusting me to share your words. And, to all those who have suffered or continue to suffer a wrongful conviction, I want you to know that I am sorry for the injustices committed against you and your loved ones. I can never give you back the years stolen from you, but I can make sure that you are never forgotten. Lastly, I want to thank my dear friend, Mr. Timmy Donald, for his friendship. I gave you my word that I would fight for you and all those wrongly convicted. I hope I make you proud.

## Kathryn M. Campbell

The opportunity to be involved in this project, outside of my own country of Canada, came as a welcome and interesting chance to explore how wrongful convictions occur and are experienced in the United States. Sadly, I saw many parallels between the havoc that a wrongful conviction can wreak on a person and their families in both the United States and Canada; however, the specter of the death penalty in the United States adds a further level of dread, fear, and anxiety. I want to thank Nicky Ali Jackson for asking me to work with her on this project, convincing me that the wrongly convicted are in fact victims and suffer in the same way as other victims of crime, and for her patience with my procrastination! I also want to thank Maggie Pate for her support in the writing of this volume and expertise in all things numerical and statistical. Finally, I am incredibly grateful to all of the wrongly convicted exonerees for their kindness in sharing their experiences with us in such a forthright and honest manner. I hope we got it right.

## Margaret Pate

This book is the culmination of much effort and hard work, and it would not have been possible without my co-authors. I would like to acknowledge Nicky Ali Jackson for the invitation to come along on this journey and for her countless hours interviewing exonerees and their families and writing many of the chapters contained within these pages. She kept us on track! I would also like to thank Kathryn Campbell for her expertise in qualitative analysis and writing and editing – our words are much more polished because of you! I would also like to thank my family for their unending support, especially by husband, Josh Pate – thank you for your support and understanding during the late nights and weekends. And to the exonerees and their families who truly made this work possible, thank you for your vulnerability and for sharing your story – your voice matters – and I hope this piece can contribute in some small way to minimize the number of victims created by the system in the future.

# PART 1

# Victimology: The Wrongly Convicted as Victims

# 1

# INTRODUCTION

## Definitions, Methodology, and Demographics

*Nicky Ali Jackson*

> "I always believed in the justice system."
>
> *Willie T. Donald*

## Timeline of a Wrongful Conviction

In 1989, Gary, Indiana, police officers took Willie T. Donald, a 20-year-old African American man, to the station suspecting he was riding in a stolen vehicle. His picture and fingerprints were taken while at the police station. Later, the owner of the car arrived and explained that he had loaned the vehicle to his nephew and Mr. Donald was a passenger. The two young men were then released.

In 1990, Mr. Donald received two traffic violations for failing to yield and failing to carry car registration. He did not appear in court to answer to these traffic violations.

On February 22, 1992, five robberies and one murder occurred in the Glen Park neighborhood of Gary, Indiana. The assailant committed all of the crimes within a one-hour window. During the fourth robbery, the assailant shot and killed Bernard Jimenez. Minutes after Mr. Jimenez was shot, the final robbery of the evening was perpetrated against a retired female Gary, Indiana, police officer and her daughter. All of the victims, including the retired police officer, described the robber as an African American male with a scarred face and slight build. Aside from being African American, none of this fit Mr. Donald's appearance.

Within days of the crime, one of the robbery victims, Rhonda Williams, called the Gary Police Department and reported that the man who robbed her was in front of her home. Willie T. Donald, who had failed to appear in court two years earlier and lived near where the robberies took place, became a suspect in the robberies and murder. It remains unclear as to why Mr. Donald was targeted as a suspect. Gary detectives then went to Mr. Donald's workplace and learned that he was at work when Williams called the police.

On March 2, 1992, multiple Gary police vehicles arrived at the home of Mr. Donald to issue a bench warrant for failure to appear in court to answer to the traffic violations from two years prior. On March 3, 1992, Gary police officers put together a photo lineup including a picture of Willie T. Donald, who was then in custody on his failure to appear charge. Robbery victim Rhonda Williams and another robbery victim, Kimberly Belinsky, whose fiancé was the murder victim, were placed in the same room at the same time to view

DOI: 10.4324/9781003121251-2

the photo lineup. Belinsky pointed to Mr. Donald's photo but said that she was not sure. Rhonda Williams picked Mr. Donald's photo out of the lineup. After Williams pointed to Donald's photo, Belinsky then confirmed Mr. Donald as the assailant. Later that day, a physical lineup was conducted. Both Belinsky and Williams identified Mr. Donald as the perpetrator. The other four robbery victims viewed the lineup as well and none identified Mr. Donald. Mr. Donald, already in custody, was then charged with robbery and homicide.

On March 4, 1992, Gary police conducted a search of Mr. Donald's home. The victims in the case consistently described a specific type of hat and jacket worn by the assailant, which were not produced during the search. In fact, no physical evidence linking Mr. Donald to the robberies and homicide was ever found.

Mr. Donald told officers that he was car shopping with his sister and her then fiancé at the time of the robberies. Car salesmen confirmed that they had seen Mr. Donald but could not confirm the time. Camera footage had been deleted by the time officers visited the various dealerships.

In June 1992, Mr. Donald was tried and convicted of two counts of robbery and one count of homicide. He was sentenced to 60 years in prison. Approximately a year after the trial, the defense learned of the witness William's call to the police saying that the robber was in front of her house prior to Donald's arrest. When she contacted the police at that time, the defense learned that the police had pursued this lead and had spoken to Mr. Donald's employer, who verified that he was with her in the break room at the time of William's call. His time card also noted that he was at work when Rhonda Williams called the police. Clearly, the man Rhonda Williams had identified as being the robber who was in front of her house was not Mr. Donald. This evidence became the basis for a post-conviction motion to vacate his conviction. The claim was that the prosecutor withheld information that would have been helpful to the defense, constituting a *Brady* [1] violation. It is unclear whether the prosecutor was given this information prior to trial. Nonetheless, Mr. Donald's post-conviction release and subsequent appeals at that time were denied.

After exhausting all of his appeals, in 2007 the Medill Innocence Project at Northwestern University Medill School of Journalism accepted Mr. Donald's case. They learned that while Rhonda Williams had identified Donald in the 1992 lineup, she later recanted her testimony, stating, "The detective convinced me I had the right guy," to members of the Innocence Project.

With this new and other evidence, and after spending over 23 years in prison, on January 25, 2016, a judge vacated the convictions against Mr. Donald and granted him a new trial. Two days later, the Lake County Prosecutor's office dismissed all charges against Mr. Donald and he was released.

This nightmare did not end upon his release. Mr. Donald continues to suffer from his wrongful conviction. Given that he entered prison at the age of 22 and exited at the age of 46, the world did not wait for him. Sadly, Mr. Donald's ordeal is emblematic of all exonerees. His case illustrates how an innocent person can fall victim to a wrongful conviction.

## What Is a Wrongful Conviction?

For the purposes of this text, a *wrongful conviction* is defined as occurring when the wrong person was convicted for a crime they did not commit. When a crime does occur, in these cases, a wrongful conviction results when a person is found guilty of a crime for which they are factually innocent. Another type of wrongful conviction can also occur when a person is convicted for a crime that never happened; that is, "no-crime" wrongful convictions. These types are in contrast to wrongful *acquittals*, where a person may be found procedurally innocent but in fact may have committed the crime. Thus, the wrongful convictions discussed in this text will include both "wrong-person" cases in which the individual was found guilty of a crime committed by someone else, as well as "no-crime" cases in which the individual was found guilty of a crime later determined to have never been a crime at all (Henry, 2020; Norris et al., 2018). Approximately one-third of all known exonerations stem from cases in which a crime was never actually committed, including cases involving allegations of abuse, shaken baby syndrome, arson, and death (National Registry of Exonerations [NRE], 2020b). Hence, the focus in this text will not be on wrongful convictions that occur through procedural errors but on cases of true, factual innocence.

Many believe that a wrongful conviction is an anomaly in the American criminal justice system, given the many existing procedural safeguards and due process rights that serve to protect defendants, and require guilty convictions to be proved beyond a reasonable doubt. Unfortunately, wrongful convictions occur more frequently than reported and point to larger systemic issues in the criminal justice system and reveal the immense pressure that criminal justice system actors are sometimes under to secure a conviction particularly in heinous crimes. At this writing, the NRE (2021) has identified over 2,900 known exonerations since 1989; however, it is difficult to quantify the precise number of exonerees as the numbers increase monthly. The NRE (n.d.) defines an *exoneration* as occurring when the government officially clears an individual who has been convicted of a crime based upon newly discovered or newly reviewed evidence that indicates the individual is innocent of the crime. Consequently, the term *exoneree*, for the purposes of this book, refers to an individual who has been wrongfully convicted for a crime and later exonerated.

The numbers of years lost through a wrongful conviction are staggering; according to the NRE, exonerees have served a total of over 24,000 years of time lost to convictions and prison sentences they never should have received in the first place (NRE, 2020a). Additionally, since 1973 over 170 individuals have been exonerated who received the death penalty (Death Penalty Information Center, 2020). Worse still is that these numbers only represent the "tip of the iceberg" or, rather, the actual *known* cases of wrongful conviction and exoneration (Naughton, 2007). It is impossible to ascertain the actual number of wrongful convictions as many cases are undiscovered and the wrongful conviction is only revealed upon an exoneration. While statistics are helpful to understand the scope of the problem of wrongful convictions, they do not adequately describe the overall experience and the concomitant losses of being wrongfully convicted. The wrongly convicted, whether exonerated or not, are victims of a system that is prone to error, despite the evidentiary and substantive safeguards built into the system, including rights such as the right to silence, right to counsel, and the requirement that guilt must be proven beyond a reasonable doubt for a conviction to stand. The purpose of this book is to provide a voice to those who have been victimized by the system through a wrongful conviction. In the same way that scholars study victimology by exploring the effects of crime victimization on individuals in order to understand how to best help them in the recovery process, this book is an attempt to understand the experiences of the wrongly convicted, who are also victims. Ultimately, they are victims of a criminal justice system that has taken away a fundamental freedom – liberty – as a result of systemic error.

## Methodology of This Study

In order to explore the experiences of the wrongfully convicted, it was important to hear their perspectives, as well as those of their families. For the purposes of this study, 24 exonerees were interviewed who had been wrongfully arrested, convicted, and incarcerated, all while innocent of the crime for which they were convicted. In order to establish trust between exonerees and the interviewers, exonerees who had previous contact with members of the research team were interviewed. No one was cold-called for an interview to ensure that everyone was ready and willing to discuss their experiences candidly. Snowball sampling allowed some other interviewees to be involved in the study.

Exoneree participants ranged in age from 19 to 41 years old at the time of their arrest and included 16 male exonerees and 8 female exonerees, 13 of whom identified as Caucasian, 8 as African American, and 3 as Hispanic. A majority of the participants were considered young adults, under 30 years old, at the time of their false arrest (79%). Exonerees were asked to identify their family's socioeconomic status at the time that they were falsely arrested on a scale of 1 to 10, with 1 being those who are well off financially and with a secure job and 10 being those who are the least well off financially and without a job/education. Most individuals ($n = 9$, 43%) selected a socioeconomic level in the middle of the scale (score of 5). Approximately 38% ($n = 8$) of the exonerees selected a socioeconomic level that was "worse off" than the middle (scores 6–10), and 19% ($n = 4$) identified their socioeconomic level as "better off" than the middle (scores 1–4). The length of time in prison for the exonerees varied considerably, as they served from between 4½ to 33 years of wrongful imprisonment.

In addition, 13 family members connected to the exoneree were interviewed. In order to maintain their confidentiality, the exonerees gave contact information to their family and friends, and these individuals contacted the research team. The family members interviewed included children, parents, nieces or nephews, siblings, and significant others (spouses, fiancés, or others in long-term relationships) to the exonerees.

Telephone interviews were used in the conduct of this study given that they are an ideal means to reach a diverse population that was geographically dispersed and to limit contact with others due to COVID-19 restrictions; the interviews took place in August 2020. This method of interviewing also allows participants to be more relaxed, speak freely, and disclose intimate information if they so choose (Novick, 2008). Interviews were semistructured, recorded with the interviewee's permission, and lasted approximately one hour. In order to better understand the exonerees' experiences, questions were asked about their experiences and the challenges they faced in prison, how they coped or "fit in" with other inmates, and how their wrongful incarceration had affected them upon release, including challenges faced since their release and support they have (or have not) received. For the interviews with exonerees' family members, questions were asked about the impact the exoneree's incarceration had on their life, their perspectives on the exoneree's innocence, whether they discussed the exoneree's incarceration and subsequent release with anyone, how the relationship with the exoneree may have changed post-release, their perceptions of what had been helpful for them or the exoneree post-release, and the greatest challenges they faced during the wrongful conviction, incarceration, or release.

All interviews were audio recorded, transcribed, and shared with all authors. The research team analyzed the interview transcripts using conceptual content analysis in order to seek themes in words or texts. Each researcher examined the transcriptions, drew inferences, and categorized interview data into themes; words and phrases frequently used by participants were coded. Through coding, researchers were able to make inferences regarding the exonerees' and their family members' experiences. Figures 1.1 to 1.6 provide data on gender, race, age of false arrest, time spent falsely imprisoned, charges for wrongful convictions, and familial relationship to the exoneree. Drawing on the data collected from the interviews, further analyses will be addressed in the forthcoming chapters.

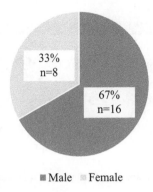

**FIGURE 1.1** Gender of Exonerees

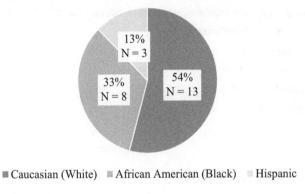

**FIGURE 1.2** Race of Exonerees

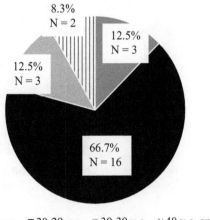

**FIGURE 1.3** Age at False Arrest

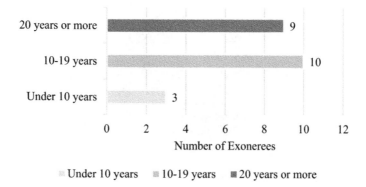

**FIGURE 1.4** Time Spent Falsely Imprisoned

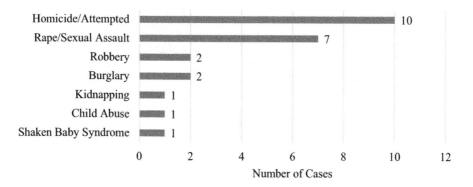

**FIGURE 1.5** Charges for Wrongful Convictions

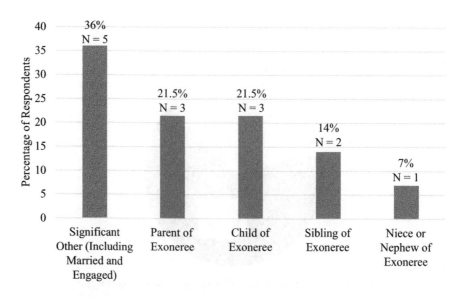

**FIGURE 1.6** Familial Relationship to Exoneree

## Book Structure

The book is organized into two sections. The first section provides a framework for understanding and situating the data received from the exonerees and their loved ones. In Chapter 2, the concept of victimology will be introduced as well as the theoretical perspectives that frame this study of the victimization of the wrongly convicted. This study of the experiences of exonerees is situated within the conceptual framework of victimology, in order to understand the short- and long-term impacts of a wrongful conviction, false imprisonment, exoneration, and reintegration back into the community. This chapter provides a historical overview of the field of victimology and the Victims' Rights Movement. Victimology discussions include both personal victimization (i.e., crimes committed or attempted against the individual) as well as the victimization that comes through institutional responses to victims. The chapter will conclude by extending the discussion of victimization to those who have been wrongfully convicted, situating these individuals' experiences within the victimology literature.

In Chapter 3, the nature and extent of wrongful conviction is discussed, including an overview of the major causes of wrongful conviction: eyewitness misidentification, false confessions, incentivized witnesses, official misconduct, and problematic forensic sciences and expert testimony. In addition, the incidence of wrongful convictions is raised, as well as the challenges encountered in establishing accurate numbers. This chapter provides a context for understanding the occurrence of wrongful convictions in the United States.

Chapter 4, written by guest authors Professor Earl Smith and Professor Angela Hattery, expands the concept of innocence and victimization beyond the experiences of the wrongly convicted and their families interviewed for this book and examines several racist and disturbing police practices that ensnare Black Americans, and especially Black men, into the criminal/legal system. By focusing on five forms of policing – (a) stop and frisk, (b) fishing expeditions, (c) killing of unarmed Black people, (d) pretrial detention, and (e) innocent defendants who are falsely convicted – the authors aim to demonstrate that much of the criminal legal system in the United States is explicitly designed to take both liberty and life from Black people. The victimization of people of color is discussed to demonstrate the significance of the unique struggles of these exonerees.

Part 2 of the book comprises chapters that examine the experiences of the many victims borne from a wrongful conviction. The data from the interviews with the wrongly convicted and their families inform most of the chapters in this section. Chapter 5 examines the victimization of the exonerees themselves, focusing on the challenges they experienced in prison, how they believe their experiences differed from those who were guilty, and how they coped with a wrongful conviction. Given that limited research has explored the experiences of female exonerees, a small but unique subset of the population of exonerees, Chapter 6 focuses on the female exonerees interviewed for this project. In Chapter 7, the data gleaned from interviews with the indirect victims of the wrongful convictions are explored, providing insights from family members and significant others' experiences regarding their loved one's wrongful conviction and exoneration.

Given that the focus of this book is on the many victims of a wrongful conviction, Chapter 8 focuses on the experiences of the "original" crime victims in cases of wrongful convictions; that is, those who are the victims of a crime for which the "real" perpetrator has not been caught and may in turn victimize others. Crime victims are revictimized through the process of a wrongful conviction: not only did they survive a frightening initial assault, but they also became victims of a system that did not bring the true perpetrator to justice. Wrongful convictions have a wide reach, and Chapter 9 will focus on so-called societal victimization. In this instance, public perceptions will be examined with regard to how the criminal justice system is viewed by members of society following a wrongful conviction and how legitimacy that is lost through these errors may be regained. The final chapter in this section focuses on the post-release experience of victimization of these individuals. Due to the many challenges they face, attempting to reintegrate into a society and into family and friend groups after many years of incarceration and the associated stigma, such experiences are a lingering form of victimization wrought by their initial wrongful conviction. The book will conclude with ideas regarding the implications of these findings on future research.

The unique character of this book is that it conceptualizes a wrongful conviction within a victimology framework, illustrating it through a new lens while also drawing on traditional research. Given that the study of wrongful convictions often focuses on examining the well-known contributing factors and the consequences of a wrongful conviction on the exoneree (Campbell, 2018; Gershman, 2014; N. A. Jackson et al., 2021; Leo, 2009; Norris et al., 2018), this volume represents "thinking outside the box" by providing a new and interesting framework from which to study this problem. Given that researchers have tended to use this list in many studies to best explain how a wrongful conviction occurs, the aim of this book is to go beyond this list and examine the experiences of the wrongly convicted as victims themselves.

## Conclusion

In order to examine the victimology of a wrongful conviction, it is essential to understand the history of victimology and its theoretical implications. The approach of recognizing exonerees as victims is as important as recognizing original crime victims themselves. Similar to the actual victim of a crime, the wrongly convicted are also victimized, in most cases through no fault of their own; they suffer unimaginable hardships and losses for crimes they did not commit or for crimes that never existed. This suffering also extends to their family members, the original victims of the crime, and society at large. This book puts a spotlight on the myriad victims borne from these miscarriages of justice.

## Note

1 The U.S. Supreme Court 1963 decision established that the prosecution has an obligation to turn over all exculpatory evidence to the defence, if it fails to do so; this constitutes a Brady violation and violates due process (Brady v. Maryland, 1963).

# 2

# VICTIMOLOGY

## Theoretical Perspectives and their Applications to the Wrongly Convicted

*Nicky Ali Jackson*

## Introduction

A large body of wrongful conviction scholarship has focused mainly on the study of causation and consequences. A missing piece within this research, however, has been the examination of the innocent people – the wrongly convicted – as victims. Similar to crime victims, they have suffered unimaginable losses. Moreover, as a result of a wrongful conviction, additional victims are created. Family, friends, co-workers, crime victims, the community, and other agents all experience indirect victimization. To this end, the purpose of this chapter is to situate the wrongly convicted, and those affected by their wrongful conviction, as victims within victimology literature. Examining the experiences of each of these individuals as legitimate victims of crime in a scholarly work can contribute toward a better understanding of the direct and indirect impacts of wrongful convictions on primary and secondary victims. In order to situate the construction of these individuals as victims, it is essential to explore the historical evolution of victimology as an area of study, including an overview of victim theories, the Victims' Rights Movement, types of victims, forms of victimization, and the costs of victimization.

## The History of Victimology: What Is a Victim?

Historically, scholarly research in criminal justice has largely been concerned with the causes of crime, focusing on offender traits as they relate to criminal behavior (Bruinsma, 2014). Victims were more or less ignored in this earlier work but unintentionally positioned in relationship with the offender. Consequently, this shifted the focus from offender to the victim. The term *victim* itself has gone through an evolution. It originated from the Latin term *victima* referring to an animal or human being offered as a sacrifice to a deity (Karmen, 2013). During the 17th century, it was used to describe people who were injured, tortured, or killed. Currently, the term victim refers to a person who suffers harm or injury in a variety of circumstances (B. S. Fisher et al., 2016; Karmen, 2013).

Early research that focused on victims, however, fostered a new branch of study, termed *victimology*, a subfield of criminology (B. S. Fisher et al., 2016). While criminologists traditionally study the social constructs of crime such as, *inter alia*, the creation of laws, who

DOI: 10.4324/9781003121251-3

breaks laws and why, and the societal reactions to criminal behavior, victimologists, on the other hand, explore the nature and extent of victimization. The primary areas of study among victimologists include the following:

1. The study of crime victims and their relationships to offenders.
2. The exploration of characteristics of victim vulnerability.
3. An examination of the plight of the victim.
4. An examination of the criminal justice system response to victims.
5. An examination of societal reaction to victimization.
6. The identification of new "victims" of behaviors not previously considered criminal.

While current research on victimology refers to "victims," the word takes on different meanings dependent on the context of the research; nonetheless, the common core in any definition of a victim is the idea of suffering. Some have argued that the term victim has negative connotations and thus have attempted to replace it with the term *survivor*, suggesting greater empowerment (Karmen, 2013). Others have argued that the term survivor downplays a victim's suffering (Papendick & Bohner, 2017). Some studies have also shown that the term victim is associated with ideas of weakness, passivity, and possibly even innocence, while survivor is thought to connote strength, fearlessness, and activity (Papendick & Bohner, 2017). For the purpose of this book, the term victim will refer to those who have been injured or harmed by criminal and noncriminal behaviors and survivors will refer to those who have experienced empowerment following victimization.

One of the first academic studies of victimology was *The Criminal and His Victim: Studies in the Sociobiology of Crime* by Hans von Hentig (1948), which examined victims of crime and their relationships to offenders. The focus of this study was not about victims specifically but rather on criminal behavior and the ways in which victims played a role in their own victimization. Von Hentig developed a victim typology that also serves as a victim–offender classification drawn from biological, sociological, and psychological factors and argues that age, gender, immigration, and mental status play a role in victimization, in particular, in increasing one's vulnerability. Another key figure in victim research was Romanian defense attorney Benjamin Mendelsohn who is recognized as the early father of victimology (B. S. Fisher et al., 2016; Karmen, 2013).

Mendelsohn developed a system of typologies of victims in the 1950s based on the level of the victim's involvement in the crime. The first of Mendelsohn's typologies is the innocent victim, who is the person who most typifies what is understood as a victim; that is, those who did not contribute to their victimization but was rather in the wrong place at the wrong time. The next is the victim with minor guilt. This person is said to not actively participate in their victimization but contributes in some minor way by possibly frequenting high-crime areas or is victimized through ignorance. This is followed by the guilty victim/guilty offender typology, or those who may engage in criminal activity together and be victimized. Next is the victim who is more guilty than the offender, who may induce the other to commit a crime. There is also the guilty victim: in such instances the victim instigates a conflict but is killed in self-defense. Finally, there is the imaginary victim, who is someone who suffered nothing but claims to be a victim and may falsify reports to make them appear as a victim (Sengstock, 1976). Mendelsohn's work was considered controversial at the time due to his strong emphasis on the victim's role in their own victimization (viewed as victim blaming), which is an attitude that is out of favor today (Sengstock, 1976).

The 1960s, 1970s, and 1980s evinced the burgeoning of scholarly research and interest in the study of crime victims and victimology, with early studies by Menachem Amir, Marvin Wolgang, and Ezzat A. Fatah. The first academic journal in the area of victimology can be traced to 1967 when *Victimology: An International Journal* was published. Shortly thereafter, the *International Review of Victimology* was published (1988), followed by a number of other journals, such as the *Journal of Victimology and Victim Justice* (1992). Approaches to victimology, which emerged from the study of victims, can be divided into three main areas: penal victimology, general victimology, and human rights victimology (Ferguson & Turvey, 2009). *Penal victimology*, also referred to as *interactionist victimology*, focuses on the relationship between the offender and the victim when a criminal law has violated. *General victimology* embraces the study of myriad victims from crime victims to those who have been injured as a result of natural disasters, wars, accidents, etc. (Dussich et al., 2003). Under a *human rights* approach to victimology, victims are considered man-made creations as a result of genocide, torture, and slavery.

## Victim Theories

Criminological and sociological theories have evolved over hundreds of years, with varying approaches attempting to understand and explain crime and delinquency, including approaches differentially emphasizing varying factors. They include, but are not limited to, deterrence and rational choice theories, biological and biosocial theories, psychological theories, social learning theories, social bonding and control theories, labeling and reintegrative shaming theories, social disorganization theory, anomie and strain theories, conflict theory, Marxist theories, radical and critical theories, and feminist theories (Akers et al., 2020). It is beyond the scope of this chapter to detail the many historical and modern criminological theories; therefore, the focus here will be on theories that help understand crime victims and victimology, specifically victim precipitation theory, lifestyle exposure theory, and routine activity theory.

### Victim Precipitation Theory

Victim precipitation theory argues that victims play a role in their own victimization, whether unknowingly or knowingly (Wallace & Roberson, 2019). As noted previously, early victimologists Benjamin Mendelsohn and Hans von Hentig outlined two different victim precipitation theories arguing that certain populations are most vulnerable to victimization. While both proposed that victims play a role in their victimization, their approach was different. Mendelsohn examined situational factors providing a scale of victim involvement from an innocent victim to a guilty victim, whereas, von Hentig explained victimization through sociological, biological, and psychological factors, associating age, gender, mental status, and race/ethnicity with victimization risks. Both Mendelsohn and von Hentig suggested that victims, through either no fault or some fault, played a role in their own injuries. In 1967, Stephen Schafer developed a further victim precipitation theory called *functional responsibility theory*. Schafer shifted away from Mendelsohn's and von Hentig's victim risk typologies to one of responsibility and posited that potential victims have dual functional responsibilities: (a) to not provoke or instigate victimization and (b) to prevent their own victimization. Like his earlier counterparts, his theory shifts blame for crime or injury onto the victim and away from the offender. Victim blaming theories position victims as responsible (wholly or partially) for their plight and is often found in how victims are conveyed in the media and in the courts, particularly in sexual assault and domestic violence cases. Furthermore, this approach may result in revictimization in courts, which happens when victims of sexual assault or violence are made to relive the experience as witnesses. In the case of rape victims, they may be represented as having provoked or instigated their assault based on their appearance, behaviors, or both. This is also seen in domestic violence cases, as well, where victims may be considered blameworthy for not escaping an abusive relationship.

Contemporary critics of these theories argue that situating victims and offenders in an interactive relationship takes culpability away from criminals and revictimizes crime victims (Karmen, 2013). This suggests that victims voluntarily entered the relationship which puts ownership on them for their victimization. Victim advocates further argue that these theories ignore offender motives and planning which ultimately affects the processing of those cases that actually make it to the courts. Specifically, if victims are held morally culpable for their victimization, it may mitigate *mens rea* (the intent of the offender), resulting in lesser sentences for defendants who have caused injury.

## Lifestyle Exposure Theory

Hindelang et al. (1978) described the lifestyle exposure theory for understanding victimization. They proposed that exposure to criminal victimization is rooted in a person's lifestyle, defined as "daily activities, both vocational (work, school, keeping house) and leisure activities" (Hindelang et al., 1978, p. 241). For them, the way people adapt in society depends on role expectations and structural constraints; role expectations are based on one's ascribed status (involuntary status assigned at birth) and achieved status (voluntary status earned through accomplishments). Hindelang et al. (1978) argued that demographic variables such as age, gender, race, income, marital status, education, and occupation help explain risk factors associated with personal victimization. Age, gender, and race (ascribed statuses) are determined at birth; thus, according to this theory, certain people are born more vulnerable to victimization than others based on those attributes. Income, marital status, education, and occupation (achieved statuses) can change over time, which may affect a person's vulnerability to personal victimization. *Structural constraints* are the economic, political, and cultural factors that limit how people can achieve role expectation.

Hindelang et al. (1978) argued that potential victimization is based on what they term "homogamy." This principle suggests that the link between victimization and offending is produced through shared lifestyle activities. Put differently, "this principle states that persons are more likely to be victimized when they come into contact with members of demographic groups that contain a disproportionate share of offenders" (Lauritsen et al., 1991, pp. 267–268). In other words, victims who share similar lifestyles with offenders are more likely to fall victim to crime. For example, young people are more likely to commit crime; thus, the people they are likely to victimize are those who are near them – other young people. Gathering in public places and going out a night are part of one's lifestyle, and those who are most likely to be victimized will be those who hang out at the same places and at the same time as offenders. In short, one's risk for victimization is affected by how people live their lives. It is not simply based on who they are but who they spend time with, where they live, and what they do.

## Routine Activity Theory

At around the same time of Hindelang et al.'s (1978) publication, L. Cohen and Felson (1979) published an article proposing routine activity theory as explanatory of victimization. Like victim precipitation and lifestyle exposure theories, routine activity theory examined the victim's role in the crime. Particularly, they focused on crime as a product of three factors: a motivated offender, a suitable target, and the absence of capable guardians converging at the same time and location. Motivated offenders are those who are willing and able to commit a crime and are searching for a suitable target, while targets are suitable as they lack capable guardians who protect them. According to this theory, people become prey if they come into contact with an offender who is ready to attack and has the opportunity to do so and the potential victim has no capable guardians (parents, teachers, etc.) offering protection at that given time and place. An intersection of these three factors must occur in order for an individual to be victimized.

## Victims' Rights Movement

The Victims' Rights Movement can be described as a social movement that was directed toward officially recognizing the suffering and consequences that occur from being a victim of crime and the need for the provision of supports. Several events in American history have played a role its development. For one, the rising crime rate in America during the 1960s was a major catalyst in sparking victims' rights advocacy. Crime victims began to volunteer at various community-based victim witness programs to raise awareness about the plight of victims (Wallace & Roberson, 2019). Given their new platform, they spoke out on various issues affecting victims; in particular, they were concerned with the lack of care and attention given to victims within the criminal justice system. As a result of the increase in crime and in part due to the pressure mounted by crime victims, America observed a new war – the "war on crime" – which essentially created a fear of crime, one that was not necessarily founded in fact. In response to the growing fear of crime and a rise in victim advocacy, President Lyndon B. Johnson established the President's Commission on Law Enforcement Assistance Administration of Justice (LEAA) in 1965 and became the first American president to address crime as a political issue. The objectives of the commission were threefold: to examine the extent of crime, to understand its causes, and to determine ways to reduce it.

The LEAA administered federal funding to state and local law enforcement agencies and funded educational programs, research, state planning agencies, and local crime initiatives as part of the so-called war on crime. Under the LEAA, the commission created the National Crime Survey, known today as the National Crime Victimization Survey, which analyzed personal victimization through its sample of American households. Their annual publication revealed that crime was more prevalent than what had been reported by the Federal Bureau of Investigation's Uniform Crime Reports, which measured arrest rates and reported crimes to the police. This was due in part to the fact that victimization surveys are often administered anonymously and hence people are more honest about their experiences, whereas police statistics only report crimes known to them. Such surveys reveal the "dark figure" of crime, representing unreported and undiscovered crimes. In response to these findings, the Commission established victim compensation programs. This changed the trajectory for crime victims by officially recognizing their injuries and acknowledging the needed for healing.

In addition to the establishment of the LEAA and increased victim advocacy, two major grassroots movements played a role in the Victims' Rights Movement: The Feminist Movement and the Civil Rights Movement. While it is beyond the scope of this chapter to do justice to the rich histories of these important social movements, they laid the groundwork for the Victims' Rights Movement. Recognizing society's patriarchal structure, feminists argued that males held most of the societal power while women struggled, particularly women of color. This imbalance in society encouraged social, political, and economic inequality between males and females. When males are placed in positions of power, women are left vulnerable. As such, women are more often victimized by sexual and/or domestic violence than are men. Specifically, at that time, feminists were advocating for greater egalitarianism in society, which allowed for women to have greater influence, as well as increased social, political, and economic equality with men. Also important to feminists was how female victims were treated by the police, prosecutors, and courts. Feminists were concerned with the criminal justice system's lack of response to sexual assault and domestic violence victims. Recognizing the need for help, during the 1970s, victim advocates created rape crisis centers and domestic violence shelters. Perhaps inadvertently, feminists' concerns for female victimization paved the way to help recognize other types of victims.

The Civil Rights Movement of the 1960s was also fundamental to the development of the Victims' Rights Movement. Given the centuries-long history of abuses (including murder), racism, segregation, and discrimination in the United States against African Americans, civil rights activists began to rise up during the mid-20th century and demand justice and equality. Activists were arrested and some faced unimaginable horrors, such as lynching, at the hands of their oppressors. African Americans were being denied their rights guaranteed under the U.S. Constitution, including the right to life, liberty, and equal justice before the law and equal employment, education, and housing opportunities, among other things. Raising awareness of the mistreatment of Black offenders and victims also showcased African Americans as victims of an unjust criminal justice system. Together, the Women's Movement and Civil Rights Movement provided the tools to push forward the first wave of the victims' movement.

The second wave of the victims' movement, during the 1980s, took on a more direct approach to addressing criminal victimization. Violent crime was a serious national problem at that time, which resulted in President Ronald Reagan establishing the President's Task Force on Crime Victims in 1982. The task force was concerned with addressing three issues – policy development, program implementation, and public awareness around crime victimization – and came up with recommendations to help victims receive the financial, medical, and legal supports needed.

Historically, victims have not been provided the same protections offered to criminal suspects. However, the enactment of two federal laws offered crime victims assistance in their recovery through federal aid. In 1984, Congress established the Victims of Crimes Act (VOCA), which had two major outcomes: one was the creation of the Office for Victims of Crime and the second was the establishment of the Crime Victims Fund, which distributed federal monies in compensation to state victim assistance programs. The task force was clear that monies collected for the fund would not come from taxpayers. Rather, federal monies collected came from criminal fines and penalties, forfeitures, special assessments, and related revenue and were to be dispersed to states. In 1984, 37 states had victim compensation programs. Since the creation of VOCA, every state now has a victim compensation program marking significant progress in providing financial reparations to crime victims.

Twenty years after the creation of VOCA, the federal Crime Victims' Rights Act was passed under the Justice for All Act of 2004. Under the Crime Victims' Rights Acts, victims of federal crimes are provided 10 fundamental rights:

1. The right to be reasonably protected from the accused.
2. The right to reasonable, accurate, and timely notice of any public court proceeding, or any parole proceeding, involving the crime or of any release or escape of the accused.
3. The right not to be excluded from any such public court proceeding, unless the court, after receiving clear and convincing evidence, determines that testimony by the victim would be materially altered if the victim heard other testimony at that proceeding.
4. The right to be reasonably heard at any public proceeding in the district court involving release, plea, sentencing, or any parole proceeding.

5.  The reasonable right to confer with the attorney for the government in the case.
6.  The right to full and timely restitution as provided in law.
7.  The right to proceedings free from unreasonable delay.
8.  The right to be treated with fairness and with respect for the victim's dignity and privacy.
9.  The right to be informed in a timely manner of any plea bargain or deferred prosecution agreement.
10. The right to be informed of the rights under this section and the services described in section 503(c) of the Victims' Rights and Restitution Act of 1990 (42 U.S.C. 10607(c)) and provided contact information for the Office of the Victims' Rights Ombudsman of the Department of Justice.

VOCA and the Crime Victim's Rights Act offer federal monies to assist direct victims of crime; however, these funds are not available to those who are indirectly affected by a crime. While making compensation available to victims is laudable, the lack of assistance for indirect victims remains problematic.

## Types and Forms of Victimization

In the three types of victimology discussed earlier, penal, general, and human rights, in each case individuals have suffered some form of injury. Drawing on these three approaches to victimology, the types of victimization may include the following:

1.  *Physical victimization*: physical acts that are willfully and intentionally committed against another that result in physical injuries ranging from minor (e.g., bruising) to severe (e.g., gunshot wounds) assaults.
2.  *Sexual victimization*: any unwanted physical or nonphysical sexual contact. Physical sexual victimization includes unwanted fondling, rape, sodomy, or forced prostitution. Nonphysical sexual victimization includes forcing a person to watch pornography, observe sexual assault, and fall victim to exhibitionists or voyeurs.
3.  *Emotional/psychological victimization*: nonphysical acts such as name-calling, betrayal, or any other acts that cause emotional injury to another.
4.  *Economic/financial victimization*: when a person knowingly and willfully controls another's money or financial assets.
5.  *Medical victimization*: intentionally withholding medical care. This may occur due to religious beliefs or for other reasons such as fear of exposing criminal behavior (e.g., not taking a child to doctor who has been physically abused).
6.  *Religious victimization*: denying a person the right to practice religious beliefs (e.g., forbidding a partner to attend religious services).
7.  *Political victimization*: lawful government acts resulting in physical and psychological injuries to certain populations (e.g., war and slavery).
8.  *Institutional victimization*: intentional harmful acts perpetrated against residents within institutional settings (schools, prisons, mental health facilities).

The majority of these types of victimizations are personal (1–7) and have received scholarly attention. Far less research focus has been on institutional or governmental abuses. Total institutions, such as prisons, are wrought with victimization, yet these institutional abuses are often ignored.

## Primary and Secondary Victims

Recognizing the suffering of crime victims has long been a challenge not only within society but also within the criminal justice system. Through the Victims' Rights Movement, great attention was directed at legitimizing the experience of crime victims and addressing their needs. While the movement focused on the direct victims of crime, it ignored others who had been indirectly affected by victimization. *Primary victims*, also called *direct victims*, are those who experience firsthand victimization, including, for example, the victim of an assault who suffer injuries as a result of their victimization. *Secondary victims*, on the other hand, also known as *indirect victims*, do not experience the victimization directly but may be emotionally and/or financially affected. Indirect victims include family members and friends of the direct victim as well as the public. An example of secondary victimization would be the following: a father is shot during a carjacking; he is hospitalized and left unable to work. His family may be affected financially (less money for food, rent, and other essential needs) and emotionally (they may develop fear, anxiety, and/or anger). Thus, indirectly, the father's family members also are victims of the carjacking, thus, becoming secondary victims of the carjacking.

## *The Consequences of Victimization: Tangible vs. Intangible Costs*

As noted above, victimization takes a toll not only on the primary victim but also on family members, friends, co-workers, and society. Primary and secondary victims experience short-term and long-term effects as a result of victimization. In the immediate aftermath of a crime, victims will experience physical and/or psychological effects – costs that are both tangible and intangible. Wallace and Roberson's (2019) four categories of the consequences of physical violence illustrate these costs. They include the following:

1.  *Immediate injuries*: bruises, contusions, cuts, and broken bones. These injuries tend to heal quickly and thus are often dismissed as being inconsequential.
2.  *Injuries that leave visible scars*: loss of teeth, loss of fingers or toes, or temporary loss of mobility. These injuries may alter a victim's life but are often not viewed as catastrophic.
3.  *Unknown long-term physical injuries*: exposure to acquired immunodeficiency syndrome or other sexually transmitted diseases. These injuries may be catastrophic as they can result in loss of life or a significant decrease in the quality of life.
4.  *Long-term catastrophic injuries*: injuries that alter a victim's physical mobility. These injuries are catastrophic in that a victim's quality of life may be forever changed.

As they outlined, the aftermath of victimization takes a toll on various aspects of a victim's life (Wallace & Roberson, 2019). Physical victimization can leave visible acute or long-term scars but at the same time create psychological consequences for victims. While these invisible injuries are often dismissed as inconsequential as they are difficult to detect and measure, their effects are often longer lasting and can have an impact on day-to-day living in myriad ways. Victims report difficulty sleeping, abuse of legal and/or illegal drugs, and increased fear, anxiety, depression, guilt, as well as a diminished interest in daily activities, fatigue, and other mental stressors (B. S. Fisher et al., 2016; Karmen, 2013; Wallace & Roberson, 2019). Victims may have a difficult time performing roles that they once were able to do.

For those victimized by crime, everyday roles may become challenging, such as a parent, partner, friend, and colleague. Day-to-day tasks may become difficult and intimate relations may also be disrupted post-victimization. Victims may struggle to continue in these roles, on both short-term and long-term bases. Work is often affected by victimization, through instances of decreased productivity, loss of wages, and increased absences. Victimization also affects social relationships as victims may distance themselves from those with whom they once shared confidences. They may no longer relate in the same manner to outsiders – those who have not been victimized – as friends cannot understand what they experienced. Moreover, secondary victims may suffer psychological consequences of victimization including loss of sleep, depression, guilt, fear, and isolation. While they may not have experienced the crime, they have been indirectly affected and, as such, they may share many similar psychological effects as the actual crime victim (B. S. Fisher et al., 2016; Karmen, 2013).

In studying the different responses people have to victimization, Bard and Sangrey (1986) developed a three-stage crisis reaction mode, detailing how victims cope with their experiences. The first stage is the *impact stage*, which occurs immediately after the crime, when the victim is in shock and cannot believe what has happened. Victims may become dependent on others for assistance during this stage as they may have problems making decisions. During the impact stage, victims may have difficulty sleeping and eating and feel a sense of helplessness. The second stage, the *recoil stage*, is when victims begin to adapt to their victimization and start to heal. It is at this stage that victims may experience denial. While some will talk feverishly about their ordeal with friends and loved ones, others may refuse to discuss what happened at all. It is at this stage that Bard and Sangrey believe that victims may also feel a sense of anger toward the offender. During these periods of denial, some will fantasize about revenge, but for most it is marked as the time that they come to terms with their victimization and attempt to rebuild their lives. The third stage is the *reorganization stage* which is a time when the victim comes to accept the victimization. During this stage, victims are often able to get back to their daily routines, and while they do not forget what happened, they have learned to cope and are able to progress in their lives.

There are numerous other costs to victimization, both tangible and intangible. Tangible costs are losses that are apparent to the senses – they are costs that may be quantified or measurable. For example, a victim who is injured and unable to work can record lost wages based on the number of days of work missed as a tangible cost of victimization. Other tangible losses would include medical bills or property damage as a result of victimization. Intangible costs, on the other hand, are difficult to measure and are not apparent to the senses as they are invisible and unidentifiable. They may include emotional responses to crime such as fear, anxiety, distrust, guilt, anger, post-traumatic stress disorder, and depression. Sleep and eating disorders, a lack of interest in intimate relationships or friendships, and fatigue are further examples of the intangible costs of victimization.

## The Wrongly Convicted, Innocent Inmate: The Forgotten Victim

Long ignored in the study of victimization is what occurs through a wrongful conviction. Those who are victimized through a wrongful conviction are most often not recognized in victim legislation as having suffered a "victimization" per se. The wrongly convicted suffer similar deprivations along with other prisoners, but it is made far worse by the injustice of their unjust incarceration. If they are fortunate enough to have their case overturned, upon release, the wrongfully convicted receive no post-release support, as do guilty inmates who are released on parole. At the time of writing, 35 states have financial compensation programs for factually innocent individuals who were wrongfully convicted and incarcerated. Unlike crime victims, however, there are no federal monies allotted to assist individuals who were wrongfully convicted of committing state or federal crimes. Moreover, exonerees are not provided rights, protections through federal legislation upon release. The wrongly convicted are ultimately victims of errors of the criminal justice system and should be entitled to the same dignity, rights, and reparations offered to other crime victims.

From a victimology perspective, another way to conceptualize the wrongly convicted and wrongly imprisoned is as an "innocent inmate." N. A. Jackson et al. (2021) defined innocent inmates as those who are factually innocent and wrongly incarcerated. While it could be argued that the term is an oxymoron, as "inmates" denote those who have been found guilty in a court of law and have had their liberty taken away through incarceration, innocent inmates are often convicted and imprisoned in most cases through no fault of their own. At the same time, the growing numbers of exonerations, as evidenced through the National Registry of Exonerations (2020a), is clear evidence that U.S. prisons and jails are filled with people who are imprisoned for crimes they did not commit, who are in fact innocent inmates. Once exonerated, these individuals deserve recognition as victims of crime, as victims of a miscarriage of justice, as do their families as secondary victims. The experiences of these ancillary victims and how they experience their victimization will be explored in later chapters.

## The Wrongly Convicted: Victims of Institutional and Personal Abuse

As noted earlier, a general working definition of victim includes those who have suffered a loss or an injury. Under this definition, wrongly convicted individuals are also victims – they have experienced loss and injury, and their suffering is immeasurable and undeniable. They have encountered institutional victimization as well as personal victimization, as the criminal justice system has created a victim by convicting and incarcerating an innocent person. In the event they are exonerated, they may also suffer continued victimization upon release.

Through the egregious error of a wrongful conviction, innocent inmates suffer while incarcerated. They suffer many deprivations that accompany the loss of liberty and may be further victimized through prison violence. It is difficult to grasp the true extent of exoneree victimization during incarceration as much research on prison victimization does not separate the experience of those who claim innocence from those who do not. This is based on a presumption that all those who are incarcerated are guilty. N. A. Jackson et al.'s (2021) research attempted to examine the prison experience of exonerees to better understand how they uniquely experienced prison life. As expected, they found that many exonerees witnessed and/or experienced violence while incarcerated. Those who *observed* violence, as bystanders, reacted in one of two ways. Some innocent inmates did not get involved as they understood that they, too, may become victimized. Their bystander role has left some with guilt while others rationalize their inaction as a survival mode. Those who did interject in violent situations argued that they felt a greater need to protect other inmates than be concerned with their own self-preservation. Moreover, those who were *approached* in a violent manner also used different techniques to handle the situation. For some, they actively fought back in an attempt to gain or maintain their reputation, while others used nonphysical approaches such as they attempted to verbally reason with other prisoners. N. A. Jackson et al. (2021) found that the exonerees they interviewed revealed that while they were incarcerated, they did not distinguish between guilty and innocent inmate as they perceived all inmates to be victims of a corrupt and warped prison system lacking in morality, humanity, and dignity.

## The Wrongly Convicted as an Ideal Victim

The late Norwegian criminologist Nils Christie (1986) developed a social construct of the ideal victim. In its purest form, Christie defined the ideal victim as "a person or category of individuals, who – when hit by crime – most readily are given the complete and legitimate status of being a victim" (Christie, 1986, p. 18). Key to understanding his model is that society will accept or reject the victim label based on a variety of factors, most prominently whether a victim's attributes are believable. Characteristics of the ideal victim are based on Christie's example of the little old lady walking home in the afternoon after caring for her sick sister when a big bad man approaches her, hits her on the head, and steals her bag in order to pay for alcohol or drugs. Christie argues that the little old lady is an ideal victim as she meets the criteria proposed in his theory. The characteristics of his ideal victim include being weak and vulnerable, carrying out a respectable project, and being where she was supposed to be, while the offender was big and bad and had no personal relationship with the victim. In his typical example, the victim was elderly and female, was on her way home in daylight, the offender was bigger than her, and they were strangers.

Thus, in Christie's model, the ideal or legitimate victim is weak, vulnerable, powerless, engaging in good work, and unknown to the perpetrator. Like his predecessors, Christie suggests that assigning the label *victim* is a social construct determined by level of involvement, association, and personal attributes (weak, female, etc.). The label may be accepted or rejected by others dependent on their perceptions of pure innocence or partial responsibility. Based on his argument, the ideal victim is not blameworthy; full responsibility for the crime falls on the shoulders of the perpetrator alone. However, those who are not ideal victims are thought to share some culpability in their victimization.

The ideal victim theory has been revisited by scholars and applied to numerous victim types (Karmen, 2013). In applying Christie's typology to the wrongly convicted, it could be argued that they are, in fact, ideal victims. The National Registry of Exonerations (2021) reported that almost 50% of exonerees are African American, while African Americans comprise only 13% of the U.S. population. The disproportionate number of African Americans within the criminal justice system reflects how they may become ideal victims of systemic abuse, as racist explicit and implicit stereotypes often lead to arresting, convicting, and sentencing of African Americans at higher rates than Whites. Consequently, this also results in far too many innocent African Americans being wrongly convicted.[1] In short, they and others marginalized by poverty, gender, and race become ideal victims as they are weak and vulnerable, like the little old lady, before the powerful criminal justice system, which in Christie's terms is "big" and "bad," holding all the power and authority.

## Victim Theory Applications for the Wrongly Convicted

As previously discussed, victim precipitation and routine activity theories provide sources of understanding about victimization. When situating the experience of the wrongly convicted within the umbrella of these theories, some interesting points can be raised. Victim precipitation theory proposes that victims play a role in their victimization. All of the exonerees interviewed for this study argued that they had no responsibility in their wrongful conviction. In fact, two exonerees described themselves as being "plucked out of society" with no cause or justification. All of the interviewees argued that they were targeted as a result of some form of official misconduct, ranging from a lack of competent investigation to perjury. According to our sample, their own actions did not have an impact on their victimization as they were innocent persons who had no shared responsibility in the crime(s). At the same time, some individuals do falsely confess to crimes they did not commit. In fact, the National Registry of Exonerations (2020a) indicated that as of March 2020, 12% of all exonerees had falsely confessed to the crime for which they were wrongfully convicted.[2] Age, mental illness, and disability were precipitating factors in these cases. The victim precipitation theory would likely apply in those cases, as someone who confesses (whether falsely or sincerely) likely contributes in some way to their conviction; however, none of the exonerees in this current study had falsely confessed.

Routine activity theory argues that every crime has to have a motivated offender, a suitable target, and the absence of a capable guardian. Applying routine activity theory to wrongful conviction positions the criminal justice system as the offender and the wrongly convicted as the victim. Police, prosecutors, and judges are motivated and pressured to solve a crime through a conviction. The innocent person becomes the suitable target to victimize (arresting and convicting the wrong person) based on a number of contributing factors, including eyewitness misidentification, faulty DNA evidence, jailhouse informant testimony, or official misconduct. In many instances, the exonerees interviewed for this book described one or more of the canonical list of factors contributing to a wrongful conviction that were present in their case. The absence of a capable guardian in a wrongful conviction would be a lack of representation by competent defense attorney or the presence of a biased prosecutor, jury, or judge. In many instances, these legal professionals did not adequately fulfill their obligations to protect the presumed innocent defendant and, in some cases, the result was a wrongful conviction.

## Conclusion

Wrongful conviction scholars have primarily examined factors that contribute to a wrongful conviction and its aftermath. Victimologists, on the other hand, have studied a number of crime victims and issues associated with their victimization. This chapter attempts to draw attention to a change in paradigm and recognizes that those who have been wrongly arrested, convicted, and incarcerated can also be recognized and understood as victims and survivors of their ordeal. Positioning wrongly convicted individuals within victimology research allows social scientists to engage in micro- and macrolevel analyses of a newly recognized victim population – that of exonerees.

## Notes

1  See Chapter 4 for more details about race and wrongful conviction.
2  https://www.law.umich.edu/special/exoneration/Pages/False-Confessions.aspx

# 3

# THE NATURE AND EXTENT OF WRONGFUL CONVICTIONS

*Kathryn M. Campbell*

## Introduction

The fact that individuals can be accused and convicted for crimes they did not commit is no longer questioned by courts and commentators. It is not uncommon to hear stories in the media about individuals who have served lengthy sentences for crimes they did not commit and who are later exonerated through DNA evidence. According to the Innocence Project, in fact, more than 375 individuals over the past 25 years have been exonerated based on DNA evidence, often years or decades after the fact. The National Registry of Exonerations (NRE), which includes cases with and without DNA, has identified close to 2,700 individuals who have been exonerated in the United States since 1989. The wrongly convicted are ultimately victims of state wrongdoing; they have been wrongfully targeted, arrested, tried, and convicted for crimes they did not commit. This chapter will present an overview of the nature and extent of wrongful convictions, as has been established through over 4 decades of research and inquiry into this problem. The extent or incidence of wrongful convictions is difficult to establish, for a number of reasons that will be discussed. What is clearer, however, are the main contributing factors to this problem, often related to evidence presented in court. A number of factors will be discussed in this regard, including witness misidentification, false confessions, misused forensic science (and expert testimony), unreliable jailhouse informants and incentivized witnesses, and government misconduct. The research has indicated that a great deal is now known about how wrongful convictions come about and how individuals become victims of state error; however, what is less known is how to rectify these life-altering mistakes.

## Extent of Wrongful Convictions

Attempting to establish the "true" extent or incidence of wrongful convictions is an unrealizable task. There are inherent difficulties attached to this exercise, often based on how one defines not only a wrongful conviction but also an exoneration. Debates in the literature as to whether the problem is "epidemic or episodic" (D. Simon, 2006) are also accompanied by very wide-ranging estimates of wrongful conviction. There are some who would count every successful appeal as an exoneration of a wrongful conviction, which would include tens of thousands of cases annually

DOI: 10.4324/9781003121251-4

(Naughton, 2005) and others who believe "… the ghost of the innocent man convicted … is an unreal dream" (Justice Learned Hand, *United States v. Garsson*, 1923). There seems to be some qualified consensus in later research around innocence scholarship in the United States of an accepted "estimate" of between "1/2 of 1% and 1%" for a general felony wrongful conviction rate (Zalman, 2012, p. 230). Zalman (2012) recognized that this judgment is subjective and based on an assessment of the overall condition of the criminal justice system in the United States presently. While the percentage is low and thus encouraging, it translates into tens of thousands of convictions annually. However, the numbers continue to vary considerably. A recent study examined the results of an anonymous self-report survey of a state prison population, and the figure for wrongful convictions among that group was 6% (Loeffler et al., 2017), whereas Cassell (2018) argued that most of the "higher" rates are overstating the risk and, through a statistical analysis, came up with a rate of between 0.016% and 0.062%.

This estimate is qualified, for a number of reasons. Primarily, studies that have proffered the estimates are often based on one jurisdiction and then taken as applicable to the entire nation of the United States (cf. Huff et al., 1986, 1996). Individual studies examining death penalty cases – which are generally not directly comparable to felony conviction cases – indicate even higher error rates (up to 2.3%), which may be in part due to the fact that there is greater scrutiny applied to these cases, post-exoneration, given the stakes involved (S. R. Gross & O'Brien, 2008). At the same time, most known exonerations are in murder and sexual assault cases, where DNA evidence is often present and in some instances can effectively exonerate individuals (S. R. Gross, 2008). Important to note is that these extreme violent crimes only make up a small fraction of all felony convictions (about 2%) and thus very little is known about wrongful convictions in the vast majority of other crimes.

At the same time, the number or incident rate is ever evasive; one can never really know how many wrongful convictions occur in a given jurisdiction. Given that this determination only occurs after the fact, at no time are all errors of justice actually caught by the inherent safeguards offered through appeal and post-conviction review. Some individuals lack faith in a system that got it wrong in first instance, so they do not bother to try a second "kick at the can" through appeal and ultimately serve a wrongful imprisonment and never attempt to overturn their conviction. Cases where individuals have avoided trial through a plea bargain, despite innocence, also escape capture by these estimates. When faced with a certain conviction and a long sentence, many innocent individuals avoid the expense and angst of a trial, plead guilty, and serve a lesser sentence. While some may attempt to overturn their conviction at a later date, having essentially offered a "plea" of guilt to a crime they are now saying they did not commit, these individuals face an uphill battle when seeking exoneration.

As Campbell (2018) noted, the debates about incidence rates are also a reflection of political divisiveness, rather than a question of mathematical precision. Those who are more sensitive to issues of wrongful conviction often endorse a position that wrongful conviction is a widespread serious problem, with damaging repercussions demanding immediate action, while those on the other end of the continuum speak of it as an irregularity – troublesome but hardly worth the attention it has garnered and unwittingly bringing the entire criminal justice system into disrepute. What exonerations reveal, in effect, are those cases that are "caught" by the system, where an error has occurred and is fortunately rectified at a later date. Even if one accepts the lower end of the estimate scale, these exonerees only reflect a small percentage of the victims of errors of justice. Further, what is most damaging for the wrongly convicted is that such error corrections often occur only after decades of incarceration and decades of fighting to get someone to listen to them. The consequent psychological, emotional, financial, and social repercussions on individuals and their families are also immeasurable.

## Evidentiary Problems: Contributing Factors

The past several decades have evinced a great deal of research into understanding the contributing factors to wrongful convictions, or what could be described as the *nature* of wrongful convictions. What innocence scholarship has revealed is that it is rarely one factor that occurs in isolation that causes a conviction in error to occur but rather a confluence of factors that co-occur and result in a wrongful conviction. Leo (2005) and Gross (2008) maintained that much wrongful conviction scholarship involves a reiteration of the causative factors that contribute to these miscarriages of justice, without placing them within a larger context, absent consideration of the structural and systemic factors that likely influence why they occur and to whom. This part of the chapter will now focus on understanding these contributing factors, not in isolation but to provide a context for the rest of the book, to understand how the wrongly convicted are in fact victimized themselves.

### Eyewitness Misidentification

The most compelling, and leading, contributing factor to wrongful convictions is eyewitness misidentification. Not only do the statistics from innocence projects demonstrate this fact but a large body of psychological research has also proven this to be correct. Eyewitnesses make mistakes: memory is not infallible, confidence does not equal accuracy, and juries are often convinced by adamant eyewitness testimony – even when incorrect. In fact, mistaken eyewitness identifications have contributed to approximately 69% (or 252 cases) of the more than 375 wrongful convictions in the United States overturned by post-conviction DNA evidence (Innocence Project, n.d.). In addition, the NRE has identified at least 450 non-DNA-based exonerations involving eyewitness misidentification.[1] Not all mistaken identifications are the same, however, and Jackson and Gross (2016) have categorized them as following: 30% of the NRE exonerations were true mistakes; the others were lies. In those cases, 26% were deliberately misidentified someone as the guilty party for a crime committed by another person and another 17% of exonerations were cases where a crime never occurred at all. While the majority appear to be true mistakes, also referred to as "wrong man" cases, what these statistics reveal is that eyewitnesses, at times, tend to lie for other nefarious reasons.

The persuasive testimony from an eyewitness at trial can have a very damning effect on an innocent defendant. Extensive psychological research has demonstrated the fallibility of human memory and the damaging effect of placing too great an emphasis on the reliability of eyewitness testimony (Campbell, 2018). At the same time, witnesses at trial are often highly believable, whether they are correct or not, and courts will seek guidance from experts regarding the malleability of human memory. The following case illustrates how these errors can happen:

> Jaythan Kendrick was exonerated in November 2020 after spending twenty-five years in a New York jail for a murder he did not commit. Kendrick was convicted of the 1995 murder of a 70-year-old woman who was stabbed during a robbery in a housing project in Queens, where Kendrick lived. While he had no criminal record, and was an Army veteran, the police pursued him as their main suspect based on a 10-year-old boy's description of the attacker. The young boy had seen the crime from over 100 feet away, out of a third-floor apartment window. The other eyewitness had told police initially he had not seen the attacker, but later changed his story to corroborate the police's version of events. The 10-year-old identified Kendrick from a subjective police lineup

—Kendrick was his "second choice", when he learned he had not initially identified the "correct" person. Aside from these witnesses, there was no physical evidence connecting Kendrick to the crime. Kendrick's exoneration came about due to the witness' recantation, new witness statements and DNA evidence. (Selby, 2020)

Early psychological research, from as long ago as the 1970s, has demonstrated difficulties with eyewitness identifications. The largest issue appears to be the problems of human memory and its fallibility. Memory does not function like a video camera; in fact, individuals pay attention to specific details, remember some and forget others, based on a whole host of intangible factors. Loftus's work has established that witnesses and their testimony can be influenced and their memory of events altered by actions occurring following the event (Loftus et al., 2008). Castelle and Loftus (2001) demonstrated that witnesses may exercise unconscious transference, which occurs when a witness views a suspect for the first time in one context and then recognizes them as having been in another context. Essentially, a witness may have seen a picture of a suspect in the media and then later pick them out of a photo or live lineup as the perpetrator but not realize where they were recognizing them from.

Further research has established that a number of specific factors may influence the accuracy of eyewitness identification; these variables can be categorized as system variables or estimator variables (Wells & Olson, 2003). *System variables* are those that are controlled by the "system" and include such things as police lineups, lineup presentation methods, and witness instructions. Police have been known to manipulate these factors in the past, either intentionally or inadvertently, ultimately resulting in erroneous identifications. *Estimator variables* can also affect the accuracy of an identification but are only assessed after the fact. They include characteristics that may affect the accuracy of an identification that are inherent to the witness, the perpetrator, the event, or the conditions surrounding the event. They include variables such as race, witness confidence, weapon presence, and the emotional state of the victim. Research has indicated that the accuracy of an identification is often dependent on how a lineup is presented (simultaneously or sequentially), to what extent the foils (non-suspects) in the lineup resemble the suspect, the instructions given to a witness about whether the perpetrator is in the lineup, or whether they chose the "right" suspect (Wells & Olson, 2003) Furthermore, researchers have also demonstrated that cross-race identification of witnesses is sometimes problematic, witness confidence has little to do with accuracy, the presence of a weapon can redirect witness focus, and highly emotional witnesses are not always accurate (Wells & Olson, 2003).

## False Confessions

While counterintuitive to common sense, at times people will confess to crimes they have not committed. Moreover, false confessions have been found to occur in an alarming number of wrongful convictions. In fact, the Innocence Project statistics from their over 370 exonerations indicate that 29% of their cases involved a false confession (Innocence Project, n.d.). In fact, of that number, 80% of the individuals falsely confessing were under 21 years of age at the time, and 9% had mental health or mental capacity issues that were known at trial. These numbers are suggestive that those with heightened vulnerabilities are more at risk of falsely confessing to a crime they did not commit. Research into why and how false confessions occur has indicated that people who falsely confess are strongly influenced and at times induced by psychologically persuasive police interrogation techniques. Kassin (2005) also believes that while interrogation practices are the most influential, a presumption of guilt also drives the conduct of such interrogations, which in turn forces interrogators to adopt a questioning style that is highly aggressive.

The Reid technique, a highly guilt presumptive interrogation method, has been used by many police forces across the United States for several decades (Moore & Fitzsimmons, 2011). This method has been commercially marketed to police departments and other law enforcement agencies with the promise that 80% of those interrogated will confess (Kozinski, 2017). While currently somewhat out of favor,[2] due in part to the fact that it has produced a number of false as well as true confessions, many police forces are currently exploring other interrogation methods. The Reid technique involves a detailed analysis of the facts of the case but its methods are also confrontational, manipulative, and suggestive (Inbau et al., 2015). Its nine-step method is aimed at soliciting a confession from the suspect. Part of the technique requires the interrogator to engage in frequent behavioral analysis in order to "read" suspect cues as indicative of guilt or innocence. Throughout the lengthy interrogation, denials are minimized, disagreements are ignored, and alternative possible solutions are proffered, and the final step involves converting an oral confession to a written one. What is further problematic about this technique is that research has indicated that police are in fact no better than laypersons at making assumptions of guilty behavior or differentiating truth from lies and in fact may be primed to assume behaviors are indicative guilt as they may be convinced of a suspect's guilt regardless of the evidence (Kassin et al., 2003, 2005).

A case familiar to many illustrates the problems with false confessions and wrongful convictions:

> An infamous case of false confessions resulting in wrongful convictions is that of the sexual assault of the Central Park jogger in 1989. A young woman was found in Central Park in 1989, brutally attacked and raped, and had no memory of her attack or attacker (s). The police quickly focused on a group of African American and Latino youth, already in custody for a series of other attacks in the park that evening. Following several hours of police interrogation, the five defendants, Yusef Salaam, Kevin Richardson, Antron McCray, Raymond Santana and Korey Wise, all between 14–16 years of age, confessed to the attacks. The boys were lied to and coerced by the police and their confessions were inaccurate; nonetheless all five were tried and convicted the following year. The prosecution presented some forensic blood and hair evidence, pre-DNA, so only similarity comparisons were entered into evidence. Santana, Salaam, and McCray were tried as juveniles, convicted of rape and assault and sentenced to five to ten years in custody. Richardson, 14 at the time of the assault, was also tried as a youth and convicted of attempted murder, rape, sodomy, and robbery. Wise, 16 years old at the time, was tried as an adult and convicted of assault, sexual abuse, and riot; he was sentenced to five to fifteen years in prison. In 2002, Matias Reyes, an already convicted murderer and rapist admitted lone responsibility for the attack. That same year, DNA evidence from the crime scene matched Reyes and the convictions of the five teenagers were overturned. (Innocence Project, 2009)

One difficulty surrounding confession evidence is that it is very compelling at trial. Essentially, confessions are statements against one's own interests, and courts regard them as highly reliable (Moore & Fitzsimmons, 2011). Once a confession has been uttered, it is very difficult to retract it or to lessen the impact it has on a jury. Psychological research has demonstrated that certain personality traits may make individuals more susceptible to falsely confessing.

Gudjonsson's research on suggestibility indicates that certain vulnerabilities, such as youth intelligence, anxiety, memory, sleep deprivation, and coping strategies, may influence this susceptibility (Gudjonsson & Sigurdsson, 2004). Moreover, further research has demonstrated that there are different typologies of those who falsely confess, based on varying vulnerabilities and motivations, although there is little consensus regarding the most accurate among them.[3]

## Incentivized Witness: Jailhouse Informants

The testimony of incentivized witness has long been recognized in the wrongful conviction literature as contributing to miscarriages of justice; jailhouse informants are one glaring example of the difficulties with these types of witnesses. These individuals are often themselves incarcerated and provide information and evidence to authorities pertinent to an ongoing investigation likely in exchange for some sort of benefit (Guilione & Campbell, forthcoming). The Innocence Project estimates that informants have played a role in one in five of their exonerations up until 2019 (at that time they had 367 exonerations; Innocence Project, 2019). These individuals are incentivized to fabricate alleged confession evidence coming from other accused persons whom they encounter while incarcerated. This evidence is often given in exchange for benefit or leniency in the charges against them. Given the harsh reality and deprivations of prison life, it is not surprising that these people come forward.

The following case illustrates how this can happen:

> James Buckley was shot and killed in 1983 in Missouri. Following the crime Ellen Reasonover approached the police about evidence connecting two men to the murder. However, the men she identified were in jail at the time of the murder. Consequently, Reasonover became a suspect, based in part as well on her timely arrival at the crime scene. Short days later, Reasonover was charged with the murder; in custody she came into contact with Mary Ellen Lyner and Rose Jolliff. These two women testified at trial that Reasonover had confessed to killing Buckley when they shared a cell; both denied receiving any benefit from the prosecutor for their testimony. Reasonover's attorney had failed to cross-examine either witness and she was convicted of murder and sentenced to life in prison. Centurion Ministries took on the case in 1993 and found considerable exculpatory evidence as well as the fact that prosecutors had withheld information about the benefits given to the informants. Due to this and other evidence, Reasonover's conviction was vacated in 1999 and she was released.[4]

When using convicted criminals as witnesses there are always going to be difficulties regarding the reliability of their testimony. These individuals may be placing themselves in danger while incarcerated as they can be exposed as informants, targeting themselves in prison; however, the opportunity for incentives may be too great to pass up. Informant testimony is often given greater weight than it deserves in the courtroom, in part due to a number of factors. They include the jury associating the testimony with the prosecution, informants presenting well as witnesses, jury ignorance of the deprivations of prison life and the incentives to lie, and the difficulty in refuting such testimony (Sherrin, 1997). Many district attorneys' offices across the United States have now developed policies to counter the problems presented when using such testimony, based in part on research in this area.

## Official Misconduct: Police and Prosecutors

Misconduct on the part of justice officials, including both police and prosecutors, can contribute to wrongful convictions. Once a person becomes a suspect in a crime, both the police and prosecution work toward gathering evidence that supports their case against them. Police are the first point of entry into the criminal justice system, and they have considerable discretionary power regarding whom to charge, what charges should be laid, the handling and preservation of evidence, and testimony at trial. At the same time, police are part of the crime control culture and may be swept up in the pressure to find and arrest a suspect quickly (Campbell, 2018). Prosecutors, on the other hand, have the responsibility of acting on behalf of the state and presenting inculpatory evidence with a focus on winning their case. They must rely on the evidence brought to them by the police in order to charge, try, and convict an accused person. There are many stages in the processes of arrest, trial, conviction, and sentencing where errors can occur; both groups have been found to be guilty of tunnel vision – which has been thought to signify "a type of willful blindness on the part of police and prosecutors" (MacFarlane, 2008, p. 31). In practice, tunnel vision functions as an overly narrow focus on a particular investigative or prosecutorial theory, which influences how information is evaluated and acted upon, while exculpatory evidence is ignored (MacFarlane, 2008).

The NRE established that official misconduct contributed to the conviction of innocent defendants in 54% of known exoneration cases since 1989; this misconduct was further broken down by profession: prosecutors contributed 30%, police 35%, forensic analysts 3%, and child welfare workers 2% (Gross et al., 2020). In their lengthy study, Gross et al. (2020) found that there were five general categories of official misconduct, including witness tampering (17%), misconduct in interrogations (57% of those with false confessions, or 7% overall), fabricating evidence (10%), concealing exculpatory evidence (44%), and misconduct at trial (23%, including perjury by law enforcement [13%] and trial misconduct by prosecutors [14%]).

Clearly, police misconduct can take many forms. It may involve losing evidence, ignoring a suspect's *Miranda* right to counsel, ignoring exculpatory evidence, and threatening and coercive behavior, among other things. Some have described this behavior as "noble cause corruption" (Caldero et al., 2018) when police use unethical and at times unlawful practices to convict a suspect, rationalizing that the ends justify the means. In these cases, police will cut corners in their investigative practices based on a belief that the individual being pursued for a particular crime is the "true" perpetrator and it is only a matter of time before they can make an arrest. MacFarlane (2008) described this as "noble cause distortion" and for him it comprises an "ends-based police and prosecutorial culture that masks misconduct as legitimate on the basis that the guilty must be brought to justice" (p. 22).

What happened to Ricardo Aldape Guerra blatantly illustrates how egregious police misconduct can result in a wrongful conviction:

> In Houston, Texas in 1982, Aldape Guerra was driving a car, when the police pulled him over; while he attempted to comply with the police, his passenger, Roberto Carrasco Flores, shot and killed the police officer. Fleeing the scene of the crime, Carrasco Flores also shot and killed another man. While searching for the two suspects, police shot and killed Carraco Flores; Aldape Guerra was later arrested and taken to the scene of the crime. During their search of the neighborhood, the police rounded up witnesses, made them lie face-down on the ground with guns pointed at their heads, and kept many overnight in the police station. While many witnesses identified Carrasco Flores as the

shooter (three did not do so quite specifically but their statements were not recorded), the police ignored exculpatory information and willfully recorded inaccurate information; many witnesses were threatened with legal action if they failed to sign statements prepared by the police. Further, police walked a handcuffed Aldape Guerra past witnesses before asking them to identify the perpetrator. While the prosecution's case was based mainly on eyewitness identification, forensic evidence indicated that there were no traces of metal from the murder weapon on Aldape Guerra's hands. At the same time, traces were found on Carraco Flores' hands, however, this information was not revealed to the defense at trial. In 1995, this gross official misconduct was revealed and Aldape Guerra was ordered released or retried. Given that much of the eyewitness testimony from the first trial would be excluded on retrial, the state dropped charges against Aldape Guerra in 1997 and he was released. (Gross, 2012)

Prosecutors, on the other hand, are entrusted with determining who will be held accountable when a crime occurs and, as a consequence, they hold a great deal of power. Working together with the police, prosecutors gather evidence in order to build a case against a suspect. If and when the case goes to trial, prosecutors must convince a jury of the guilt of the suspect. Ultimately, it is their job to seek justice and present the judge and jury with facts and legal arguments that result in the conviction of the guilty defendant (California Innocence Project, n.d.). At the same time, prosecutors come from a culture where winning cases helps keep them in elected office; this pressure at times can result in acts of misconduct. In Berger v. United States (1935), Justice Sutherland explained prosecutorial misconduct as "overstepp [ing] the bounds of that propriety and fairness which should characterize the conduct of such an officer in the prosecution of a criminal offense" (para. 2).

The most common area of "overstepping" the bounds of propriety for prosecutors has to do with the disclosure of information of materials that come to their attention that are favorable or exculpatory to the defense. While prosecutors have a legal obligation to disclose exculpatory evidence to the defense at a criminal trial, at times such evidence is withheld. In 1963, in the case of *Brady v. Maryland* the court held that "suppression by the prosecution of evidence favorable to the accused ... violate[s] due process where the evidence is material either to guilt or to punishment" (para. 87). Failure to disclose this information is described as a *Brady* violation. While there is some debate as to what constitutes materiality, there are also other rules that govern discovery in criminal cases as well as rules of professional conduct for prosecutors that require the disclosure of evidence favorable to criminal defendants (Gross et al., 2020). Regardless, this continues to be a contributing factor in wrongful convictions.

The case of Michael Morton illustrates what happens when prosecutors intentionally withhold exculpatory evidence from the defence.

In 1986, Morton's wife was bludgeoned to death in her bed. Morton ultimately spent 25 years in prison for her murder and was released in 2011, officially exonerated when DNA evidence implicated another man that same year. Morton was convicted in large part due to the fact that a great deal of exculpatory evidence was withheld from the defence at trial, including: the fact that Morton's three year old son was present at the murder and specifically stated that his father was not home at the time; a bloody bandana discovered at a construction site 100 yards from the home that was not forensically tested; evidence of a suspicious green van in the area that was not investigated; and jewelry and credit cards from the crime scene later recovered at a nearby store. At trial, the prosecutor claimed it had turned over all exculpatory evidence to the defence; it had not. While still incarcerated, after many attempts to have exhibits tested for DNA evidence, Morton was finally successful in having the bandana and hair tested in 2011 which indicated it contained the DNA of another, unknown male. In 2013, Mark Norwood was convicted for the murder of Christine Morton and sentenced to life in prison. (Innocence Project, n.d.)

Moreover, prosecutors engage in other forms of misconduct that can result in a wrongful conviction. They include permitting perjury, lying in court, and making improper statements in closing arguments or cross-examination (Gross et al., 2020). Lawyers, whether prosecutors or defense attorneys, are not permitted to lie in court; in fact, it goes against bar association rules, and when prosecutors are aware a witness is lying, they must disclose that information to the defense. Nor are prosecutors permitted in leading testimony that they know is a lie. At the same time, when they make improper statements in closing or in cross-examination, while they may be less blatant forms of misconduct, they may mislead nonetheless. Examples would include inflammatory arguments, discussing discredited evidence, or making statements regarding knowledge or certainty of guilt (S. R. Gross et al., 2020).

Given the impact that official misconduct, from both police and prosecutors, can have on the outcome of a trial, it raises questions as to how these individuals are able to behave so unprofessionally, with impunity. In only very rare cases are officials ever held accountable for their actions, and in most instances the worst that can happen is some form of disciplinary action. In even rarer cases, criminal charges may result; however, convictions are even rarer still. This is due to a number of factors. Primarily, it takes a great deal of time to bring actions of this nature forward (disciplinary or otherwise), and even when misconduct is proven, police and prosecutors are seldom disciplined.[5] Similarly, such cases are difficult to prove as, unless the actions are blatant, government officials can justify their actions as being "necessary" in the line of duty and hence protected through qualified statutory immunity in many states.

## Problematic Forensic Sciences and Expert Testimony

The presentation of forensic evidence in courts has been found to contribute to wrongful convictions. In their many DNA exonerations, the Innocence Project discovered that difficulty with the presentation of this evidence was seen in nearly half (45%) of them and also found in one-quarter (24%) of all exonerations in the United States (Innocence Project, n.d.). Consistently, courts are relying on more and more sophisticated forensic scientific evidence in criminal cases. Given that lawyers and judges are not trained in the hard sciences and are unable to make sense of much scientific evidence on their own, courts are also increasingly relying on experts to provide testimony to courts in order to explain scientific languages, probabilities, frequencies, and research results.

Difficulties interpreting the evidence are often based on the fact that, save for DNA evidence (National Academy of Sciences, 2009), there is little to no consensus in the scientific community about the validity and reliability of much forensic evidence. A number of previously accepted forms of forensic evidence are no longer acceptable in a court of law as their reliability has not been sufficiently established in a systematic fashion, including hair microscopy, forensic odontology, and fiber evidence. There is little standardization of many scientific research methodologies; there are few large, well-designed studies to rely on; and scientists may overstate, exaggerate, or oversimplify research results or similarities (Innocence Project, n.d.). Further, conclusions may be based on very small numbers, and without proper cross-examination, the nuances in scientific findings may be lost and erroneous conclusions made – conclusions that can result in a wrongful conviction. It is important to note, however, that despite the fact that many types of evidence may not have great evidentiary value, at the same time they have value to law enforcement and potentially "provide probative information to advance a criminal investigation" (National Academy of Sciences, 2009, p. 127).

The case of Steven Barnes illustrates the difficulties associated with forensic evidence:

> Steven Barnes was convicted for the murder of Kimberly Simon in 1989 in New York state. His conviction was based on a number of factors that are now known to contribute to wrongful convictions: problematic eyewitness misidentification, faulty forensic science, and jailhouse informant testimony. Several eyewitnesses claimed to have seen his car or him walking on the road near where the victim was found. While Barnes was initially questioned and released without charges, two years following the murder he was asked to submit blood, saliva and hair samples to the police. Shortly thereafter Barnes was charged with rape, sodomy and murder. While serological evidence (blood type) was introduced at Barnes trial, it was found to be inconclusive. The criminalist at trial testified to using a photographic overlay to test fabric print evidence and determined fibres found at the crime scene were similar to those found on Barnes; she also testified that hairs from Barnes' truck were microscopically similar to that of the victim. Soil samples taken from Barnes' truck were compared to dirt from the crime scene and they were also considered similar to each other. Each of these three means of forensic testing have not been validated scientifically, as there is clearly not enough empirical data for any of these categories, hence "the analyst's assertion that these items of evidence were consistent or similar is inherently prejudicial and lacks probative value." The jailhouse informant at Barnes' trial ultimately received a one-year sentence on forgery and larceny charges. Barnes was convicted of rape and murder and sentenced to 25 years to life. The Innocence Project was involved with post-conviction efforts to help exonerate Barnes, but early DNA testing was inconclusive. In 2007, however, DNA revealed that Barnes could not have committed the crime; he was released in 2008 and charges dropped in 2009. (Innocence Project, n.d.)

Forensic evidence plays a role in both police investigations and criminal prosecutions. It can take many forms, and there appears to be little agreement as to what the term *forensic evidence* covers. Physical scientific forensic evidence generally includes fingerprints, trace evidence (hair), firearm and toolmark identification, and arson investigations (Campbell, 2018). Forensic biological evidence includes forensic pathology, toxicology, serology, DNA analysis, forensic entomology, forensic odontology, and forensic anthropology (Wecht & Rago, 2007). Pollanen et al. (2013) have identified what they term the nine "core" forensic disciplines: forensic pathology, forensic anthropology, forensic odontology, forensic nursing, forensic entomology, forensic physical evidence, forensic toxicology, forensic biology, and forensic psychiatry.

Experts are the only witnesses who are permitted to provide opinion evidence at trial. As a consequence, expert testimony is admissible in the courtroom, but case law has attempted to provide parameters to this form of testimony. The case of Frye v. United States (1923) established that expert testimony was admissible if it had been generally accepted in the relevant scientific community. Over 70 years later, in Daubert v. Merrill Dow Pharmaceuticals, Inc. (1993) the courts affirmed that experts could be used at criminal trials and their reliability safeguarded through screening by the trial judge, cross-examination, and the presentation of contrary evidence, essentially a "reliable foundation" test (Campbell, 2018,

p. 174). Later, in Khumo Tire Company Ltd v. Patrick Carmichael (1999), it was established that the scientific method was not essential for all forms of expertise as not all are based on science. Questions related more to whether the expert had developed a specialized knowledge that was sufficiently reliable (Pacciocco & Stuesser, 2015).

Not surprisingly, problems with expert testimony, particularly around forensic sciences, have also resulted in wrongful convictions, problems that emanate not from the science itself but from the conduct of the expert. Sometimes, one expert can function for many years providing testimony at trial and wreak havoc over many convictions and many lives.

> One example of a discredited expert is Steven Hayne, a quasi-official medical examiner from Mississippi who performed a number of criminal autopsies, without having the proper credentials and regularly testified in court as a forensic expert. In the case of Christopher Brandon, who was charged with the killing of his girlfriend's fifteen-month old son, Hayne had testified that the child had the symptoms of shaken baby syndrome – a controversial and largely debunked syndrome– whereas Brandon claimed the child had struck his head while falling off a bed. Brand was convicted and sentenced to life in prison. Hayne was the only expert to testify and on appeal it was discovered that he relied on false information and lied on the stand. This is not the first time Hayne attracted controversy regarding his medical practices and testimony at trial, as his testimony contributed to the wrongful convictions of Kennedy Brewer and Levon Brooks, as well as a number of other controversial convictions including Cory Maye, Jimmie Duncan and Tyler Edmonds. (Innocence Project, 2014)

While forensic evidence has the potential to provide clarity around complex, scientific phenomena, research and case law on wrongful convictions has revealed that it must be treated cautiously and necessarily supported by testimony from reliable experts in order to help the triers of fact in a criminal trial.

## Conclusion

This chapter has attempted to provide an overview of the nature and extent of wrongful convictions in the United States. While understanding the "extent" of wrongful convictions is truly an impossible task, an overall acceptance that these errors do occur and that the victims of wrongful convictions suffer as a result is important. Given that it is impossible to know how often wrongful convictions happen, simply recognizing that they do happen at all is an appropriate step toward addressing and ultimately preventing them. Presenting research and case law examples regarding the factors that contribute to wrongful convictions provides an appropriate framework for understanding how individuals become victimized by the criminal justice system in this manner.

## Notes

1 http://www.law.umich.edu/special/exoneration/Pages/Eyewitness-Identifications.aspx
2 In 2017, Wicklander-Zulawski & Associates, a consulting group that has worked with the majority of U.S. police departments training them on the Reid technique, announced it will no longer be using this method. This decision was based in part on academic research showing that it could procure false confessions, as a method that is "too risky," and that "confrontation is not an effective way of getting truthful information" (Hager, 2017).

3 See Campbell (2018) for a discussion of the many typologies.
4 https://www.law.umich.edu/special/exoneration/Pages/casedetail.aspx?caseid=3564
5 S. R. Gross et al. (2020) found that in only 2 of 727 cases of prosecutorial misconduct was a prose-cutor convicted criminally, whereas for police 127 officers were prosecuted out of 843 cases of misconduct (S. R. Gross et al., 2020, table 24).

# 4

# VICTIMIZING THE INNOCENT

## Racism, Wrongful Convictions, and Exonerations of Black men in the Criminal Legal System

*Angela Hattery and Earl Smith*

UNIVERSITY OF DELAWARE, CENTER FOR THE STUDY AND PREVENTION OF GENDER BASED VIOLENCE, NEWARK, DELAWARE, USA

"… the United States did not face a crime problem that was racialized; it faced a race problem that was criminalized."

*Anderson (2016, p. 137)*

## Introduction

It is difficult to estimate how many innocent Black men are currently imprisoned, but there are some numbers regarding those who have been exonerated of crimes for which they were wrongly convicted. The National Registry of Exonerations (NRE) has identified 2,783 exonerations since 1989 as well as 24,915 years of life lost. Many of these victims of injustices are innocent Black men; in fact, the statistics reveal that of the 2,783 exonerations approximately 1,337, or 50%, are Black men. In this chapter, the ways in which innocent Black men are victimized by the criminal legal system[1] will be explored. Further to that, the concept of innocence will be expanded beyond those who are wrongfully convicted and later exonerated to include a discussion of several racist and disturbing police practices that ensnare innocent Black Americans, and especially Black men, in the criminal legal system. This will be demonstrated by focusing on five forms of policing: (a) stop and frisk, (b) fishing expeditions, (c) the killing of unarmed Black people, (d) pretrial detention, and (e) innocent defendants who are falsely convicted. It will also focus on the fact that much of the criminal legal system in the United States is explicitly designed to take both liberty and life from Black people. This chapter will conclude with a discussion of history, arguing that by expanding our conceptualization of innocence beyond those who are identified through exoneration illuminates the interlocking elements in the criminal legal system that must be addressed, individually and collectively, to ensure that we deliver on the promises of the Constitution to *all* Americans.

## Why This Matters

This chapter is an analysis of the ways in which innocent Black men are victimized by the criminal legal system. The concept of *innocence* is expanded beyond those who are wrongfully convicted and later exonerated to include those innocent Black Americans, especially Black

DOI: 10.4324/9781003121251-5

men, who have been ensnared by several racist and disturbing police practices in the criminal legal system. Whereas other research, notably Hattery and Smith (2021) and that of Gross et al. (2017) has documented the racialized and racist causes of wrongful convictions and exonerations, this chapter moves beyond this very small but important set of cases and articulates the much more common experience of innocence in the criminal legal system and the ways in which Black men become victims of a set of racialized and racist policies, practices, and processes. As Anderson (2016) argued, the United States faces, and in fact created, deliberately and by design, a criminal legal system that criminalizes race and, more specifically, Blackness. Designing a criminal legal system based on White supremacy sets into motion the inevitable and deliberate victimization of Black people, especially Black men.

The United States prides itself on being a nation conceived in freedom and equality, of promising "liberty for all," of being one of the first nation-states to experiment with implementing the principles of democracy and serving as a role model for those around the world to emulate. As argued by Hattery and Smith (2021), in fact, the United States was founded on White supremacy and patriarchy and all of its social, political, and economic institutions were built to further the expansion of these interlocking systems of oppression. Not long after the founding of the United States, the mode of production evolved into full-blown capitalism, which, based on its core principle of exploitation and the extraction of surplus value, was easily incorporated into the foundation on which this new country was conceived and built. The criminal legal system in the United States, as Alexander (2010) and Hattery and Smith (2021) have persuasively argued, was explicitly created and designed to remove Black bodies from the social political economy, regardless of their guilt or innocence.

In this chapter, the myriad ways in which the criminal legal system has been designed and weaponized will be examined through a series of race-based policies and practices including stop and frisk, "fishing expeditions," pretrial detention, police killings of unarmed Black people, and a legal system that values punishment over innocence, such that tens of thousands of innocent Black bodies are denied liberty but also life. Too many unarmed, innocent Black people are killed by the police annually, while tens of thousands more experience civil, legal, and social death (Patterson, 1982) as they sit, never convicted of any crime, or wrongly convicted, serving time in the hundreds of jails and prisons that comprise what has been termed the Prison Industrial Complex (Hattery & Smith, 2021). They are the most recent victims of White supremacy in a long history of oppression and subjugation.

## A *Very* Brief History

Hattery and Smith (2021) argued that the history of "policing" in the United States begins with the slave patrols. Because the enslaved body held incredible value for the planter, the enslaved person who dared run away and seek freedom or the enslaved person who had the audacity to buy their own freedom or the freedom of another was defined as "stolen property" to the extent "it" should be returned to its rightful owner (Oshinsky, 1997). Slave patrols served just that function. Following emancipation, Whites feared both the economic loss as well as the possibility that the formerly enslaved might take up arms and demand justice.

The Black body, then, needed to be surveilled and controlled. Slave patrols continued and they were enhanced by Black Codes, a series of laws that allowed police officers to arrest Black people for crimes of freedom, including loitering and curfew violation. These Black bodies were then remanded to the Department of Corrections where they could be incarcerated in plantation prisons like Parchman Farm, the Mississippi State Penitentiary, or Angola in Louisiana (Oshinsky, 1997). These institutions were leased out for a pittance as plantations, known as the convict leasing system, to engage in the same agricultural work performed when enslaved or leased out to build roads and railroads and to work in turpentine production occurring throughout the state of Georgia (LeFlouria, 2016). The basis of incarceration was never really about guilt or innocence; rather, the focus was on reducing fears, ensuring the safety of White people, and providing the labor needed to sustain, at huge profit, the Southern plantation economy.

The Black Codes, sometimes called Black Laws, were early laws governing the conduct of African Americans. The best known of them were passed in 1865 and 1866 by Southern states, after the American Civil War, in order to restrict African Americans' freedom and to compel them to work for low wages. In 1832, James Kent wrote that

> in most of the United States, there is a distinction in respect to political privileges, between free White persons and free coloured persons of African blood; and in no part of the country do the latter, in point of fact, participate equally with the Whites, in the exercise of civil and political rights. (p. 258)

What these early examples illustrate are the roots of modern-day racial oppression, over-incarceration, and racist criminal justice and policing practices.

## Critical Race Theory and Intersectionality

Critical race theory and intersectionality are two frameworks for analyzing the data presented in this chapter. Critical race theory was originally developed by legal scholars such as Richard Delgado and Jean Stefancic (2017) as a framework for exposing the role that social structures, and White supremacy in particular, played in shaping the legal foundation on which the United States was built. Critical race theorists argued that every social institution in the United States, from public education to health care to the legal system, must be interrogated through a lens focused on illuminating the role that White supremacy played in not just creating but also in maintaining these structures. Critical race theory requires an examination of the role that power and privilege play in the founding of the United States as well as in the development of policies and practices that facilitate the removal of Black bodies from the social political economy (Bonilla-Silva, 1997).

The most fundamental assumption that supports the arguments presented in this chapter is the assertion that the "carceral state" is, in structure and formation, built entirely on the system of racism and White supremacy. Though his research is not focused on prisons, sociologist Victor Ray's work on "racialized organizations" is important to an interrogation of the criminal legal system as a set of racialized structures. Ray (2019) argued:

> Race is constitutive of organizational foundations, hierarchies, and processes [and comprises] ... four tenets: (1) racialized organizations enhance or diminish the agency of racial groups; (2) racialized organizations legitimate the unequal distribution of resources; (3) Whiteness is a credential; and (4) the decoupling of formal rules from organizational practice is often racialized. I argue that racialization theory must account for how both state policy and individual attitudes are filtered through—and changed by—organizations. Seeing race as constitutive of organizations helps us better understand the formation and everyday functioning of organizations. Incorporating organizations into a

structural theory of racial inequality can help us better understand stability, change, and the institutionalization of racial inequality. (pp. 27–28)

Intersectionality is also a useful concept for situating the discussion in this chapter. It was Black feminist theorists like bell hooks (2003) and Hill Collins (2016) who first illustrated the concept of intersectionality with the image of a matrix. Hill Collins called this the "matrix of domination" (Hill Collins, 2016, p. 227). The matrix is composed of various systems of domination: racial domination, patriarchal, class domination (capitalism), heteronormative domination, ableism, religious superiority – all are woven together in a mutually reinforcing structure.

In her latest text, Hill Collins and co-author Bilge (2020) extended the concept of intersectionality as an analytical tool beyond the image of the matrix of domination. They argued that in order to use intersectionality to understand contemporary social issues, intersectionality must be conceived of as being composed of several core ideas: relationality, social context, power, inequality, and social justice. In other words, when examining any phenomenon, attention must be focused on the social context in which it exists, the ways in which inequality is structured and distributed, which groups put the current structures in place (power), and how they benefit from the current structures (relationality). Lastly, intersectionality is not merely an analytical tool; it is a call to action (social justice).

Consequently, Hill Collins (2016) underscored that intersectionality is relational. In 1952, Fanon wrote about the relational context of slavery: there can be no slave without a master, but there can also be no master without the slave. Oppression does not exist in a vacuum; every act of oppression benefits someone, and every benefit is also the direct result of an extraction or exploitation. The plantation owner's wealth is created by the exploitation of the enslaved person's labor as well as the ownership of the enslaved body as a commodity that can be traded and sold. In modern terms, dozens of multinational corporations, including Victoria's Secret and McDonald's, increase their profits by exploiting the labor of incarcerated Black bodies. White, wealthy politicians fill up the seats in congress, making policy that reduces access to food stamps, student loan debt relief, and health care, in part because of the felony disenfranchisement of Black voters. An intersectional framework therefore advances an understanding of the experiences of Black people, Black families, and Black communities because it illuminates the oppression experienced by Black people alongside the privileges that are simultaneously accruing to Whites – individuals, families, and the broader White community. Quite frankly, if White supremacy were toppled and racial equality became a reality, White people and White communities would lose not only wealth but also the power and control to dictate the terms of literally every aspect of the lives of those living in the United States, from policing practices to college admissions to voting restrictions to mortgage lending. White people and White communities have a vested interest in maintaining the criminal legal system and the racialized order that the United States was founded and built upon.

## The Modern-Day Carceral State

It has been argued that beginning in and around 1980 up to today, the criminal legal system in the United States has been harnessed to victimize Black people by removing them from full participation in the social political economy (Alexander, 2010; Hattery & Smith, 2021). Beginning with President Nixon's declaration of a "war on drugs," through President Reagan's expansion of the war on drugs and then President Bill Clinton's signature on the 1994

"Crime Bill" (Violent Crime Control Act and Law Enforcement Act of 1994, 1994), the U. S. government has been waging a thinly disguised war on Black people. Black men are the main victims in this war.

There has long been speculation that the so-called war on drugs targeted Black people, but until the spring of 2016 there was no convincing proof. In research for a book, Baum (2016) attempted to answer the question, "How did the United States entangle itself in a policy of drug prohibition that has yielded so much misery and so few good results?" In Baum's interview with John Ehrlichman, who had been Nixon's domestic policy advisor when the original war on drugs began, Erlichman's response was the following:

> "You want to know what this was really all about?" he asked with the bluntness of a man who, after public disgrace and a stretch in federal prison, had little left to protect. "The Nixon campaign in 1968, and the Nixon White House after that, had two enemies: the antiwar left and Black people. You understand what I'm saying? We knew we couldn't make it illegal to be either against the war or blacks, but by getting the public to associate the hippies with marijuana and blacks with heroin, and then criminalizing both heavily, we could disrupt those communities. We could arrest their leaders, raid their homes, break up their meetings, and vilify them night after night on the evening news. Did we know we were lying about the drugs? Of course we did." (Baum, 2016)

As a result of the war on drugs, in 2021, nearly 2.5 million Americans are incarcerated, with as many as 8 million more under the supervision and control of the criminal legal system vis-à-vis parole, probation, and electronic monitoring ("e-carceration"). And, despite making up only 6% of the total U.S. population, Black men account for *half* of all those incarcerated or otherwise under the control of the criminal legal system in the United States. In other words, Black men are 8.5 times more likely to be incarcerated, on parole or probation, or wearing an ankle bracelet relative to their representation in the population. The war on drugs has effectively removed millions of Black people from the social political economy, first through incarceration and second through a series of policies that place significant limits on the rights of individuals with a felony record, a status held by perhaps one-third of Black men, including 70% of Black men without a high school diploma. In reality, Nixon's thinly veiled war on Black people has been highly effective.

Furthermore, the Innocence Project and other legal scholars (for example, Gross et al., 2017) researching "mass incarceration" estimate that, at a minimum, as many as 6% of all persons who are incarcerated are factually innocent. In other words, on any given day there are likely 120,000 to 160,000 innocent men and women confined in jails and prisons throughout the United States and likely tens of thousands more serving supervised time on parole, probation, or e-carceration (Garrett, 2011). Consistent with prison statistics cited above, that translates into tens of thousands of Black Americans who are wrongly convicted.

## The Innocent Victims

Given that the focus of this book is on the victimology of wrongful convictions, part of this chapter will examine the ways in which wrongful convictions and the exonerations that attempt to rectify them are racialized. At the same time, this chapter will also broaden the umbrella and consider the fact that most innocent people who are incarcerated or under the supervision and control of the criminal legal system will never be exonerated. Some may never even be convicted, and yet they serve days, weeks, months, and even years in the worst jails and prisons in the United States – indeed, in the world. Their stories are an important and often neglected part of the larger discussion of innocent victims behind bars. The following practices illustrate how this comes about.

## Stop and Frisk

As part of the war on drugs, many police departments instituted a practice known as "stop and frisk." Stop and frisk not only allowed but indeed encouraged police officers to stop people they think might possess drugs or weapons and search them for contraband. A series of court decisions upheld this practice until 2013 when it was repealed in New York City after it was discovered to be racially discriminatory. For the years it was in place, however, thousands, and perhaps tens of thousands, of Black people, mainly teenagers and younger men, had their bodies subjected to the surveillance of the criminal legal system through this practice. And, as Justice Sotomayor argued in Utah v. Strieff (2016), even if one is not found to be carrying drugs or weapons or is acquitted at a later time, much of the damage has already been done.

In the case of Utah v. Strieff (2016), Mr. Strieff was leaving a suspected drug house and an officer followed him to a local convenience store where he initiated a "stop." The officer asked Mr. Strieff for his driver's license so that he could verify his identity, and when he ran his ID, he discovered a warrant for an unpaid traffic ticket. Based on this discovery, the officer searched Mr. Strieff and found a small amount of methamphetamine and he was arrested and charged with felony drug possession. Mr. Strieff argued that the arrest was illegal because the search, without a warrant, violated the Fourth Amendment. Writing in the dissent, Justice Sonia Sotomayor argued:

> The Court today holds that the discovery of a warrant for an unpaid parking ticket will forgive a police officer's violation of your Fourth Amendment rights. Do not be soothed by the opinion's technical language: This case allows the police to stop you on the street, demand your identification, and check it for outstanding traffic warrants—even if you are doing nothing wrong. If the officer discovers a warrant for a fine you forgot to pay, courts will now excuse his illegal stop and will admit into evidence anything he happens to find by searching you after arresting you on the warrant. Because the Fourth Amendment should prohibit, not permit, such misconduct, I dissent. (*Utah v. Strieff*, 2016, para. 12)

Justice Sotomayor went on to argue that unwarranted searches are humiliating and that they more often than not target Black bodies and others from communities of color. She further stated:

> The officer's control over you does not end with the stop. If the officer chooses, he may handcuff you and take you to jail for doing nothing more than speeding, jay-walking, or "driving [your] pickup truck ... with [your] 3-year-old son and 5-year-old daughter ... without [your] seatbelt fastened." ... At the jail, he can fingerprint you, swab DNA from the inside of your mouth, and force you to "shower with a delousing agent" while you "lift [your] tongue, hold out [your] arms, turn around, and lift [your] genitals." ... Even if you are innocent, you will now join the 65 million Americans with an arrest record and experience the "civil death" of discrimination by employers, landlords, and whoever else conducts a background check.

And, of course, if you fail to pay bail or appear for court, a judge will issue a warrant to render you "arrestable on sight" in the future. This case involves a suspicionless stop, one in which the officer initiated this chain of events without justification. As the Justice Department notes, many innocent people are subjected to the humiliations of these unconstitutional searches. The White defendant in this case shows that anyone's dignity can be violated in this manner. ... But it is no secret that people of color are disproportionate victims of this type of scrutiny. ...

For generations, black and brown parents have given their children "the talk"—instructing them never to run down the street; always keep your hands where they can be seen; do not even think of talking back to a stranger—all out of fear of how an officer with a gun will react to them. (*Utah v. Strieff*, 2016, para. 12)

And, as Justice Sonia Sotomayor confirmed in her dissent, these policies target Black bodies, and they continue to contribute to locking up Black people far away from mainstream culture and economic opportunity, thrusting them, their families, and their communities further into peril. Furthermore:

By legitimizing the conduct that produces this double consciousness, this case tells everyone, White and black, guilty and innocent, that an officer can verify your legal status at any time. It says that your body is subject to invasion while courts excuse the violation of your rights. It implies that you are not a citizen of a democracy but the subject of a carceral state, just waiting to be cataloged. We must not pretend that the countless people who are routinely targeted by police are "isolated." They are the canaries in the coal mine whose deaths, civil and literal, warn us that no one can breathe in this atmosphere. They are the ones who recognize that unlawful police stops corrode all our civil liberties and threaten all our lives. Until their voices matter too, our justice system will continue to be anything but. (*Utah v. Strieff*, 2016, para. 12)

### Racial Profiling: AKA Fishing Expeditions

Extant literature documents the fact that Black people are disproportionately represented as victims in traffic stops (Pierson et al., 2020). Black people have always known that their communities are overpoliced (see, especially, the National Advisory Commission on Civil Disorders, known as the Kerner Commission, 1968), and not necessarily because there is more crime in Black communities. However, the U.S. Department of Justice (2015) report, which was conducted after the murder of Mike Brown and the protests in Ferguson, Missouri, provided insight into just how much overpolicing occurs in the Black community of Ferguson. According to the report:

Ferguson uses its police department in large part as a collection agency for its municipal court. Ferguson's municipal court issues arrest warrants at a rate that police officials have called, in internal emails, "staggering." According to the court's own figures, as of December 2014, over 16,000 people had outstanding arrest warrants that had been issued by the court. In fiscal year 2013 alone, the court issued warrants to approximately 9,007 people. Many of those individuals had warrants issued on multiple charges, as the 9,007 warrants applied to 32,975 different offenses. (U.S. Department of Justice, 2021, p. 55)

This investigation conducted in Ferguson also revealed a long-standing, widespread, but often invisible practice of using ticket quotas to fund local law enforcement agencies. Quite simply, officers were charged with writing a certain number of traffic tickets each shift in order to generate revenue for their departments. According to the Council of Economic Advisors (2015) report,

> In a high-profile example of this practice, a Department of Justice investigation of the Ferguson Police Department in Missouri showed that the town of Ferguson set revenue targets for criminal justice fines and fees of over $3 million in 2015, covering over 20 percent of the town's operating budget. (p. 2)

Hayes (2017) revealed even more insidious practices that target Black bodies and police them in order to extract monetary resources in his book. He stated:

> The model of cops as armed tax collectors didn't stop with simple traffic stops for speeding: the entire municipal court system was designed to function as a payday lending operation. Relatively small infractions quickly turned into massive debts. Many traffic citations required the ticketed person to make court appearances, but the local court would hold sessions only three to four times a month for just a few hours. Because of the limited hours, the court couldn't process everyone who came for their court date. Those left outside were cited for contempt for failing to appear. Not coming to court triggered another fine, and failure to pay that fine counted as its own form of contempt, adding to the total. (Hayes, 2017, p. 84)

According to Hayes, the Department of Justice report identifies one woman who ended up owing nearly $1,500 for a $151 parking ticket because of the payday lending apparatus operated by the municipal court in Ferguson, Missouri. Clearly, some of the people who are cited for traffic violations are guilty, but as Epp et al. (2014) revealed, many of the traffic stops that Black citizens endure do not, in fact, result in an arrest or the seizure of drugs or weapons, nor do they constitute a "legitimate" traffic stop. What this unmistakably reveals is victimization based on race.

Based on more than a thousand interviews, the careful research by Epp et al. (2014) revealed that police stops fall into two categories: legitimate stops and "fishing expeditions." Legitimate stops involve stops for speeding 10 to 20 miles over the speed limit, stops for erratic driving, patterns that might signal distracted driving, running stop signs and stop lights, and the like. In fact, there were very few racial differences and no racial disparities in legitimate stops in terms of either the likelihood of being stopped or the way drivers experienced the stop. Both Blacks and Whites who reported on these kinds of stops indicated that they were over quickly: usually the officer simply wrote a ticket and the driver was allowed to go on their way.

In sharp contrast, fishing expeditions were highly racialized in terms of both the likelihood of being stopped and the driver's experience of the stop. When President Obama proclaimed after the death of Philando Castile that Blacks are 30% more likely to be pulled over, he was referencing these fishing expeditions. And, in fact, this is exactly what Epp et al. (2014) argued took place in the case of Philando Castile. Fishing expeditions involve officers pulling over people they suspect might be engaged in criminal activity (with "might be" being a very loose term). As these authors argued, because the officer has no legitimate reason to stop the motorist, the driver often becomes suspicious and agitated. The "warrior police officer," engaging their "killology," approaches the driver, who is already suspect of the police officer's motive, and the violence escalates rapidly, too often tragically, resulting in the officer taking the life of the motorist (Epp et al., 2014).

Some would argue that this practice allows police officers to preemptively stop people who might be engaged in criminal activity. But as the data in the 2014 study by Epp et al. revealed, in fact the person stopped is rarely engaged in any criminal activity. While White motorists are pulled over less often than Black drivers and they are less likely to be subjected to having their vehicle searched, White drivers are 20% more likely to be discovered with evidence of criminal activity, such as drugs or stolen goods, than Black drivers. In other words, police officers "get it right" 20% more often when they pull over White drivers, but they pull over White drivers 30% less frequently. This raises numerous questions: How many White people engaged in criminal activity are missed in these racially motivated fishing expeditions? And how many Black bodies are policed and even murdered over fishing expeditions that had no basis in reality and ended in unnecessary tragedy? Is this the most efficient use of police resources? There are few businesses that would be profitable with this high level of false positives and missed positives. It is not surprising that Black people often report feeling harassed by the police. Sadly, those interviewed in the study by Epp et al. reported that when they saw the blue police lights flashing in their rearview mirrors, they hoped it was for a legitimate stop, even though that meant a fine, instead of a fishing expedition, which could result in them being beaten, tased, or even killed.

In short, fishing expeditions, like stop and frisk, are deliberate strategies that target Black people under the guise of policing. And, though these practices may result in some drugs and weapons being taken off the streets, more often than not it is innocent people who are stopped and pulled into the criminal legal system. These individuals then find themselves having to navigate a complex system that, in cases like Ferguson, make it incredibly difficult to pay a simple traffic ticket; these individuals may find themselves locked up on contempt or failure to pay charges, which can result in them having to find the funds to make bail. These are funds they would have used to pay the original ticket if they had just been allowed to send in the check through the mail, the way millions of Americans pay all kinds of bills each month. At the extreme, as the study by Epp et al. (2014) revealed, these fishing expeditions can escalate quickly and the person who is pulled over allegedly for a burned-out taillight or expired license may wind up dead, as both Sandra Bland and Philando Castille did.

## Police Killings of Unarmed Black people

Tragically, too many Black people (mainly men) who are both unarmed and innocent are killed at the hands of the police; they are victims of police homicide. As Hattery and Smith (2021) argued, most often Black people are killed either because the violence escalates during a fishing expedition or because police officers invoke stereotypes of Black people, Black men in particular, that paint them as monsters. As noted, both Sandra Bland and Philando Castille died as a result of police violence that escalated during a fishing expedition. Neither had been convicted of a crime; both were legally innocent. In fact, fishing expeditions, though most often associated with traffic stops, are also a feature of stop and frisk. Conceptualized in this way, this includes many more police killings of unarmed Black people, including George Floyd, Eric Garner, Alton Sterling, and even Breonna Taylor, who was the victim of a fatal shooting during the execution of a botched no-knock warrant (Oppel et al., 2021).

Other innocent Black people are killed by the police because the police perceive them – or so they claim – as a threat. In the deposition police officer Darren Wilson gave after the murder of Mike Brown, he described Mike Brown as being "like the hulk." Wilson and Brown are about the same height, and though Brown outweighed Wilson by 60 or so pounds, Wilson is also a big man, standing 6 feet 5 inches, and reportedly weighing 210 pounds at the time of the murder. And yet, according to documents from the grand jury hearing, published by National Public Radio, Wilson claimed, "And when I grabbed him, the only way I can describe it is I felt like a 5-year-old holding onto Hulk Hogan" (Calamur, 2014, para. 9). The police officer who killed 12-year-old Tamir Rice said after the murder that he feared for his life. Rice was a child of 12 years, playing with a toy gun as so many children do every day in their backyards or in local parks or on playgrounds. George Zimmerman, the police surrogate who killed Trayvon Martin, also believed he (and his community) were being threatened. Whether or not any of these statements are in fact true, what remains true is that police kill unarmed, innocent Black people.

## Overrepresentation of Black Accused Persons in Pretrial Detention

Many people assume that only guilty people are incarcerated, while, in fact, not only are innocent people convicted and incarcerated for crimes they did not commit but estimates are that 20% to 30% of all people incarcerated in American jails and prisons are incarcerated because they cannot afford to pay a fine or a fee. The most common case is that seen in the numbers on pretrial detention. Those on pretrial detention include as many as a half a million (20% of 2.5 million) people who are confined in jails not yet having been convicted of a crime; they are legally innocent. Contrary to what many people may believe about pretrial detention, the majority of people who are confined prior to trial are not violent criminals; rather, they are the poor, and are disproportionately Black, who simply cannot afford bail. Unable to make bail, they sit in jail awaiting their day in court.

In her book, Buser (2015) detailed her time working as a mental health specialist in the notorious Rikers Island jail and offered a personal account of an inmate she worked with named Hector Rodriquez:

> Most of the boroughs have their own jailhouse, but because of the huge number of people arrested, most are held here at Rikers. The thing is, the smaller jails are closer to home, easier for family visits. … I was confused. Hector Rodriquez has been arrested and charged with a crime that he may or may not have committed. He had yet to have his day in court. But, in the interim, because he couldn't make bail—for lack of a few hundred dollars—he was remanded to an inaccessible island. His pretrial incarceration was not a question of guilt or innocence—it was a question of money! (pp. 120–21)

Having one's liberty restricted represents a serious human rights violation, and, just as with an exoneree, one's innocence does not protect one from the torture and trauma of jail. Of equal concern is the fact that pretrial detention is a significant driver of mass incarceration because those held pretrial are far more likely to accept deals and plead guilty, even if they are not, simply to reduce their overall sentence.

Stevenson's (2018) research on the impact of pretrial detention on the risk of pleading guilty, fines and fees, and length of sentence in Philadelphia confirmed what research in Los Angeles and other jurisdictions has found:

I find that pretrial detention leads to a 13% increase in the likelihood of being convicted, an effect largely explained by an increase in guilty pleas among defendants who otherwise would have been acquitted or had their charges dropped. Pretrial detention also leads to a 41% increase in the amount of non-bail court fees owed and a 42% increase in the length of the incarceration sentence. I find large gaps in the pretrial detention rate across the race and neighborhood wealth levels of defendants, partially accounted for by differences in the likelihood of posting monetary bail. *If black defendants posted bail at the same rate as non-black defendants, their average detention rate would decrease by 6 percentage points, or half of the entire race gap in detention.* (n.p., emphasis ours)

Buser (2015) also shared an account from a prisoner that affirmed Stevenson's overall finding that pretrial detention "encourages" accepting a guilty plea:

"I must have been nuts to think I was going to trial. In the time it takes to sit here and wait for trial, I could serve the same time upstate and go home. It just doesn't make sense. If I had the money for bail, it would be a different story—I could wait it out. But I don't." Hesitating for a moment, he added, "I know I'll have to take a felony, Miss B. But there's nothing I can do about it. I'll lose my job, but I'll get something else. I'll find something." (p. 175)

As stated, clearly, being innocent does not protect incarcerated people from the trauma of jail. Two cases that illustrate the devastating consequences of pretrial detention on incarcerating people who have never been convicted of a crime, and are therefore presumed innocent, are those of Sandra Bland and Kalief Browder.

Ms. Bland was stopped on a stretch of road leading to Prairie View College in Prairie View, Texas. The violence escalated quickly, and she was restrained, arrested, and placed in a jail cell. She was found dead on July 13, 2015, 3 days after being jailed. The coroner in Waller County, Texas, ruled the death a suicide, though her family and many others have disputed that claim. Extending the analysis of the study by Epp et al. (2014), it is likely that Sandra Bland was the victim of a fishing expedition, or what otherwise might be termed as "driving while Black," in a neighborhood where she was not expected to be but otherwise was doing nothing wrong. The violence in this case escalated rapidly, and Sandra Bland died as a result. Essentially, Sandra Bland died quite simply because she couldn't pay the $500 bail that would have set her free. In the HBO documentary *Say Her Name* (2018), her family members express the grief they feel over their loved one's death. Sandy, as they called her, died because she was too poor to afford bail; she was legally innocent and had not been convicted of a crime. She died an innocent person in police custody. Such a senseless death raises the question as to what price an innocent person should have to pay.

Kalief Browder, who was 17 at the time he was arrested, was incarcerated at the notorious Rikers Island jail for allegedly having stolen a backpack. He spent 3 years locked up on Rikers Island, including more than 400 days in solitary confinement. Shortly after his release, he committed suicide. Moreover, in the wake of George Floyd's death at the hands of the police, his brother, Philonise Floyd, testified before the United States Congress and said, "I am asking you, is that what a black man's life is worth? Twenty dollars?" (The Hill Staff, 2020). In the context of pretrial detention, such a question becomes "Is that all a Black person's life is worth—the $500 of bail money?"

It also raises the question as to why the families of Sandra Bland and Kalief Browder did not pay the $500 bail or the required 10% ($50) plus $500 in property to secure the loan to a bail bondsperson to get their loved ones released. The answer is that they simply did not have the money. While this might be surprising, when the incredible racial wealth gap is considered, such disparities are revealed to be commonplace.

## The Racial Wealth Gap

On average, White families have ten times more wealth than Black families. The average White family has $170,000 in wealth (assets minus debts) compared to an average of only $17,000 for Black families. Digging more deeply, when we examine just the poorest, those in the bottom 40% of the income distribution, not only does the racialized gap in wealth remain but poor Blacks have no wealth—not even enough to pay the bail bondsperson $50. The bottom 20% of the income distribution – in other words, the poorest 20% of people living in the United States – have almost zero wealth, and there isn't even a bar for poor Blacks. Estimates are that the poorest Whites have just a few hundred dollars and the poorest Blacks have negative wealth – in other words, they have debt that exceeds anything they own.

While it is difficult to conceptualize how one could have negative wealth, if individuals rent and do not own property and vehicles, have substantial personal debt, and are living hand to mouth, then it is possible to declare negative wealth. Moreover, in such instances it would be impossible to find $50 for a bail bondsman, plus collateral to secure a $500 bond. Innocent people like Sandra Bland and Kalief Browder not only had their liberty and their freedom denied but also lost their lives, over $50.

## Wrongful Convictions and Exonerations

Wrongful convictions, it can be argued, are the most egregious form of racialized victimization in the criminal legal system. Jackson et al. (2021) demonstrated that a wrongful conviction denies an innocent person their liberty (and in some cases their life) and results in people serving decades in prison for crimes they did not commit, more than half of whom are Black men. It is clear that

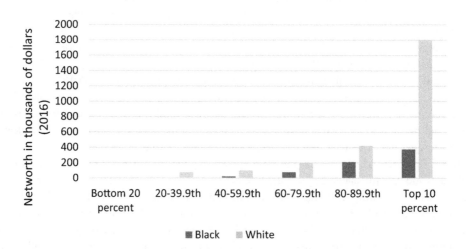

**FIGURE 4.1** Median Net Worth by Household Income and Race. Courtesy Hamilton Project (2020), Brookings Institution.

wrongful convictions and exonerations are highly racialized (Smith & Hattery, 2011) and are the result of the racist practices discussed above. Innocent Black men are victims when they are stopped and frisked and literally "fished out" of their homes and communities, dragged into police stations, interrogated for hours, denied counsel, coerced into confessions, and tried, convicted, and sentenced to prison for decades, often for life, and sometimes even sentenced to death.

As research has demonstrated, Black men are even more overrepresented among the innocent who were wrongfully convicted and later exonerated than they are in the criminal legal system more generally (Gross et al., 2017; Hattery & Smith, 2021). Gross et al. (2017) revealed that

> African Americans are only 13% of the American population but a majority of innocent defendants wrongfully convicted of crimes and later exonerated. They constitute 47% of the 1,900 exonerations listed in the National Registry of Exonerations (as of October 2016), and the great majority of more than 1,800 additional innocent defendants who were framed and convicted of crimes in 15 large-scale police scandals and later cleared in "group exonerations."
>
> (p. 1)

In their analysis, Hattery and Smith (2021) included an examination of 2,706 of the NRE exonerations as of January 2021 and found that adding more cases to the population magnifies rather than diminishes the power of race. Of all exonerations to date from 1989 through 2020 there have been approximately 2,706 exonerations, and native-born Black Americans (mostly men) account for 1,337 or 50%, yet they account for only 13% of the total U.S. population, or approximately 40 million people. Young Black men of the age when most crimes are committed (early 20s-early 30s) account for approximately 2% of the U.S. population and yet represent 50% of all exonerations. Understood differently, Black men, outside of the crime of homicide – committed against each other – are no more criminal than men of all other races/ethnicities in the United States (Gross et al., 2017).

As with every other phenomenon discussed in this chapter, wrongful convictions and exonerations are a story about victimization and race. But unlike the stories that illustrate the racial bias in stop and frisk or even in the killings of unarmed Black people, the racialized story of wrongful convictions and exonerations is one that illuminates the deepest, darkest parts of American history. Although Black men are overrepresented among exonerations, and presumably among wrongful convictions as well, they are not overrepresented proportionally in all crimes. Instead, exoneration clusters and Black men are significantly overrepresented among just two types of crimes: rape and homicide. Gross and colleagues (2017) found that innocent Black men are *seven times* more likely to be wrongfully convicted of homicide than White men.

Further analyses revealed that exonerations cluster around wrongful convictions in one particular type of crime: cases where Black men have been convicted of the rape and/or murder of White women (Figure 4.2).

Early exoneration research that was more legally oriented paid little attention to the role that race played in exonerations. Scholars such as Hattery and Smith interested in the racialization of exonerations built a unique data set using a variety of sources, including data provided by the Innocence Project (New York City), data from University of Virginia law professor Brandon L. Garrett, data from the Centurion Ministries, and data from the NRE at the University of Michigan Law School.

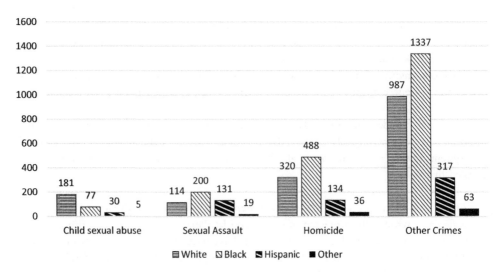

**FIGURE 4.2** Exonerations by Race and Crime. Courtesy of the Innocence Project (2021).

Moreover, they researched the profiles of exonerees and searched the local newspapers where the crimes had originally occurred for any additional data, particularly data on the race of the victim, which was often not reported in the case summary published by the Innocence Project or contained in other data sources. Despite that fact that exonerations continued to occur, a decision was made to "close" the data collection at the end of 2014; ultimately their data set contains 1,358 cases of Black men convicted of rape and/or murder of White women and later exonerated (Hattery & Smith, 2021).

Perhaps what is most interesting about exonerations is that they often cluster in cases that are otherwise extremely uncommon. Unfortunately, Hattery and Smith (2021) were unable to always confirm the race of both the victim of the crime and the person exonerated from their sample, likely due to one of two reasons. First, if most of the research is conducted by legal scholars who are less interested in racial patterns than the facts of the case, they may not report the race of the victim in the case summaries and databases that they develop. Secondly, in cases of rape where the victim is not murdered, rape shield laws protect the identity of the victim, including her name and race. Thus, in many cases where the race of the exoneree was evident, it was sometimes difficult to identify the race of the victim. As a result, when examining the clustering of exonerations that focused on the interaction between the race of the victim and the race of the exoneree, there were a smaller number of cases (504), to analyze, which is a statistically meaningful sample size, given such a relatively rare phenomenon, from a total of only 1,358 cases with which to work.

Though most crimes are *intraracial*, especially violent crimes like murder and rape, the vast majority of exonerations occur in cases of *interracial* crime. Even more troubling is that there is one particular interracial configuration that is disproportionately represented among exonerations: despite the fact that Black men murdering White victims accounts for only 7% of all homicides, it accounts for 56% of all exonerations. Exonerations thus follow a pattern that is the exact opposite of the pattern of actual crimes committed. Black men commit only 16% of the rapes perpetrated against White women's bodies, and yet the rape and/or murder of a White woman by a Black man is the most common crime for which there are wrongful convictions and subsequent exonerations. A crime that rarely occurs accounts for the majority (87%) of the exonerations examined by Hattery and Smith (2021). In other words, Black men are 5.4 times more likely to be exonerated for raping White women compared to the number of times they actually commit this crime (Figure 4.3).

This clustering of exonerations has been found by other scholars, and when death penalty cases were analyzed, the most common case where a death sentence was handed down is the murder of a White person by a Black man (Baldus et al., 1983). Black bodies, whether they are victims or perpetrators, rarely get justice; Black bodies are always undervalued. When Black people perpetrate crimes, it is comparatively easier to send them to the death chamber, and when Black bodies are the victims of violent crime, the perpetrator is held "less" accountable. The message behind these trends is that when a violent crime is perpetrated on a Black body, it is somehow less serious than a violent crime perpetrated against a White body. When Black people kill other Black people, there is often no investigation at all, the assumption being that the homicide is gang related or that the Black person's life is not important enough to investigate or that they will not even be missed.

## Case Studies: The Central Park Five and Darryl Hunt

On April 19, 1989, while jogging in the park at approximately 9 o'clock in the evening in New York City's Central Park, Trisha Meili, a 28-year-old White woman investment banker at the financial firm Salomon Brothers, was brutally beaten, raped, sodomized, and left for dead (Meili, 2003). For several weeks after the assault, Trisha Meili lay in a coma from a loss of blood, having had her head bashed in, and suffering from hypothermia, and her left eye

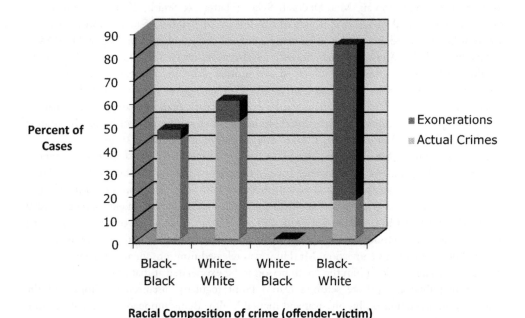

**FIGURE 4.3** Exonerations in Relation to Crimes Committed

was removed from the socket. During this time, New York City police conducted their investigation of the crime and initially identified six suspects (later reduced to five) who had been in the park at the same time as the victim.

Five *teenagers of color* – including Antron McCray, Kevin Richardson, Raymond Santana, Khory Wise, and Yusef Salaam – were arrested, and soon thereafter four, except for Salaam, confessed to committing the crime. Despite no concrete evidence connecting any of the youth to the crime, emerging doubts by those associated with the case, a lack of forensic evidence, and contradictory eyewitness accounts, the police and prosecutors continued to pursue the prosecution of these innocent young Black men. And in the case of the Central Park jogger, much like the murder of Deborah Sykes (discussed below) in Winston–Salem, there was tremendous pressure on the police to make an arrest. During the case, former president Donald Trump, at that time a real estate mogul in New York City, took out a full-page ad in the New York Times calling for the death penalty in this case. What mattered little was whether the police had the right suspect(s).

Like most cases in which eyewitnesses misidentify suspects or prosecutors conduct their business in ways that are at best unprofessional and at worst unethical, the real perpetrator(s) remained free to continue to ravage innocent people.[2] In this case, the real perpetrator, who was a lone rapist in the case of the Central Park jogger, remained free for several years. In 2002, while in prison for other unrelated crimes, convicted serial rapist and murderer Matias Reyes, a Puerto Rican–born man serving a life sentence for other crimes, confessed to being the Central Park rapist. Antron McCray, Kevin Richardson, Raymond Santana, Khorey Wise, and Yusef Salaam were exonerated later that same year.

The case of Darryl Hunt was, in the words of his attorney Mark Rabil, the quintessential southern crime: Darryl Hunt was a Black man who was wrongly convicted of the rape and murder of a White woman, Mrs. Deborah Sykes (Hattery & Smith, 2021). Moreover, the case tore at the racial divide that is part of the history of Winston–Salem, North Carolina, where it had occurred, just as it is in so many southern communities. On August 11, 1984, a copy editor for the Winston–Salem *Sentinel*, an afternoon newspaper, 26-year-old Deborah Brotherton Sykes was found brutally raped and murdered behind an apartment complex in downtown Winston–Salem. She had been attacked on her way to work in the early morning hours. In September 1984, Darryl Hunt, a 19-year-old Black man, was arrested and charged with her rape and murder. One year later, Hunt was tried and convicted; he barely escaped the death penalty and was sentenced to life imprisonment at the age of 19 years.

From the moment Mr. Hunt was arrested, a handful of local residents who were convinced from the very beginning of his innocence banded together to advocate for him. After Mr. Hunt had spent nearly 20 years in prison, an investigative journalist at the *Winston–Salem Journal* began what turned out to be a nearly year-long investigation that culminated in an eight-part series that ran in December 2005. Based on her work and some other evidence in the case – including DNA testing of Mr. Hunt and another man who was suspected of being the real perpetrator – nearly 2 decades after his conviction, Mr. Hunt was released from prison, and in February 2006 he was exonerated, making him the 150th person to be exonerated at that time.

In both public and private settings, Darryl Hunt regularly discussed the impact of the trauma of incarceration on his physical and mental health. Being innocent did not shield him from the violence of incarceration. He endured death threats from skinheads and correctional officers who believed he had raped a White woman. He spent hundreds of days in solitary confinement. All of this took a significant toll. And, sadly, fewer than 10 years after regaining his freedom and working to rebuild his life, Mr. Hunt took his own life. In the words of his attorney, Mark Rabil, Mr. Hunt's death sentence was finally executed.

The stories of Darryl Hunt and the Central Park Five share much in common, and these cases are more the norm than the exception. What occurred in Mr. Hunt's case is evidence of a pattern, one that is visible in many other cases: a Black man is wrongfully convicted of the rape and/or murder of a White woman and he spends decades in prison until a team of people identify his case, find the real perpetrator, and he is set free and exonerated. Black men, including Antron McCray, Kevin Richardson, Raymond Santana, Khorey Wise, Yusef Salaam, and Darryl Hunt are all victims of the racist criminal legal system.

More recently, the case of Eddie Lee Howard, the first exoneree of 2021, followed the pattern discussed above. Mr. Howard, who is Black, was sentenced in 1994 to death for the rape and murder of an 84-year-old White woman by the name of Georgia Kemp, in Columbus, Mississippi. After 26 years in prison, he finally received his freedom. Typical of other similar cases, it is yet one in a long line of Black men wrongfully convicted for the rape and murder of White women. What made Howard a target in this case was the problematic testimony of Dr. Michael West, a so-called forensic dentist. At trial, West testified that Eddie Lee Howard's teeth marks were similar to the markings found on the body of the victim. Just before Howard's exoneration, it came to light that the forensic odontology evidence proffered by Dr. West was vilifying, lacking in scientific credibility, and considered inherently subjective.

This outcome of racialized offender/victim wrongful conviction and exonerations, a bizarre pattern whereby something that happens so rarely in reality has emerged as one of the most common types of cases that leads to wrongful convictions and exonerations, raises significant questions. Hattery and Smith (2021) argued that the reason it is so common is due to the crime itself, the rape and/or murder of a White woman by a Black man, as it precisely fits the trope of a lynching (Kendi, 2020). Consequently, these cases evoke the same behaviors that characterized tens of thousands of lynchings that took place across the United States, mostly in the South, but certainly other regions of the country were not immune, from the time of Emancipation until today.[3]

Other scholars detail the history of lynching in the United States, and all arrive at the same conclusion: it is the stereotype of the Black man as hypersexual, as desiring White women, as being "animal like" that was among the thing Whites feared the most (including Davis, 1983; Patterson, 1982; Yancy, 2020, among others). In order to manage their fears, White people turned their imaginations into action; they accused Black men of raping (and sometimes of murdering) White women, and they took justice into their own hands. Vigilante mobs often stormed jails where an accused Black man was being held, dragged him out of his cell, and lynched him in front of a crowd, often including women and children and led by local ministers. The message was clear: White people control the justice system, and they can and will not only accuse any Black man of rape but they will execute him as well, without due process, without evidence, without trial, without judge or jury.

For those who assume that "justice" is the goal of the criminal legal system, wrongful convictions and exonerations may be troubling, and they should be. The history of lynching in the United States reveals that they were never about justice; they were never even about crime. They reflected the fear of the Black man, his masculinity, his sexuality, and the fact that he might gain access to the power that White men had, not just to marry White women but to control every aspect of the social political economy. In this way, lynchings were not about "getting it right" or extracting justice; instead, they were about sending a message to the Black community: "If you dare to dream too big, dare to demand your rights, you may be lynched."

Even today, when a White woman is raped or murdered by a Black man, it is clear from the data that there is no intention of "getting it right" or of delivering "justice." Rather, the criminal legal system is harnessed toward lynching; whichever Black man does the time for the crime is not the issue. What matters is that *a* Black man is held accountable. In fact, cases like those of Antron McCray, Kevin Richardson, Raymond Santana, Khorey Wise, Yusef Salaam, and Darryl Hunt may have a bigger impact on the local Black community precisely because the system did get it "wrong." One of the rallying cries in the Black community in Winston–Salem agitating for "Justice for Darryl" was "if it can happen to Darryl it can happen to you, to your son, to your husband, to your brother." Given that in reality it can and does, this sends a message of fear that reverberates throughout entire Black communities.

Moreover, even in the cases of exoneration – and most people who are wrongly convicted will never be exonerated (Gross et al., 2017) – the person who is exonerated may get his liberty back, but he does not get his life back, because he continues to experience the social death of incarceration and living with a felony conviction. While a Black exoneree may not have been physically lynched, he was *judicially* lynched and further victimized by the racist criminal legal system.

Evidence supports the fact that White people know this. In the spring of 2020, just before New York City went on lockdown in response to the global COVID-19 pandemic, Amy Cooper, a White woman walking her dog (off leash) in Central Park called 911 and reported that she had been confronted by a Black man, Christian Cooper (no relation), who asked her to leash her dog (Nir, 2019). On the 911 call she can be heard screaming that she feared for her life, that she was being attacked by a "Black man." Amy Cooper invoked, almost without thought, as reflexively as any activity engaged in routinely, the oldest trope in the book. She was, in essence, accusing a Black man of attempting to rape her.

Again, at the end of 2020 in New York City, another White woman, Miya Ponsetto, accused an innocent Black teenager, Keyon Harrold, Jr., who happens to be the son of a prominent jazz musician, Keyon Harrold, of stealing her cell phone. Her cell phone was later returned by an Uber driver, who found it after he dropped her off at the hotel, as she had apparently left it in his car (Coleman, 2021). Ponsetto, who falsely accused Keyon Harrold, Jr., did what so many White people do: falsely accuse Black people, more often men than women, for their own misdoings, just as Susan Smith famously did when she accused a Black man of car-jacking her minivan. She invented this story to cover up the fact that she drove her car into a lake, her two young sons strapped in their car seats, and left them to drown (Coleman, 2021).

Amy Cooper and the others did not come up with this idea on her own. It was not her imagination working in overdrive. She invoked this trope because White people – women and men – have been doing so for 400 years. Sadly, most of the time, it works.

## Concluding Remarks

As Anderson (2016) has argued, the United States does not have a racist criminal justice system; rather, the United States is built on the system of White supremacy that criminalizes race. Specifically, the criminal justice system, criminalizes Blackness (Hattery & Smith, 2021). Given that then-President Nixon acknowledged that the true intent of the war on drugs that began in the 1970s was to wage war against Black people, effectively criminalizing them for being Black (Lopez, 2016) it stands to reason that the current policies and practices that target Black people and take away their liberty are not incompatible with this earlier goal. At the extreme end, wrongful convictions remove individuals' liberty and, for all intents and purposes, their life as well. Anyone convicted, guilty or innocent, experiences civil, legal, and social death. And even those lucky few who are ultimately exonerated may get their liberty back, but they can never have their rights or their life fully restored. They (re)enter society with a felony conviction and face all of the obstacles any other returning citizen does (Hattery & Smith, 2010). If they are among the fortunate, they will get a payout – a settlement – but no amount of money can make up for the years lost while in prison or the trauma experienced during incarceration.

As discussed, it is not simply the racialized wrongfully convicted who suffer; rather, tens of thousands of Black people experience constant surveillance by law enforcement every day in America; they are regularly stopped and frisked and caught in the net of fishing expeditions. On this matter, U.S. Supreme Court Justice Sotomayor wrote in her dissent in Utah v. Streiff (2016):

> It says that your body is subject to invasion while courts excuse the violation of your rights. It implies that you are not a citizen of a democracy but the subject of a carceral state, just waiting to be cataloged. (para. 12)

And once cataloged as a risk, this increases the possibility not only of loss of liberty but also the concomitant loss of civil, legal, and social rights.

For those caught up in the dragnet of stop and frisk and fishing expeditions, once arrested, and lacking funds to make bail, liberty is immediately suspended – sometimes indefinitely. Wrongly accused, Kalief Browder, and tens of thousands like him, spent 3 years in prison never having been convicted of a crime. Much like the wrongfully convicted, he lost his teenage years and was never able to graduate from high school, pursue college or a job, or start a family. And, just like Darryl Hunt, the traumas he experienced while incarcerated were too much for him to handle and he ultimately took his own life.

Both Stevenson (2018) and Buser (2015) illustrated that those innocents who are detained because they cannot afford bail are far more likely to plead guilty than those who arrive as free persons to their court hearings and trials. Removing the liberty of the legally innocent practically ensures that they will spend even more time in jail or prison, their legal, civil, and social death not only guaranteed but their successful (re)entry blocked by all of the societal barriers erected for those who carry the stain of a felony conviction.

When the fortunate few wrongly convicted are exonerated and finally leave prison, they are often victimized again. As of this writing, only 32 states have compensation statutes for the wrongly incarcerated. Even in those states that have some form of compensation, it is not robust. States such as Illinois and Ohio compensate the wrongly convicted, but accessing payment is often tied up in expensive litigation for years and requires that stringent criteria be met (that they are innocent!) and/or the compensation received is only a partial sum of what is owed. In the more "progressive" states, including Kansas, exonerees seeking compensation must engage in a lengthy legal process and demonstrate multiple prongs of innocence (Gutman & Sun, 2019).

In the state of New Jersey, for example, A. Jabir Nash was charged with the sexual abuse of a child and received a sentence of 22 years. The sentence was based on the testimony of the victim, a 12-year-old boy named "JB," who was a special education student diagnosed with schizophrenia. JB testified that on three occasions Nash sexually assaulted him in the school bathroom and that Nash threatened to harm his mother if he told anyone. Following his exoneration, when it was established that Jabir Nash did not commit a crime, he applied for reinstatement in his job and back pay was denied. His case is similar to hundreds of Black men who spend years in prison, are exonerated, and then cannot receive compensation (Possley, 2014).

The Center for Wrongful Convictions at Northwestern University estimated that between 1989 and 2011, upwards of $300 million has been paid in compensation by the State of Illinois, with the bulk of the money coming from the city of Chicago (Anyaso, 2011). Unfortunately, in cities like Chicago, which are already hovering near bankruptcy, many exonerees, like Christopher Coleman, who was finally released from prison in 2013 after serving 20 years for a crime he did not commit, find out after the fact that their compensation has been indefinitely delayed simply because the city has run out of money. There is no timeline as to when compensation will be paid to Christopher Coleman and others like him. Given that wrongful convictions are often the result of state errors or state crime, government bodies representing states or municipalities should not be allowed to default on compensation to those they so terribly wronged. Most of these people are also Black bodies ripped out of their homes and communities, locked up for decades and then undervalued (Hattery & Smith 2021).

In ending this chapter, we are reminded that wrongful conviction injustices continue to occur. For example, since the exoneration of Darryl Hunt, number 152 on February 6, 2004, there are now over 2,800 exonerations; of these, 1,384 are African American (NRE, 2020a). These data inform us that it is at the first point of contact with the police that Black Americans are unjustly arrested, convicted, and incarcerated for crimes they did not commit.

As discussed, Justice Sotomayor wrote:

> We must not pretend that the countless people who are routinely targeted by police are "isolated." They are the canaries in the coal mine whose deaths, civil and literal, warn us that no one can breathe in this atmosphere. They are the ones who recognize that unlawful police stops corrode all our civil liberties and threaten all our lives. Until their voices matter too, our justice system will continue to be anything but. (*Utah v. Strieff*, 2016, para. 12)

We must start to listen to the canaries.

## Notes

1  Throughout this chapter, the term "criminal legal system" will be used instead of "criminal justice system" to emphasize that the system is not concerned with justice, per se. This includes the actors in the criminal legal system who are police, lawyers, judges and the processes that occur in the system itself through the courts, prison, parole and probation.

2  In 2000, Stanley Mozee and Dennis Allen, both Black men, were sentenced to life in prison for the murder of a Texas pastor who had been stabbed 47 times at a store he owned. It turns out that the former lead prosecutor in the case, Richard E. Jackson, who is White, was found by the State Bar of Texas to have withheld evidence during the trial. Jackson was forced to surrender his law license and was effectively disbarred – a relatively rare consequence in the realm of wrongful convictions. According to a 2020 report from the NRE, researchers found that prosecutors across the country committed misconduct in 30% of the 2,400 exoneration cases studied at that point, including behaviors such as "concealing of exculpatory evidence and misconduct at trial, and a substantial amount of witness tampering." Among those, only 4% received any form of formal discipline. According to the NRE, Mr. Jackson is only the fourth prosecutor to lose his license over a wrongful conviction (Fazio, 2021).

3  This connection has also been commented on by others, in particular in the Central Park Five case, and by Mr. Hunt's attorney, Mark Rabil, who referred to what happened to his client as a "modern-day lynching" (Rabil, 2012). We are not the first to recognize this connection: Mr. Hunt's attorneys and many who commented on the Central Park Five referred to these cases as modern-day lynchings.

# PART 2

# The Many Victims of a Wrongful Conviction

# 5

# THE EXONEREE AS VICTIM

*Nicky Ali Jackson*

"The justice system threw me away because they didn't think I was worth anything. ..."

*White male exoneree*

## Introduction

The person most affected by a wrongful conviction is the individual falsely suspected, arrested, convicted, and incarcerated. The objective of this chapter is to highlight the experiences of innocent men and women who were convicted of crimes that they did not commit and, subsequently, wrongly incarcerated, as they are the direct victims of this miscarriage of justice. Given that the vast majority of research on wrongful convictions has focused on the contributing factors, research on the effects of a wrongful conviction on the wrongly *convicted* is more limited (Campbell & Denov, 2004; Norris & Mullinex, 2020). Only recently have studies begun to examine the prison experience and post-release effects of the wrongly convicted (N. A. Jackson et al., 2021; Konvisser, 2012; Westervelt & Cook, 2008, 2018). While these studies represent a contribution to the literature around the experiences of the wrongly convicted, a further neglected area in wrongful conviction research recognizes the wrongly convicted individual, from both theoretical and practical viewpoints, as a *victim*, similar to other crime victims. The pioneering work of Westervelt and Cook (2010) studied death row exonerees as victims of state crime. This chapter expands on their work by examining the wrongly convicted themselves as victims of crime.

## The Victimization Process

In order to understand the victimization process, it is important to understand how innocent people become labeled as criminals and, ultimately, if they are fortunate, labeled as exonerees. Once they enter the criminal justice system, the wrongly convicted experience the harsh realities for that system. Here, an exoneree describes his experience at the sentencing hearing and his arrival at the prison:

DOI: 10.4324/9781003121251-7

*I was sitting in the courtroom on that day ... my vision was blurred. I don't know if I had an anxiety attack or panic attack. I don't know what I would call it but it was terrifying at that moment because I realized my life was over. I couldn't hear anything. And all of a sudden, one voice and that was my mom I heard scream, and when I heard her scream in the courtroom, that's when I was sentenced. I realized I had to toughen up. I couldn't lose it. At that point, that's when I told myself I had to toughen up and get prepared for what I'm about to experience. ...*

*As we approach the prison, I realized that it was like a horror house, like this was some big horror house with big gates and when the bus pulls in, the gate squeaks. And while the gate was squeaking, it's like my whole life. I don't even know how to explain it. But I realized that was the most fear I have experienced in my life. Getting off that bus and walking through the prison was so shocking to see all the men. They walked us through the prison and it was like war was out on the streets. I guess they was (sic)having lunchtime or whatever time it is and they begin to yell foul language and stuff at all the new guys coming in. And I was like, "Oh, my goodness, how am I going to survive this?" What I done (sic) was I started praying within myself. And I realized I hadn't even got really in the population of the prison yet and I was already shaking. There's so much fear but I have to realize that I can't go in with this because of the things you hear about, you can't go in afraid. Well, let people know you are here. My mind went to an area I've never thought about before: I was making weapons to defend myself. And then I realized I was turning myself into somebody that I wasn't. When I first got to prison, I had a single cell. As I was locked in the cell, I begin to talk to myself. It's just crazy how you become this person that really talks to yourself.*

After moving to a shared cell:

*Oh, that was more ridiculous, because now you have to share a cell with someone you have no idea what they were about. You have to adjust to being in the cell with another man and there was only one toilet. You had to compromise, or you hear about a lot of fights and at that everybody was equipped with weapons. Everybody was considered dangerous. And here you are innocent saying 1,000,000 prayers. You never even thought about stuff like this. I feel that I was a pretty nice guy before prison. I've always been a nice guy. One day when we were walking to chow, somebody got badly stabbed or something like that. I went to help him as he is laying on the ground and another guy pushed me. I turned around. He told me I can't help nobody (sic)unless I want to become that person on the ground. And you know what he meant so you got to get with the program and keep walking. So I had to step over this guy. He told me don't go around; step over him as that shows you are not afraid. This is how they live. (African American male)*

Victimization is the process of making a victim, and the process of becoming a victim of a wrongful conviction occurs throughout the criminal justice system. Police, prosecutors, legal experts, and/or judges, intentionally or unintentionally, can all play a role in wrongful convictions. All too often, mistakes occur in a case, leaving innocent people vulnerable to a harsh criminal justice system. At the same time, the system creates its own victims, the wrongly accused. And, worse still, in some cases, the system creates a victim when no crime has taken place at all (Henry, 2020). *No-crime cases,*[1] also referred to as *fictitious crimes* and *phantom crimes*, are crimes in which people are arrested and convicted for crimes that never took place. Females are disproportionately wrongly convicted in no-crime cases. The most common phantom crimes are homicide, shaken baby syndrome, and sexual assault. The following case of Kristine Bunch illustrates how a phantom homicide can occur.

On June 30, 1995, Kristine Bunch and her son, Anthony, were sleeping in their Indiana home when a fire broke out in the middle of the night. Tragically, her 3-year-old son, Anthony, succumbed to the fire despite her attempts to rescue him. Six days later, police arrested Kristine based primarily on a state arson investigator's claim that the fire had been intentionally set in two locations. At her trial, the 22-year-old then-pregnant mother was found guilty of murder and sentenced to 60 years for murder and 50 years for arson. In 2007, the Center for Wrongful Conviction at Northwestern University of Law, with the help of three fire experts, concluded that the evidence in that case indicated there was no arson. Kristine Bunch was exonerated after serving 17 years in prison for an accidental fire where no crime had taken place. In Ms. Bunch's case, there was no crime; the fire that killed her son had been accidental.

Regardless of whether an actual crime occurred or whether it was a fictitious crime, innocent people suffer as a result of a wrongful conviction. They are ultimately victims of mistakes in the criminal justice system, whether intentional or not, who experience physical and psychological trauma at each stage within the criminal justice system. The next section will examine the roles that police, courts, and correctional agencies play in the victimization process.

## The Impact of Criminal Justice System Actors on Victimization Through a Wrongful Conviction

### Police

The actions of law enforcement can often be traced to the roots of a wrongful conviction. Police discretion provides officers legitimate authority to make decisions that, ultimately, can affect a citizen's life. Tyler (2016) argued that police act on behalf of the community; therefore, it is appropriate for them to use their judgment to resolve conflicts and enforce rules. Making an arrest is a life-changing event for the arrestee as once an officer makes an arrest, an individual enters the formal criminal justice system. When an arrest is wrongful, however, it is often at this stage where errors can occur that could result in a wrongful conviction. A number of law enforcement–initiated factors can have an impact on contributing to a wrongful conviction, including failures in criminal investigations, perjured testimony, faulty lineups, and coerced confessions. Moreover, when there is an error in a criminal investigation, any contaminated evidence will follow the arrestee throughout the criminal justice system (Findley & Scott, 2006). For example, tunnel vision may lead police to focus solely on one suspect and ignore exculpatory evidence. Tunnel vision can be practiced by prosecutors and judges as well. What can occur also is what Dror and Stoel (2014) termed the bias snowball effect, which refers to how one piece of biased evidence may contaminate another piece of evidence. In these instances, one piece of evidence influences another and greater distortion occurs, leading to more evidence being misinterpreted, and so on, the outcome of which may lead to a wrongful conviction.

Law enforcement initiates the victimization process of the wrongly convicted in other ways as well. Much research has pointed to how psychologically manipulative police interrogation practices can influence some suspects to falsely confess to a crime they did not commit (Drizin & Leo, 2004; Gudjonsson, 2003; Kassin, 1997, 2005; Ofshe & Leo, 1997). Certain individuals are thought to be more vulnerable to suggestibility and falsely confessing often due to age, psychological state, or intoxication (Campbell, 2018). While different researchers have attempted to classify different types of false confessions, based on varying social structural and environmental factors, Kassin and Wrightsman's (1985) three categories of false confessions are as follows: voluntary, coerced compliant, and coerced internalized confessions.

- *Voluntary confessions* are said to occur when an individual provides a self-incriminating false statement without police pressure. This may occur based on a desire to protect another individual, due to a desire for infamy, or due to guilt based on other undiscovered criminal activity or the result of mental illness (Leo, 2009).
- A *coerced compliant confession* is when an individual falsely confesses in an attempt to exit an aggressive interrogation. The suspect is desperate to stop the interrogation; therefore, they admit to the crime while knowing they are innocent. Some coerced compliant suspects may falsely confess to be obedient to authority, whereas others may falsely confess as they attempt to bargain for leniency (Ofshe & Leo, 1997).
- A *coerced internalized confession* is when a vulnerable individual inaccurately believes he or she committed the crime and confesses to it, when in fact they did not. Through psychological interrogation tactics, the police are able to obtain a false confession and, ultimately, get their suspect to question his or her own innocence (Kassin, 2007).

## Prosecutors

A common misconception regarding the role of the prosecutor is that their primary function is to obtain a guilty verdict. In Berger v. United States (1935), however, the Supreme Court held that a prosecutor is

> the representative not of an ordinary party to a controversy, but of a sovereignty whose obligation to govern impartially is as compelling as its obligation to govern at all; and whose interest, therefore, in a criminal prosecution is not that it shall win a case, but that justice shall be done. (para. 16)

The Court recognized that prosecutors face a heavy burden in seeking justice. As noted in a 1940 article by Attorney General Robert H. Jackson "The prosecutor has more control over life, liberty, and reputation than any other person in America," and he goes on to say even more power than the president of the United States (as cited in Bellin, 2019, p. 187). Whether or not Jackson's statement is to be believed, it is undeniable that prosecutors have great discretionary power in the criminal justice system. While police are the gatekeepers into the criminal justice system, prosecutors have the ultimate power on whether to indict or dismiss a case. Prosecutors' decisions impact innocent suspects and also affect whether or not an innocent person is tried or convicted. There are specific factors in the hands of the prosecutor that can lead to a wrongful conviction: *Brady* violations, perjury, and improper closing arguments.

- *Brady* violations: In the landmark case of Brady v. Maryland (1963), the Supreme Court argued that prosecutors have a duty to seek truth and fairness in criminal trials rather than achieving a win at any cost. Toward this end, prosecutors are obliged to disclose any and all exculpatory evidence to the defense. Failure to do so is regarded as a *Brady* violation and can lead to a conviction being overturned. The Supreme Court did not provide definitions of what constitutes favorable evidence; however, it is understood that any evidence that could help the defense establish reasonable doubt on a charge falls under the category of a *Brady* violation (Daughety & Reinganum, 2018).

- Perjury: *Perjury* refers to the act of intentionally making false statements. In Mooney v. Holohan (1935), the Supreme Court held that prosecutors cannot knowingly present perjured testimony as it is a violation of due process and is, therefore, unconstitutional. The use of perjured statements or falsehoods may indirectly or directly sway judges and juries and result in a conviction that is in error.

- Improper closing arguments: Closing arguments are argued to be the most important part of a criminal trial as they allow prosecutors and the defense the opportunity to make a final summation on the evidence presented that would prove or disprove the defendant's guilt. According to Cicchini (2018), prosecutorial misconduct is rampant during closing arguments as prosecutors, at times, have been known to make inflammatory and untrue statements. At the same time, they have been known to misrepresent evidence as facts and misstate laws (Broyles & Lynn, 2018). Cicchini provided two explanations for this type of misconduct: "they know that improper arguments are highly effective, stirring jurors' emotions and inviting them to convict for reasons other than proof beyond a reasonable doubt" and "prosecutors have learned that this form of misconduct is virtually risk free" (p. 888). It is very difficult to establish that a prosecutor acted maliciously and, given that they have qualified immunity, even more difficult to hold them to account for their misconduct. Consequently, a win at any cost without foreseeable sanctions leaves innocent suspects vulnerable to prosecution.

## Judges

Judges' roles in miscarriages of justice are often ignored in wrongful conviction literature. While police and prosecutors have been highlighted as contributing to wrongful convictions (Campbell, 2018; Norris et al., 2018; Sherrer, 2003), judges' actions have not been extensively investigated in this regard. Nonetheless, judges do play a role in wrongful convictions; they have been found, at times, to act in a biased manner around the admissibility of evidence, directions to the jury, and use of screening mechanisms for charges (Campbell, 2018). Exoneree-turned-attorney Jeffrey Deskovic (2020) argued that judges are favorable to prosecutors as many are former prosecutors themselves. He further suggested that judges can be complicit by suppressing evidence that would be helpful to the defense's case and allowing unlawful evidence to be presented by the prosecutor (Deskovic, 2020).

## The Impact of a Wrongful Conviction on Direct Victims

The consequences of a wrongful conviction are convoluted and multifaceted. Throughout the interviews undertaken for this volume, the exonerees shared the many challenges of their wrongful conviction with a focus on their wrongful incarceration, describing the psychological and physical trauma resulting from their many years of wrongful confinement. Before discussing how the wrongly convicted coped with a wrongful imprisonment, it is instructive to first discuss the impact of incarceration for all prisoners more generally. Since the 1970s, the United States has incarcerated more inmates than any other nation in the world (Travis et al., 2014). The statistics are shocking. The United States has the highest prison population in the world with the highest per capita incarceration rate: for every 100,000 persons in American society, there are 665 in prison. That translates into almost 2.3 million people in 1,833 state prisons, 110 federal prisons, 1,772 juvenile correctional facilities, 3,134 local jails,

218 immigration detention facilities, and 80 Indian Country jails, as well as in military prisons, civil commitment centers, state psychiatric hospitals, and prisons in the U.S. territories (Sawyer & Wagner, 2020).

One very obvious consequence to mass incarceration is prison overcrowding. The overarching prison experience is challenging in itself; however, overcrowding exacerbates many of the problems inmates already face (Kreager & Kruttschnitt, 2018). Even so, little research has been conducted on the physical effects of incarceration (Cobbina et al., 2012; DeLisi et al., 2011; Duwe & Clark, 2013). The few studies that do exist focus primarily on physical health and mental health implications. Although these areas are of legitimate concern, there are other consequences of incarceration that also result from institutionalization.

## Physical Consequences of Incarceration

### Adapting to Prison Life

An early American sociologist, Erving Goffman (1961) provided characteristics of what he coined "total institutions." While his essay focused on asylums, the concept has been expanded to prisons. Goffman described a *total institution* as "an isolated, enclosed, and highly structured space of work and residence that strips individuals of self-expression and promotes conformity to norms and rules" (cited in Ellis, 2021, p. 176). Individuals entering prison are forced to adhere to their new society's rules and culture. Adapting to prison life "involves modifying oneself (or objects) for a new use or purpose" (N. A. Jackson et al., 2021, p. 12). As described by an exoneree, "I had to eat when they told me to eat, I had to shower when they said I could shower, and I had to turn in [go to bed] when the guards told me." Being commanded to engage in basic privileges at specific times that many take for granted is difficult for new inmates. The challenge of living in closed spaces with a complete stranger was noted by a male exoneree: "Now you have to share a cell with someone you have no idea what they were about. You have to adjust to being in the cell with another man and there was only one toilet." Adjustment includes learning how to live in a controlled environment with complete strangers, both inmates and guards.

### Deprivations

Inmates are deprived not only their freedom but also of privacy, dignity, and activity while incarcerated. One of the greatest deprivations of inmate privacy is that exercised against their own person, specifically, their bodies. Inmates are routinely strip searched. Not only have they lost their right to privacy but they also lose their dignity during these invasive searches. The purpose of strip searches is to seize contraband; in reality, it is often used as a means to humiliate, control, and degrade prisoners. In 2011, Warden Melody Hulett of the Lincoln Correctional Center in Illinois ordered a mass strip search on 200 female inmates. They were ordered to the beauty shop and bathroom adjacent to the gym, where they were forced to stand for up to seven hours, shoulder to shoulder, and ordered to strip and remove sanitary products if worn. They were then ordered to lift up their breasts, spread their legs, and show their body cavities. Blood spilled onto the floor and other women had to step on menstrual blood as they got dressed. Those menstruating were not given new feminine products to use when they were getting dressed. During the search, male and female guards were watching. In addition, other female inmates and staff were able to view the search as it was not conducted in privacy. This mass strip search was not conducted due to safety concerns but rather as a training exercise for new guards on how to properly conduct a strip search. Consequently, the prisoners challenged this barbaric violation through the courts, and it made its way to the Seventh Circuit Court with all 12 judges participating (*en banc*; A. Mills, 2020). In this case, Henry v. Hulett (2020), the Court found that the female inmates' right to privacy had been violated. The Court did not, however, bar strip searches. Rather, it barred *mass* strip searches. Regardless of their purpose or how they are conducted, strip searches dehumanize and demoralize individuals.

Another consequence of incarceration is boredom. Inmates have the choice, at times, to engage in two types of recreation: passive and active. *Passive recreation* is when an inmate is the recipient of entertainment such as listening to music, watching television, and reading. Active recreation occurs when the activity requires physical or mental action, for example, playing cards, chess, ping-pong, pool, gardening, and playing instruments (Frey & Delaney, 1996; Roberts, 2001). Other active recreational activities involve basketball, walking, lifting weights, and yoga. At times, excelling in an activity grants an inmate recognition and honor. One exoneree spoke about his basketball skills,

> *I'm not trying to be boastful, but I was really good at basketball. Everyone wanted me on their team. My being good kept me out of trouble because no one wanted to mess with me. I was kind [of] like a celebrity in there when it came to basketball.*

A strong implication from the exoneree's statement is that those who do not excel in sports are considered weak and vulnerable. Active recreations are severely limited in most institutions, due to staffing shortages, safety concerns, and little funding for recreational pursuits leaving inmates with inactivity for long periods of time. Passive recreation fills the boredom gap but ignores the physical health of inmates.

## Separation From Family and Friends

Sykes (1958) introduced the concept of the pains of imprisonment where he argued that physical separation of inmates and their families creates significant strains on familial relationships. The pain suffered by inmates who struggle to maintain family contacts is a true hardship among all prisoners. Among the exonerees interviewed for this book, all mothers reported the most difficult part of being locked up was being apart from their children. Moreover, this was exacerbated by knowing someone else was raising their children. As one woman reported,

> *My kids did not know me. … they were very young when I was sent here. If I was lucky enough for them to come see me, it was even more hurtful when they left. They did not know me as their mother.*

A male exoneree further stated, "I did not want my kids to see me in prison so I did not allow them to come. I wanted to protect them from this wicked place." While some scholars have argued that visitation has positive effects (Cochran & Mears, 2013) and inmates report that visitation can be beneficial, it can also prove to be quite painful. An exoneree shared, "[My] mom used to come visit me until it got too hard for her to get here, so I didn't have a visitor after my first few years in prison." Prison visits may be difficult for family and friends due to travel, health issues, economic constraints, or a combination of these factors. Guards can make visits challenging for inmates as a form of punishment. When an inmate is viewed as noncompliant, correctional staff may restrict familial visits for a period of time.

## Isolation

In prison, inmates are, at times, placed in administrative segregation, also known as solitary confinement; for inmates, it is referred to as "the hole." Although it is unimaginable for an inmate to be placed in "the hole" for any length of time, inmates may languish there for extended periods of time. In fact, they can remain in segregation for days or years. It is difficult, however, to accurately assess the length of confinement due to the barriers to accessing this sensitive prison data. Those in solitary confinement are remanded to their cells anywhere from 22 to 24 hours per day. At times, that may be confined even longer when prisons are short-staffed and unable to escort inmates to showers or recreation (Nolan & Amico, 2017).

## Violence

Prison violence is a legitimate concern for inmates as victimization may occur at the hands of other inmates or guards. There is scant research on the types, sources, and patterns of violence in prisons (Wolff & Shi, 2009). Much of the limited prison violence research focuses on sexual victimization (Beck & Harrison, 2007; Hensley, Castle, & Tewksbury, 2003; Hensley, Tewksbury, & Castle, 2003; Wolff & Shi, 2011). In a study by Wolff and Shi (2009), they found that males were more likely to be sexually assaulted by a guard, whereas female inmates were more likely to be sexually victimized by another inmate. Their study also found that the most common type of sexual assault reported by males and females was inappropriate touching. Violence, in general, was a concern for exonerees in this study. As innocent people who had not been previously incarcerated, their image of prison is much of what the media has portrayed and thus many were afraid for their own safety.

## Forced Slavery

While slavery has a long history in the United States, it was officially abolished when President Lincoln issued the Emancipation Proclamation on January 1, 1863. Inmates, however, report that slavery not only exists but persists. In fact, Pereira (2018) argued that prisons share operational characteristics of slave plantations. An interesting observation Pereira made is that many American prisons are in the exact locations where slave plantations once existed. Expanding on her thesis, the following highlights similar characteristics among slaves and prison inmates:

- Slaves' lives are determined by their owners. Prisoners' lives are determined by their guards.
- Slaves and prisoners are controlled (punished) by their owners/guards with little oversight.
- The aim of slavery was to strip away the slaves' connections to others. Prisoners are separated from society.
- Slaves are required to follow slave codes. Inmates must follow formal and informal prison rules/codes.
- Slaves and prisoners are forced to work in jobs that they do not electively choose.
- Slaves and prisoners earn, if any amount of money, a meager hourly or daily rate.

A White male exoneree interviewed for this study believed that slavery continues to exist in the penal system. He argued that inmates, regardless of race, were forced into prison labor. "I was forced to work in a job out in the fields. I was young, skinny, weak and they made me work long hours until my hands bled and my feet could no longer hold up my frail body."

An African American male exoneree said that he had not understood what his ancestors – victims of slavery – endured until he was wrongly sent to prison. Once incarcerated, he felt bonded with them as he also saw himself as a victim of slavery. He shared that he never thought he would be picking corn out in a field as his ancestors had, but there he was, enslaved in a carceral state, forced to pick corn.

## Food Quality and Portions

Prison food is notoriously bad, malnutritious, not fresh, and prepared in mass quantities. No one interviewed for this study reported satisfaction with food quality or portions. Many reported that some prisons were known for better food choices than others, but that does not suggest that the food was actually better but possibly only slightly healthier and served in bigger portions. A female exoneree described a Thanksgiving meal she will never forget: her unit was the last one to be served, and by the time she got up to the line, all that was left was a piece of bread and gravy.

While most prisons have a great deal of freedom with their food service, there is little oversight on what is served and how it is served. One inmate described how he refused to eat the canned meat that was regularly served,

> I had a friend who worked in the cafeteria. He said that on the can of meat they used to serve us, it said "Not for human consumption." He would not touch it, so I knew not to eat it myself. How do they get away with trying to poison us?

It is impossible to verify this claim, but his statement was similar to other exonerees who shared that food served was not appropriate for humans. As prisons feed approximately 2.3 million people daily, it would appear that the goal is to feed the inmates with little concern for nutrition or food handling guidelines. According to the Centers for Disease Control, food-borne illness affects prisoners at a rate six times higher than the general population (Marlow et al., 2017). It would be difficult to deny that the quality of food and portions given to prisoners are a form of neglect. In the free world, parents are prosecuted for starving children or not offering adequate nutrition. In prison, these are legitimate and acceptable practices.

## Cell Temperatures

Consistently throughout the course of interviews, each exoneree described prison temperatures as unbearable. In the winter months, it was freezing while during the summer months, there was no ventilation, and some described their experience as "being fried like an egg." One exoneree reported telling guards that he had to use the bathroom throughout the night simply to get out of his cell as the bathrooms were located in an area where temperatures were more tolerable. Another exoneree shared her experience during menopause:

> I was having hot flashes, but they became unbearable as the air conditioning either didn't work or didn't exist. I don't know which one it was, but I felt like I was going to have a breakdown. It was sheer torture.

Exonerees reported windows not being able to close, which caused ice to build up in cells:

> Everything was frozen in my cell. I was wearing everything I owned to keep warm. Hats, gloves, blankets, jackets – anything I could put on top of me to keep warm, I did. Even the toilet water was frozen. That meant we couldn't flush our toilets. It was pure torture.

## Health

Due to prison temperatures, overcrowding, prison violence, lack of ventilation, poor nutrition, inadequate medical and dental care, and poor hygiene, inmates develop many health difficulties during their confinement. Not surprising, inmates have higher rates of disease compared to the general population (Cloud et al., 2014). Common health issues include infectious diseases (i.e., tuberculosis, HIV, COVID), respiratory illnesses, and heart disease. Lack of proper medical and dental care leaves inmates vulnerable to health problems that go either undetected or untreated (Greifinger, 2007).

## Psychological Consequences of Incarceration

The toll of incarceration is not limited to an inmate's physical well-being. Psychological effects of imprisonment such as depression, mood disorders, anxiety disorders, and mental health issues may also surface during confinement (Campbell & Denov, 2004; Schnittker, 2014). Difficulties with mental health are a serious concern in American prisons, where the rate of mental illness is higher among prisoners than among the general population (Fazel & Baillargeon, 2011). At the same time, prisons do not have adequate treatment programs to treat mental illness, resulting in more serious side effects, such as self-harm, delusions, hallucinations, and even suicide. Haney (2002) found that inmates suffer from a myriad of psychological effects, including a diminished sense of self-worth, social withdrawal, hypervigilance, and suspicion. As one exoneree described, "I stayed to myself. I didn't trust no one). I didn't talk to people. I was a loner." Loneliness, helplessness, and sadness are traits that many inmates describe (N. A. Jackson et al., 2021). Ultimately, the invisible scars can be more damaging than the physical scars of incarceration.

## Effects of Incarceration on Innocent Inmates

Prison does not distinguish between who belongs there and who does not: all inmates experience the same daily physical constraints and many of the same psychological effects. However, there are some challenges that are unique to the wrongly convicted. Those challenges are not necessarily physical, as they all experience the same physical constraints.

> We are all the same in prison – Black, White, Brown, it doesn't matter. It doesn't matter if you are innocent or guilty; we all go through the same hell every day. We are told when to wake up, when to eat, when to shower, when to sleep. No one cares if you are innocent or not. (White male exoneree)

What is unique to wrongly convicted individuals, however, are a myriad of psychological effects that they experience. Although research on the psychological effects of a wrongful conviction during incarceration is sparse (Campbell & Denov, 2004; Grounds, 2004; N. A. Jackson et al., 2021), through the exonerees' interviews, the following were identifiable psychological consequences experienced by innocent inmates.

## Psychological Consequences Unique to Innocent Inmates

### Broken Trust

As one exoneree shared, "Growing up, I believed in the police and the criminal justice system. That all changed when I was placed under suspicion. The police focused on me like a predator focuses on a child. I became the prey" (Caucasian male). Consistent with the exoneree's view of police, A. D. Fine et al. (2020) found that White youth had more positive impressions of police than African American and Latino youth. While race may impact one's perceptions of the police, the people interviewed for this volume shared that it plays little role in an exoneree's prison experience. The exonerees in this study consistently reported that racial stratification does not exist in prison in the same way it does in society. While it is undeniable that African American people are disproportionately suspected, questioned, arrested, and incarcerated at significantly higher rates than Whites (D. A. Harris, 1997; Lundman & Kaufman, 2003; Nellis, 2016), in prison, the inmate experience appeared to be similar regardless of race.

Another Caucasian male exoneree expressed his lack of trust in the criminal justice system, not just in the police:

> I can't believe how corrupt and crooked the system is … full of liars and cheats who are in this for personal and political gain. It just blows my mind that these people are in this business. They're nothing but a bunch of liars. … You believe so deeply in these things and these people that it just blows my mind. … Why do people believe so much in these people?

In this study, African Americans were less shocked at being incarcerated for crimes that they did not commit than were Whites. Although they were initially traumatized when they entered prison, they were not surprised that this happened to them, as African Americans are more often targeted by the police than are Whites (Epp et al., 2014; McGlynn-Wright et al., 2020).

### Stigma

Wrongly convicted individuals experience damage to their reputations upon exoneration (Burnett et al., 2017). They are stigmatized by society, and while incarcerated are stigmatized even among other inmates. Suspicion raises doubt while a conviction confirms guilt. Exonerees often find themselves in a position where others do not believe in their innocence (Konvisser, 2015). One male exoneree described his shock at how his former friends and family members believed he was guilty.

> Once I was convicted, none of my friends or my brothers and sisters came to see me. Only my mom and dad visited. They did not want to hurt me, but I knew that others thought I was guilty and wanted nothing to do with me. They thought I was a criminal. I think the pain of that was worse than being locked up in this cage.

A female exoneree shared that her kids were "brainwashed" to believe that she killed their father.

> My kids were little when their dad died. When I was arrested, his family took them. They didn't bring them to see me. They brainwashed my kids into believing I killed their dad. Being away from my young kids was so hard, but it was even harder to know that they thought I was a killer.

## Guilt

Exonerees reported feeling guilt at having been wrongly convicted. Some reported that they could not understand how this had happened to them. At times, they questioned their own involvement in their wrongful conviction (Westervelt & Cook, 2010). This was particularly true in cases of false confession. While scholars provide explanations as to why people falsely confess, there is no existing literature on the psychological toll this takes on a wrongly accused person. Exonerees in this study took ownership for their wrongful conviction even when they were coerced into a confession.

> *I just couldn't take it anymore. No matter what I said, they would not listen. It got to a point where I was sitting in this room hungry and had to go to the bathroom that I just said whatever they wanted me to say. I just wanted to get it over with because I had to go to the bathroom and I needed something to eat.*

Leo (2009) described this type of false confession as a coerced-compliant confession. The exoneree reported feeling weak, vulnerable, and partially responsible for his wrongful conviction. Had he not succumbed to the pressure, the outcome may have been different.

## Wrongly Convicted Individuals: Similar Traits to Other Crime Victims

The individuals interviewed in this study shared many of the psychological, emotional, social, and financial consequences of their wrongful imprisonment that have found parallels in the experiences of other victims. Here the similarities between the experiences of prisoners of war and battered women will be juxtaposed with that of the wrongly convicted.

### Prisoners of War

Kauzlarich et al. (2001) defined state crime victims as "[i]ndividuals or groups of individuals who have experienced economic, cultural, or physical harm, pain, exclusion, or exploitation because of tacit or explicit state actions or policies which violate law or generally defined human rights" (p. 176). Kauzlarich et al. noted many types of victims of state crime, including civilians and soldiers in war, populations targeted for genocide, and persons who suffered from racism, sexism, and classism, to name a few. Drawing on their working definition, wrongly convicted individuals could be considered as victims of state crime. Ultimately, it is the state that wrongly convicted an innocent person. Westervelt and Cook (2010) studied the experiences of the wrongly convicted as victims of state harm in their study that focused specifically on death row exonerees.

While this concept will be discussed in greater detail in Chapter 9 regarding societal victimization, in this section, the similarities between their experiences and that of the wrongly convicted will be outlined. Westervelt and Cook (2010) explained the relationship between six characteristics of the experiences of state crime victims, established by Kauzlarich et al. (2001), as they applied to death row exonerees.

1.  Victims of state crime tend to be among the least socially powerful actors.
2.  Victimizers generally fail to recognize and understand the nature, extent, and harmfulness of institutional policies. If suffering and harm are acknowledged, it is often neutralized within the context of a sense of "entitlement."

3.  Victims of state crime are often blamed for their suffering.
4.  Victims of state crime must generally rely on the victimizer, an associated institution, or civil social movements for redress.
5.  Victims of state crime are easy targets for repeated victimization.
6.  Illegal state policies and practices, while committed by individuals and groups of individuals, are manifestations of the attempt to achieve organizational, bureaucratic, or institutional goals.

The six characteristics model can be extended to all those who are wrongly convicted. In the end, they are victims of state harm, whether intentional or not. Criminal justice actors are powerful and have resources to convict individuals, whereas the targets of wrongful convictions historically lack the power and means to fight the system. Consequently, they become victims and are at the mercy of the state (1). The criminal justice system fails to understand or recognize the harm it has done to the wrongly convicted and, in cases where they are aware, an apology is rarely forthcoming for the suffering they have caused (2). In addition, society may blame the wrongly convicted for their suffering. For example, the community may believe that the exoneree was wrongly convicted due to their own false confession without understanding the context in which the confession was given, in particular in situations of duress (3). Redress is traditionally offered in one of two ways: through a lawsuit or via compensation. Regardless of which path is taken, the exoneree must rely on the same agency, institution, or governmental entity that contributed to their wrongful conviction in the first place for reparations (4). Exonerees are vulnerable to future victimization as they may become targets of retaliation by police and prosecutors in new criminal investigations (5). During interrogations, police use aggressive techniques to obtain a confession. Some suspects are tortured by their police interrogator until a confession is given. These tactics are unlawful; however, they yield the end departmental goal – a confession (6).

Drawing on one state crime victim population, prisoners of war, Table 5.1 provides a list of shared physical and psychological consequences to the wrongly convicted.

## Battered Women

The women's movement of the 1970s sparked awareness of domestic violence issues with a particular focus on battered wives (Hanser, 2007). Lenore Walker's (1979) book, *The Battered*

**TABLE 5.1** Physical and Psychological Consequences Shared by Wrongly Convicted and Prisoners of War

| Physical | Psychological |
| --- | --- |
| Confinement | Depression |
| Health issues | Fear |
| Humiliation | Suicidal ideation |
| Boredom | Anxiety |
| Separation from family | Mental health issues |
| Physical abuse | Psychological abuse |
| Poor food quality/ration | PTSD |
| Sleep deprivation | Lack of trust |
| Deprivation of physical intimacy | Deprivation of emotional intimacy |

**TABLE 5.2** Physical and Psychological Consequences Shared Among the Wrongly Convicted and Battered Women

| Physical | Psychological |
|---|---|
| Violence | Lack of self-worth |
| Isolation | Depression |
| Health Issues | Fear |
| Humiliation | Anxiety |
| Sleeping problems/nightmares | PTSD |
| Sexual difficulties | Gaslighting |

*Woman*, introduced readers to the psychological effects of domestic violence, specifically examining physical and sexual abuse. Since her pioneering work, domestic violence has been studied among victimologists, psychologists, sociologists, and public health organizations. Scholars have studied a myriad of domestic issues, including the types of physical and psychological injuries suffered by victims, how the courts deal with this issue, and the reasons why it is so underreported (Gelles, 1987; N. A. Jackson, 2007; N. A. Jackson & Oates, 1998; Straus, 1980).

When comparing the experiences of battered women to that of victims of a wrongful conviction, the common thread among perpetrators of domestic violence and the criminal justice system is control. Batterers attempt to control their victims through a variety of techniques, often using fear (N. A. Jackson, 2007). Similarly, the criminal justice system controls vulnerable populations through its discriminatory law enforcement practices, among other things. Coercive control techniques allow batterers (whether intimate partners or criminal justice actors) to be in a position to batter. These control tactics include grooming their victims in order to better control them, making promises they do not intend to keep. For battered women, their intimate partner grooms them by giving them false promises. For the wrongly convicted, police tell suspects that they know that they are good people who may have accidentally made a mistake. They lie to the suspect and explain that if they tell the truth, nothing bad will happen and they can go home, knowing all too well that this is not the case. Both victims share similar physical and psychological consequences from their ordeals, a list of which can be found in Table 5.2.

## Conclusion

This chapter highlights the victimization process of the wrongly accused, convicted, and incarcerated. The role that police, prosecutors, and judges play in wrongful convictions helps to better understand the victimization process. As exonerees are the direct victims of a wrongful conviction, they suffer from the physical and psychological effects of incarceration and false imprisonment. This chapter also drew comparisons of exonerees with victims of state harm and battered women to highlight the similarities between these vulnerable groups. The wrongly convicted, like other victims, deserve recognition and redress similar to crime victims.

## Note

1 These "no-crime" wrongful convictions will be discussed in greater detail in Chapter 6.

# 6

# FEMALE VICTIMS OF A WRONGFUL CONVICTION

## Continual Marginalization

*Kathryn M. Campbell*

## Introduction

There is a growing body of literature that examines wrongful convictions from the perspective of those experiencing it – the wrongly convicted person himself (cf. Campbell & Denov, 2004; N. A. Jackson et al., 2021; Westervelt & Cook, 2012). The gender designation of "him"-self in the previous sentence is intentional as there is very little academic literature that presents the perspective of the wrongly convicted *female*. [1] Similar to research that has demonstrated that women's experiences in the criminal justice system have differed considerably from that of men (Bruckert & Law, 2018), presumably the experiences of women who are imprisoned for crimes they did not commit will differ from those of wrongly convicted males. Thus, the purpose of this chapter is to explore the data collected from the wrongly convicted women who were interviewed for this volume and situate their experiences within the context of the other limited data that are available for this evasive population, mainly from the National Registry of Exonerations (NRE) and the Innocence Project. Theoretical considerations will also be explored, examining how feminist theory can shed light on these women's experiences within broader social structural frameworks. The issue of race will also be briefly examined, as despite what statistics reveal about the overrepresentation of African Americans in the criminal justice system[2] and among the populations of exonerees,[3] we were only able to interview one racialized (Latina) woman for this study. Finally, to situate this chapter within the context of the wrongly convicted as victims of errors in the criminal justice system, the women's experiences will be highlighted.

## Women in the Criminal Justice System

The study of women in the criminal justice system was a relatively neglected area for many years, due in part to their smaller numbers, until Carole Smart's (1977) seminal book, *Women, Crime and Criminology: A Feminist Critique*. This pioneering work brought attention to the lack of treatment of and attention to women in mainstream criminology, as well as the neglect of women as victims in the criminal justice system. A great deal of work has followed this book, and now feminist criminology thinking is evident in other disciplines where women are studied as offenders, as victims, and as workers in the criminal justice system, in

DOI: 10.4324/9781003121251-8

disciplines such as criminology, sociology, law, or feminist and gender studies. What has been discovered. is that the patriarchal structures existing in society that denigrate and suppress women's voices and women's experiences in society, in positions of power and in the home, can find parallels in the criminal justice system.

Wrongly convicted women, and women generally in the criminal justice system, have often become victim to failed stereotypes, whereby their behavior (often due to circumstances of race, poverty, and marginalization) does not comply with tropes about good mothering – which embodies ideas of selfless sacrifice directed toward nurturing and protecting children (Hays, 2003). A consequence of this is that such stereotypes are often used to justify and rationalize how women are perceived and treated once they enter the system. Moreover, as will become apparent in this chapter, there are certainly parallels in how women are treated in the criminal justice system and routinely subjected to gendered and racial biases and inequalities (cf. Bruckert & Law, 2018) that can be found in patterns among wrongfully convicted women.

## Women and Wrongful Convictions

The innocence movement has long been a driver of social change with respect to criminal justice policy and wrongful convictions; however, it has been slow to "pay explicit attention to women's cases of wrongful conviction, or the ways in which gender might meaningfully shape the types of cases for which women (and men) are wrongfully convicted" (Webster & Miller, 2015, p. 978). While much more is now known about women in the criminal justice system, revealed by early feminist scholars such as Smart (1977, 1995), Daly and Chesney-Lind (1988), and, more recently, scholars such as Bruckert and Law (2018) and Comack and Balfour (2004, 2014), as well as developments in feminist criminology (Britton, 2000; Renzetti, 2013), there has been little attention paid to the experiences of *wrongly* convicted women.

Webster and Miller (2015) explained this "androcentrism" as resulting from disproportionate attention in innocence scholarship paid to serious violent crimes involving strangers, and in most cases perpetrated by men, overturned through DNA forensic analysis, which arguably overlooks many women's cases (p. 979). Two wrongful conviction lawyers, Karen Daniel and Judy Royal, from the Centre on Wrongful Convictions at Northwestern University Law School have examined a number of women exoneree's cases and found specific issues that set women's cases apart from that of men. First of all, it seems that women are more difficult to exonerate due to the lack of DNA evidence in the majority of their cases. Given that men perpetrate the most reported rapes and murders of strangers – crimes that are more likely to leave behind physical evidence that can rule out innocent suspects – women are not included in these numbers. Secondly, when women commit murder, the victim is most often someone close to them, where the presence or absence of their DNA is irrelevant as evidence (Redden, 2015). In fact, according to Selby (2021), only 11 women on the NRE have been exonerated through DNA. This is compounded by the fact that most innocence projects rely on DNA for their exonerations; thus, in many women's cases, given that DNA is not a factor, the help of such projects is unavailable to them.

The third and most problematic aspect of Daniel and Royal's investigation was that in the majority of women's cases – in fact, 63% of them – it turned out that there was never a crime committed to begin with – the death of the victim was actually a suicide or an accident. Conversely, that was true in only 21% of the men's cases. More recently, Henry (2020) describes these "no-crime" wrongful convictions as particularly problematic for women. It would seem that exonerated women were especially susceptible to convictions involving the intentional killing or physical harming of a child or other loved one, reflecting gender stereotypes about women and crime (Lewis & Sommervold, 2015). Not only do these women violate societal norms by behaving outside of what is traditionally expected of women by committing crimes per se, but they are also said to "shirk their duties" as women and caregivers (Lewis & Sommervold, 2015, p. 1046). In fact, Henry (2020) has classified these no-crime wrongful convictions of innocent people as falling into the following areas: suicides mislabeled as murders, mechanical malfunctions misidentified as homicides, illnesses or natural deaths misdiagnosed as shaken baby syndrome (SBS)[4] or murder, and accidental fires misclassified as arsons.

These no-crime cases, to be discussed in more detail later, are particularly revealing as to not only why women are more likely to be wrongly convicted in these cases but also why these cases are especially difficult to overturn. It seems that

> attorneys have a much easier time getting a wrongful conviction reopened when they can point to the real culprit. Yet if a woman is wrongly convicted for an accident that kills her child, there is no crime to solve, no "real-killer" and probably no alibi.
>
> *(Redden, 2015)*

Such cases are very difficult to overturn, requiring proof that forensic evidence was misused, misunderstood, or withheld. In many of these cases, the evidence is highly technical and at times controversial, requiring the hiring of expensive expert witnesses to battle it out in the court (cf. Goudge, 2008).

The final factor that Daniel and Royal found in their study that set exonerated women's cases apart from their male counterparts was that sexist stereotypes were often used to fabricate a motive for the alleged crime (Redden, 2015). Often these stereotypes, based on ideas about motherhood, career, and disinterest in raising children, are used to justify murder, when in fact they have no basis in reality. In most cases, these stereotypes also have nothing to do with the crime committed, if one was in fact committed at all. Women's care taking – whether of children/partners/elderly – comes with a cultural expectation that it be done selflessly, with social pressure on women to perform it (Dodson & Zincavage, 2007). The fact that these ideas are unrealistic and often take a heavy toll on women's mental and physical health is ignored, and when women's behavior deviates from such normative expectations, the consequences for them can be grave. Moreover, such responsibilities are firmly embedded in cultural practices and power relations, where women can become particularly marginalized (Fine & Carney, 2001).

## Prevalence of Women Among Exonerees in the United States

The NRE for the United States is the most comprehensive database in existence regarding the nature and extent of wrongful convictions and exonerations. In fact, it collects, analyses, and disseminates information about all known exonerations of innocent criminal defendants in the United States, from 1989 to the present day (NRE, n.d.). In terms of understanding how women fit within the statistics gathered by the NRE, they generally follow a gendered pattern. Statistical analyses done on the data set in 2014 revealed that approximately 8% to 9% of exonerees are female, which is consistent with the proportion of female prison inmates in the United States. Of the female exonerees, 40% were exonerated for crimes with child victims (compared to 22% of males), 30% of female homicide exonerees were convicted of killing children (compared to only 17% of male exonerees), 22% of female exonerees were convicted for child sexual abuse, and 63% of female exonerees were convicted for crimes that never occurred, which is three times the rate of men (21%; Jackson & Gross, 2014).

A further analysis undertaken by Webster and Miller (2015) of the NRE data set from 1989 to 2014 attempts to understand how race and gender intersect and

> feed this process of tunnel vision by providing criminal justice actors with particular kinds of cultural scripts through which they interpret real or perceived criminal events and come to make decisions about which actor or actors they believe are responsible and why.
>
> *(p. 982)*

Their research supports an intersectional approach to this task as from the outset, they believed that neither gender nor race could account for these patterns on their own. Their results, through an examination of 126 cases of female exonerees, reveal a number of interesting findings regarding how women come to be wrongly convicted and for what types of crimes.

The racial distribution of men's exonerations closely paralleled racial disparities in men's incarceration rates; in the case of women, however, White women made a larger proportion of exonerees than their representation among incarcerated women more generally (Webster & Miller, 2015). This overrepresentation of White women in the data set may have to do in part with their increased numbers among the child sexual abuse hysteria cases of the 1980s and the 1990s. It should not be surprising and is rather consistent with what is already known about women convicted of crimes that harms or perceived harms against children account for the largest number of women's wrongful convictions. Moreover, women were more likely than men to have been exonerated for nonviolent crimes. In terms of the "no-crime" wrongful convictions, discussed earlier, Henry's further analysis of the data set found that 70% of female exonerees were convicted of a crime that never happened (Henry, 2018, 2020).

Webster and Miller (2015) also found significant racial disparities in the types of crimes among female exonerees. It appeared that while half of the White women exonerees were convicted of crimes against children, partners, or other family members, they were also more than twice as likely than African American women to have been wrongly convicted of property or White-collar crimes. Whereas half of African American women exonerees' wrongful convictions involved drug cases or street crimes (defined as violent crimes such as murder, robbery, home invasions that target strangers and occur outside the home). It appears that almost half of all women, of any race, are wrongly convicted of domestic crime scenarios, which refers to the identified crime taking place or believed to have taken place in the context of women's familial relationships and/or caretaking roles. In fact, 43% of exonerations of women in the NRE are of this nature (Webster & Miller, 2015). Across race and crime type, however, crimes involving child victims predominated in the domestic crime scenarios. In these 27 cases (15 for murder, 1 manslaughter, 1 assault, 5 child abuse, 5 sexual abuse), the prosecutorial narrative focused on tropes of "bad" mothering.

In their study, Webster and Miller (2015) found that only 31% of the cases involved intimate partners as victims or presumed victims. What was interesting about this number is that only four women exonerees had been convicted for self-defensive acts against a violent partner or former partner. When battered women are convicted of killing in self-defense, they may in fact have been wrongly convicted but are strangely underrepresented among the exonerated. Webster and Miller (2015) believed this may be the result of successful advocacy on behalf of battered women mainly taking the form of seeking clemency and not through efforts at exoneration, which reflects an important gendered feature of miscarriages of justice more broadly. There is a great deal of literature that has examined how the criminal justice system has dealt with women who kill their abusive partners; however, American courts appear reticent to treat their actions as self-defense (Linklaters LLP, 2016).

## *Interview Data*

While demographic information was sought and collected from the women interviewed for this book, further to that, their personal experiences of coping with a wrongful conviction were also explored. As a result, these data are far richer than those found in the NRE or the Innocence Project as they convey how the women coped with a wrongful conviction, the greatest challenges they faced, and the ways in which their experiences were different from so-called guilty prisoners. Of the entire sample of 24 exonerees interviewed for this book, 35% (8) were female. Moreover, they were older than their male counterparts at the time of arrest, as the average age of females was 27.88 years, whereas the average age for males was 20.80 years. Many were mothers upon entry into prison, and that in and of itself posed unique challenges. This group of female exonerees was also more often convicted of crimes involving harming children or loved ones, including crimes such as child molestation, SBS, and murder/manslaughter of children or boyfriends. By contrast, the male exonerees were often wrongly convicted for sexual crimes such as rape and sexual assault. The majority of the female exonerees in the sample were also Caucasian (7 of 8, 88%), while the majority of the males were African American (53%). The women interviewed also spent less time on average in prison (W = 13.75 years) than did the men (M = 20.67)

## *Interview Themes*

Though the numbers in this study are small and very little can be gleaned regarding patterns of female wrongful convictions from them, they are nonetheless instructive in understanding more about the women's overall experiences as victims of a wrongful conviction. In terms of the types of crimes the women were charged and convicted of, as illustrated in Figure 6.1, the most common crime was murder (in five of the women's cases). In the three other cases that were not murders, two were convictions for aggravated sexual assault. In a fifth case, the child victim was allegedly killed through SBS. In the three other cases, two were for aggravated sexual assault and one was another case of SBS, but the child did not die.

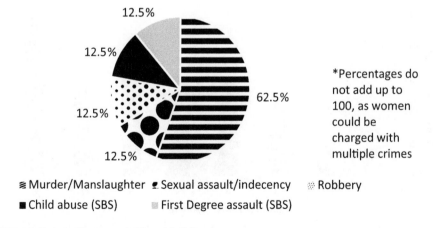

12.5%

12.5%

12.5%

12.5%

62.5%

*Percentages do not add up to 100, as women could be charged with multiple crimes

≋ Murder/Manslaughter  ♣ Sexual assault/indecency   ∷ Robbery
■ Child abuse (SBS)     ▒ First Degree assault (SBS)

**FIGURE 6.1** Female Exonerees' Charged Crimes

In terms of sentencing and time served, as noted in Figure 6.2, the women received a range of sentences: death (1), life without parole (2), 20 years to life (1), 20 years with good behavior (1), and 15 years (3).

Many of the women served a great deal of time for the crime for which they were wrongly convicted, and the number of years served prior to exoneration was largely based on the efforts of innocence projects (in six cases) or dedicated lawyers. As observed in Figure 6.3, the women served from 4.5 years up to 22 years in prison, for a total of 102.5 years lost to a wrongful conviction, with an average of 13 years.

Following the telephone interviews undertaken for this study,[5] a qualitative content analysis was done on the transcripts to ascertain whether any recurring themes emerged from the data. A series of questions had been asked not only regarding demographic information but also about the women's experiences of being wrongly convicted. These questions explored

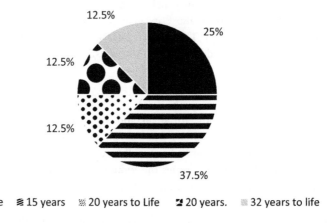

**FIGURE 6.2** Female Exonerees' Sentence Lengths

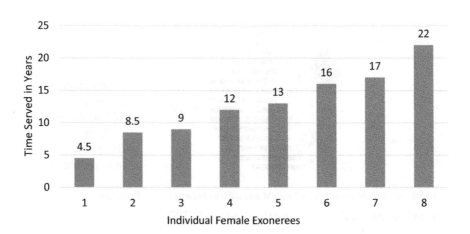

**FIGURE 6.3** Female Exonerees' Time Served

themes of their feelings upon entry into prison, the greatest challenges of being incarcerated, the experience of being innocent and locked up with the guilty, and how they coped with being wrongly incarcerated.

Upon entry into the criminal justice system at their conviction, may of the women felt dazed or stunned. For all of these women, this had been their first arrest and conviction and thus their first experience as a defendant in the criminal process. Some described themselves as feeling "shocked, fearful, dehumanized" or "scared out of my wits" and the police interview as being "surreal." One interviewee felt she was very inexperienced about everything:

> *[I felt] shock ... it didn't seem like it was possible. ... I was really young, naïve, at some point through all of that I realized that nobody was going to be able to help me, like no one can help me.*
>
> *(6f)*

One interview described her complete incredulity about the experience and the process:

> *It was a nightmare, unimaginable. ... I don't want to say I was in denial of the situation, but all the way up to the guilty verdict, I was quite sure that everyone was going to see that I was innocent. After the guilty verdict came, it was a hard slap in the face. You pretty much go into survival mode and start the appeal process.*
>
> *(5e)*

Given that all of these women experienced prison as wrongly convicted persons, questions were asked about how this experience differed, in their view, from that of their guilty counterparts. Some viewed it as completely different and had a different perspective about the system:

> *I didn't have a chip on my shoulders, like the guilty inmates. ... I didn't feel guilty because I wasn't guilty.*
>
> *(2a)*

> *Being innocent, I trusted the system ... guilty people would accept the charges and would have taken a plea bargain ... guilty people don't follow the rules, innocent are model prisoners.*
>
> *(2b)*

Others shared some of the difficult challenges that being innocent in a sea of guilty people posed:

> *I knew that if I had gone in there and said "I'm innocent and I don't belong here" that I would create a further division between myself and them. I went in with the mindset that I needed to find common ground as much as possible if I was gonna make 10 years in there, so I just didn't share with anybody.*
>
> *(3c)*

> *[It was the] worst possible thing that could ever happen. [I] felt angry, let down by the system. I knew what was true. ... Trying to get help was stressful, caused anxiety. ... Had to watch my back because others were envious my family took care of me. Had to be on guard. ... Psychological torture – "Why*

*me?" I was crucified by the victim's family and media. … I couldn't say I was sorry because I didn't do it. This made me look bad.*

(4d)

*Everybody does the same time. It wasn't as if they said, "Oh, she may be innocent so let's give her cupcakes and everyone else, you know, nothing."*

(5e)

*Well, we're all guilty of something. Some made a huge mistake and that's why they were there. Not everyone was bad. I met some really nice women. I really just wanted to be left alone.*

(3c)

When queried about their experience more generally, most shared the pain of being imprisoned, which was likely experienced by most (rightfully convicted) imprisoned women:

*It hurts even today.*

(2b)

*You lose your identity and are assigned a number – you are informed that you are now the property of the state.*

(5e)

*I wasn't trying to get comfort in there, I was trying to get out.*

(5e)

*Being away from children was so hard on all of us. Prison is a very rigid, hard environment.*

(8h)

It was important to explore the challenges that the women faced throughout their incarceration in order to have a sense of their experiences and how they managed them. Many women expressed feelings of denial, depression, guilt, devastation, and feeling overwhelmed; being separated from their children was especially hard.

*My identity was taken away, my freedom was taken away, [I was] no longer me, but a number.*

(1a)

*Especially challenging was personal hygiene, family separation, and being another person.*

(2b)

*I didn't speak their language… they came from the streets. I could not speak their street language. Like I didn't know what 'suck socks' meant. I learned that it meant be humble.*

(3c)

*Being separated from my children and family and trying to continue the relationship as best as possible as I could in there. Pretty much every day was a battle, like fighting administration, fighting, you know, the processes and policy … to maintain the strongest relationship with my kids as I could.*

(6f)

*Keeping your sanity, dealing with the terrible stress, a terrible thing. … It's pretty awful dealing with it … all these people [staff] yelling at you all the time.*

(7g)

Coping with a wrongful imprisonment is a challenging process. As Campbell and Denov (2004) pointed out: "Maintaining one's innocence can, within the context of the judicial process, be perceived and experienced as a 'burden' or liability" (p. 141). In their earlier study, they found that the men they interviewed employed creative and resourceful strategies in coping with their wrongful imprisonment, effectively diverting their energy and attention away from the devastation of their present situation. In the interviews undertaken for this study, the women shared the many ways they adapted to their trying circumstances; some found solace in religion, others by helping fellow prisoners:

*After 5 years I had a religious encounter with God – now I was surviving.*

(1a)

*[I had] religious beliefs. … [I] followed the prison rules and inmate rules – two sets in prison and had to follow both.*

(1a)

*[I coped] in little chunks … cross stitch … watched a lot of football … walked a thousand miles and lost a lot of weight.*

(3c)

*Once people realized I could type and was educated, they came to me for help. I probably helped over 1000 women.*

(3c)

*I kept as busy as possible, did legal research. I helped men and women with their cases. I started a choir. I helped build a church. Drum and bugle camp prepared me for this – I slept on gym floors, no personal space, diverse population in camp, and I had to overcome obstacles. I think this helped prepare me for prison life.*

(4d)

*I came to believe it was my mission in life to go there – I was able to change the laws from inside the prison. … We're all damaged, whether we admit it or not … anyone who served more than 5 years is damaged, but you know they have different kinds of damage … but we are all severely damaged … we all have PTSD [post-traumatic stress disorder], we all have issues.*

(7g)

As opposed to the research on men's imprisonment (Jackson et al., 2021; Trammel, 2012), few of the women discussed experiences of violence. Rather, some women shared what they termed as more subtle forms of manipulation, or what they termed as "mind games," or situations of strife, jealousy, or envy.

Release from a wrongful conviction is often sudden. This is contrary to the experiences of those who exit prison on parole or statutory release, who may have access to supports in place in the community to help them adjust, such as halfway house residency, parole officer support, and family involvement. For the wrongly convicted, their release routinely occurs with little notice, and while there is often extensive press coverage of some high-profile cases immediately upon release, very little support follows the individual. As Norris (2012) noted, a lack of re-entry assistance to the wrongly convicted, may be due to shortcomings in the existing statutory remedies for them. Moreover, one former exoneree has undertaken a study to ascertain the number of exonerees who have symptoms of PTSD, both male and female, and the difficulties adjusting post-release, given the lack of support that many exonerees experience (Michaels, 2016).

While some receive compensation from the state, it is far from automatic, and most wrongly convicted persons struggle in the community, financially, psychologically, and socially. Many women shared their struggles upon release with us:

> Everything was like the Twilight Zone. I hadn't been in a car. I didn't know cell phones.
>
> (1a)

> Learned to control my feelings, learned the Internet. Relationships have changed, I have trouble setting long-term goals.
>
> (2b)

> There were a lot of challenges on release … you lose a lot while you're incarcerated. There's a trickle effect. I wasn't the only one that was incarcerated. My siblings were, my nieces and nephews were, my parents were, my grandparents were.
>
> (5e)

> They literally just kick you out without anything, an apology or anything. Anyone who has experienced some type of post-traumatic stress. So, you're gonna need mental health, you're going to need regular medical health, you're gonna need dental – things that you were deprived of in there.
>
> (5e)

> You know, it's kind of like having your leg amputated in a car accident. You know you can go and do really well and deal with your trauma, but it changes your life forever.
>
> (7g)

Upon release, however, some women have attempted to use their experiences to help others. Some shared with us that they returned to prison to speak to the other women, to give them hope for release, while another created a handbook for exonerees and shadows them upon release to provide support; others work with innocence projects. All of the women, however, emphasized the importance of raising awareness about wrongful convictions due in part to the fact that the public does not understand that "clear-cut, DNA exonerations" are few and far between. In fact, none of the women we interviewed were exonerated via DNA. One said:

> I do a lot of public speaking, at local schools, local organizations – people need to know that this can happen to anyone and there doesn't even have to be a crime committed.
>
> (5e)

The findings in this chapter mirror some of what Konvisser (2015) found in her larger study of female exonerees, undertaken from her perspective as a trauma researcher. In her interviews with 21 formerly wrongly convicted females, Konvisser's findings were similar to what the interviewees in this book shared: for most it was their first involvement in the criminal justice system; prison was a culture shock; many suffered from the "pains of imprisonment" and later showed evidence of PTSD and had nightmares, depression, and anxiety; many suffered from grief and loss of relationships; and most developed creative coping strategies in prison. Upon release, again similar to the interviewees in this chapter, most had adjustment problems adapting to the new realities of technology, disconnections from families and friends, and difficulty finding work opportunities. As one of the exonerees, Barb, recalls that she "wasn't prepared to leave prison any more than I was prepared to go in" (Konvisser, 2015, p. 349).

One of the best means to helping individuals cope with release from a wrongful conviction is financial support. However, it is not an automatic process in most states, not every state provides compensation, and the assistance offered varies tremendously. In fact, only 35 states, the federal government, and Washington, DC, have laws to compensate the wrongfully convicted (Innocence Project, n.d.). Moreover, variations exist with regard to amounts awarded, standards of proof for eligibility, processes of adjudication, and offset provisions with respect to federal and/or civil awards and settlements. In terms of the women interviewed, only three of them received compensation from the state; the others were barred from doing so due to the circumstances of their case.

Interestingly, and what some of the interviewees shared with us, was that their case was not included in the NRE, as they were not in possession of what they referred to as an "innocence" certificate. While no such legal certificate exists *per se*, what they may have been referring to is the fact that a court has not pronounced an acquittal on their case. The NRE defines their criteria for classifying cases as exonerations[6] based on official actions taken by courts and other government agencies. There are a number of legal outcomes for the wrongly convicted that could bar a wrongly convicted individual from declaring they are factually, legally innocent, despite not having committed the crime in question, and therefore they are excluded from the registry. One instance would be when the case is resolved through an *Alford plea*. What that entails "is when a defendant maintains his innocence but admits that the state has sufficient evidence to convict him and agrees to be treated as guilty" but is then released from prison. (*N.C. v. Alford*, 1970). Other instances would involve charges being dropped and the case being dismissed, leaving a defendant essentially in legal limbo, or cases where DNA may exonerate the individual but for bureaucratic reasons has been neither pursued nor tested. Some of the interviewees expressed the belief that the NRE numbers were inaccurate for these reasons and could likely be at least 20% higher, if the criteria for inclusion were expanded. At the same time, given that the NRE data set includes as exonerations all crimes in which the person is officially cleared, it may include individuals who are legally but not necessarily factually innocent (Webster & Miller, 2015). Moreover, the consequence to not being fully exonerated, in some cases, results in the withholding of compensation.

## "No-Crime" Wrongful Convictions

As discussed, previous research by Henry (2018, 2020) has underlined a significant problem in wrongful convictions: that up to one-third of all exonerations involve the wrongful conviction of an innocent person for a crime that never happened. What little research exists in this area points to three main factors that contribute to this phenomenon: official misconduct (police lies, aggressive policing tactics, and prosecutorial malfeasance), mislabeling of a non-criminal event as a crime, and outright fabrications by informants and nongovernmental witnesses with motivations to lie (Henry, 2018). These "no-crime" wrongful convictions revealed themselves in the cases of five (63%) of the women interviewed for this study.

In one instance, an exoneree was accused of murdering her husband, in what turned out to be a suicide. Another involved false accusations of child abuse, which became part of an alleged but fabricated case of Satanic ritual abuse, involving three other defendants. For three other women interviewed, there was a misdiagnosis of shaken baby syndrome (SBS), whereby new medical evidence later emerged that exonerated all three women. These are just of the tip of the iceberg of SBS cases, now known as abusive head trauma as in the previous three decades there was a preponderance of such cases where the law was clearly outpaced by science and people who have committed no crime were imprisoned (Findley et al., 2019; Tuerkheimer, 2011).[7] In the interviews for this study, the exonerees were convicted on a now "widely discredited theory that violent shaking of infants can produce immediate and extreme neurological damage or death without external or skeletal injuries. It now appears that these deaths and injuries were caused by unrelated accidents or undiagnosed pathologies" (Jackson & Gross, 2014, para. 10). Two of the women shared their experiences about being convicted for SBS:

> *They were accusing me of [causing the] bleeding in my nephew's brain and the doctor automatically said that he was shaken because there was no other evidence of any other type of trauma.*
>
> *(5e)*

One blamed a massive scientific agenda dedicated to upholding the diagnosis of SBS as solid science:

> *There is a whole organization dedicated to making sure all of this information and pamphlets and booklets and videos and everything are in hospitals across the nation, even worldwide. If their diagnosis is not right, then they lose these grants and they lose everything that they've built their careers on. I remember one of my attorneys telling me that out of all the doctors that I could have had against me for this particular diagnosis in the country, I had some of the worst ones – like they have staked their whole careers on this false diagnosis and so I was just another one of their victims.*
>
> *(6f)*

## Contributing Factors

As Webster and Miller (2015) pointed out, women are often wrongly convicted for one or several of the contributing factors found in men's cases, including eyewitness misidentification, use of jailhouse informant testimony, official misconduct, problematic forensic science, and false confessions. However, they noted that for these factors, what differs in men's and women's cases is often "criminal justice actors' cultural assumptions about gender and race" (Webster & Miller, 2015, p. 981), about what constitutes appropriate feminine behavior, in particular, how a "good" mother should act. Other researchers, however, point to the fact that given that most women's wrongful convictions are for crimes against children, the most problematic contributing factor tends to be false or misleading forensic evidence around child death (Selby, 2021). In the data examined by Selby (2021), 87 of the women exonerees had been wrongly convicted due to "errors in forensic testing, information based on unreliable or unproven forensic methods, fraudulent information or evidence, and forensic information presented with exaggerated and misleading confidence." When a child dies, it would seem that most are quick to blame the mother, as she is likely the person in closest proximity to the child, and regardless of the strength of the forensic evidence, most medical personal and forensic experts tend to "think dirty" and point to the mother as the perpetrator (Goudge, 2008).

During the interviews, information was gleaned regarding the factors that had contributed to the wrongful convictions and crimes for which they had been convicted, including convictions where no crime took place. Perjury or false accusations were evident in five cases, and misleading forensic evidence was presented in four cases. Official misconduct was evident in two cases, and one case each demonstrated evidence of a false confession, a murder that was actually a suicide, and inadequate defense counsel. What is also interesting and consistent with the literature in this area is that four of the cases involved crimes against children, and all four cases were in fact crimes that never actually happened. Three involved false accusations of SBS, and one was the victim of an accusation of Satanic ritual child abuse. The latter accusation was retracted on appeal, and in the SBS cases, the science that was used to convict was later debunked on appeal.

## Racial Divide?

The racial divide existing among the prison population in the United States is no longer a matter of debate. According to the Prison Policy Initiative, systemic racism is evident at every stage of the system, from policing to prosecutorial decisions, pretrial release processes, sentencing, correctional discipline, and even re-entry (Sawyer, 2020). Data have consistently demonstrated this disproportionality. For example, prison incarceration rates in the United States for 2018 indicate that per 100,000 population, 2,772 Black men were incarcerated in state and federal prisons, whereas the number for White men was 392. The numbers for women for that same year are a little less disparate: per 100,000 population, 88 Black women and 49 White women were incarcerated (Sawyer, 2020).

Among the wrongly convicted, however, the racial divide is somewhat confounding and unpredictable. In Webster and Miller's (2015) study, racial minorities (predominantly African Americans) were nearly two-thirds (62%) of the male exonerees, whereas for the women exonerees only 35% were women of color (again, predominantly African Americans). Therefore, of the cases of 126 women exonerees examined in their study, 82 were White, 34 were African American, 7 were Latina, 2 were American Indian, and 1 was Guyanese (Webster & Miller, 2015). The women exoneree's numbers are inconsistent with the numbers of women in the prison population more generally, where African American women represent over half of the prison population. As discussed earlier, the larger number of White women in the exoneree data set may have to do with their greater numbers in the child abuse hysteria cases of earlier decades. Among the women interviewed for this study, similar disparities were evident: the majority of women were Caucasian (7), with one Latina woman. No African American women responded to our call to be interviewed for this study, which may be consistent with the NRE data set and likely reflective of the differential way in which gender is treated in the criminal justice system, even in cases of wrongful conviction.

## Women in the Criminal Justice System: Theoretical Considerations

Historically, feminist theory has helped to situate the problem of women in the criminal justice system within larger structural frameworks. Liberal, radical, and socialist feminisms all have contributed to understanding the ways in which laws are written using language that marginalizes women, that laws and legal institutions do not impact on all women in the same way, and that law itself is a "site" of struggle and not only a "tool" of struggle (Smart, 1995). Put differently, while early feminists viewed the law as an apparatus in the battle against normative patriarchal structures that served to marginalize them, feminists later came to realize that indeed law is not neutral – it is inherently political and is, in and of itself, a place where struggle occurs. More recent feminist theorists employ the language of law as a "gendering" practice and one that "... intersects with other institutions and discourses in the construction of woman" (Chunn & Lacombe, 2000, p. 18). Thus, feminist criminology and intersectionality help in understanding how structural inequalities are produced, reproduced, and resisted through social action (Webster & Miller, 2015). By employing an intersectional approach to the study of women who are wrongly convicted, what must be undertaken is an investigation of "micro-level processes, namely how each individual and group occupies a social position within interlocking structures of oppression" but frames those in relation "to macro-level connections linking systems of oppression such as race, class and gender" (Hill-Collins, 2015, p. 8).

It is clear that gendered and racial biases play fundamental roles in creating the crime and typification that takes hold in many cases of wrongful convictions. Given existing institutional arrangements, community structures, and even family systems, criminal justice system actors are positioned to reinforce further dynamics of stratification, hierarchy, and power (Webster & Miller, 2015). Social inequalities come to be reinforced and reproduced within structures of gender and racial inequality (Hill-Collins, 2015). From this perspective, what becomes useful for understanding how the wrongful conviction of women occurs is accepting that cultural ideologies about gender, race, and intersections are embedded in social life. Consequently, much research has demonstrated how particular gendered and racialized individuals come to be identified as suspects in a given crime scenario and, furthermore, how particular racialized and gendered crime narratives come to be constructed and vehemently believed (Webster & Miller, 2015). Such ideologies and stereotypes shape and influence how a wrongful conviction happens and, drawing on them, allows women to be held "criminally accountable for accidental and natural deaths, crimes committed by others and their efforts to protects themselves from serious harm" (Webster & Miller, 2015, p. 1030). Such scripts continually repeat themselves given that normative societal expectations reinforce patriarchal hierarchies.

## Conclusion: Wrongly Convicted Women Are Victims

As Campbell and Denov (2004) noted, "The wrongly convicted are fundamentally victims of errors of the criminal justice system. Like other victims, they also suffer a secondary victimization at the hands of agents of the criminal justice system" (p. 157). Their victimization is further exacerbated by the unjust nature of their incarceration. Not only were the women in this study victimized by a system that relied on stereotypes of how women should behave and how a "good" mother should act but, in many cases, they were blamed for a crime that did not even occur. They are again victimized in prison, a system that does not accept their innocence and, once exonerated, in more than half the cases, are released without any support and left to fend for themselves. Clearly, the women interviewed for this study have been victimized by a failed justice system that is quick to blame them and accepts the stereotypes about women's behavior that played a large role in their original, wrongful, conviction.

The data set analyzed in this chapter should serve as a warning – women are routinely wrongly convicted for crimes they did not commit, particularly crimes involving children as victims. These miscarriages of justice will continue to occur if actors in the criminal justice system continue to fall victim to tunnel vision, view women's behavior through a gendered lens, and fail to question the science around child death. The Prison Policy Initiative has recently pointed out that are there over a quarter of a million incarcerated women current in American prisons and jails (Kajstura, 2019). If one accepts that likely 8% of them are wrongfully convicted – which is likely a conservative estimate – that translates to over 18,000 women possibly incarcerated for crimes they did not commit. Moreover, this number is growing; in fact, women's incarceration has grown at twice the pace of men's incarceration in recent decades (Kajstura, 2019). While extrapolating the correct number of wrongly convicted women from the prison population is an impossible task, regardless, the effects of these growing numbers of imprisoned women are far-reaching given that women are the primary care givers of their children. According to the Vera Institute (2016), incarcerated women tend to be single parents or primary caretakers more often than incarcerated men, whereas the Prison Policy Initiative reports that more than 60% of women in prison have children under the age of 18 and nearly 80% of women in jail are mothers (Kajstura, 2019). Accordingly, more and more children will end up in foster care or be adopted out to other families, which is accompanied by a whole host of emotional and psychological consequences. In this way, children become victims of the system as well.

Stopping the cycle of victimization that occurs through a wrongful conviction requires concerted and mutually supported efforts on the part of criminal justice officials, policy-makers, and governments. For women generally, and women marginalized by race and poverty more specifically, a wrongful conviction comes about due to a failure to recognize and acknowledge their unique struggles but also by accepting world-weary stereotypes about women's roles in society as caregivers. What is required is a greater acknowledgment that such errors can and do occur, greater and more careful scrutiny around scientific evidence presented in court, greater challenges of tropes about women and motherhood, and a greater societal effort to provide the social, emotional, and financial supports many of these women need, which could prevent such miscarriages of justice from occurring in the first place.

## Notes

1 Except for the ground-breaking work of Konvisser (2012, 2015), who explored the experiences of wrongly convicted women from a trauma perspective.

2 Despite making up only 29% of the U.S. population, African Americans and Latinos comprise 57% of the U.S. prison population (Carson, 2018).

3 Statistics from the National Registry of Exonerations indicate that African American *males* make up 13% of the U.S. population but are 47% of known exonerations.

4 The NRE defines shaken baby syndrome (or SBS) as a condition first articulated in 1971 … said to arise when an infant is shaken so hard that the brain rotates inside the skull, causing severe and potentially deadly brain injury, but often without any external signs of harm. SBS is said to involve a telltale 'triad' of symptoms—brain swelling, brain hemorrhaging, and retinal hemorrhaging. When present in an infant who has no outward signs of abuse, this triad of symptoms indicates that the child has been violently shaken. …"

However, more recent medical evidence has debunked this so-called syndrome and now points to the fact that it is physically impossible for such severe brain damage to be caused by shaking alone, without visible injuries to the skull or spine. There was also increasing evidence that other injuries, including short falls and the lingering effects of birth trauma, can produce the diagnostic "triad" of symptoms that is said to prove SBS (Gross, 2018).

5  See Chapter 1 for more details on the methodology of this study.

6  The registry considers a person to have been exonerated if he or she was convicted of a crime and, following a post-conviction reexamination of the evidence in the case, was either (1) declared to be factually innocent by a government official or agency with the authority to make that declaration or (2) relieved of all of the consequences of the criminal conviction by a government official or body with the authority to take that action. The official action may be (1) a complete pardon by a governor or other competent authority, whether or not the pardon is designated as based on innocence; (2) an acquittal of all charges factually related to the crime for which the person was originally convicted; or (3) a dismissal of all charges related to the crime for which the person was originally convicted, by a court or by a prosecutor with the authority to enter that dismissal. The pardon, acquittal, or dismissal must have been the result, at least in part, of evidence of innocence that either (1) was not presented at the trial at which the person was convicted or, (2) if the person pled guilty, was not known to the defendant and the defense attorney and to the court at the time the plea was entered. The evidence of innocence need not be an explicit basis for the official action that exonerated the person. A person who otherwise qualifies has not been exonerated if there is unexplained physical evidence of that person's guilt (NRE, n.d.a).

7  There continues to be controversy around SBS/abusive head trauma as a scientific diagnosis. See, for example, the dissent in Cavazos v. Smith (2011) and Moreno and Holmgren (2013, p. 1362), where they refer to the debates as "manufactured controversies."

# 7

# FAMILIES AS VICTIMS OF A WRONGFUL CONVICTION

*Margaret Pate*

"I think they forget about us. ..."

*Daughter of an Exoneree*

## Introduction

As discussed in Chapter 5, exonerees face a number of challenges, many of which involve their families. Their struggles include attempts to stay connected to them throughout incarceration and rekindling relationships post release. While conclusions can be drawn about the effects of incarceration on the family from previous literature, almost nothing is known about how the families of the wrongly convicted cope. The purpose of this chapter is to provide the perspective of the family coping with the wrongful conviction and incarceration of their loved one by reviewing the data collected through interviews with 13 people, including three parents, two children,[1] five romantic partners, and three relatives (siblings and a niece) of the exonerees whose experiences were detailed in Chapter 5. As indicated in previous chapters, these individuals are referred to as *indirect* or *secondary victims*, as they also suffer victimization. In fact, in a study by Jenkins (2013), the family and friends of the wrongly convicted identified themselves as secondary victims and believed they, too, were victims of the wrongful conviction. As victims of miscarriages of justice, parents, partners, and children are left to struggle with psychological consequences, financial hardships, fractured relations, belief in their loved one's innocence, and practical life constraints associated with an incarcerated family member.

## Psychological Consequences

### Initial Reaction

Many secondary victims report that with a wrongful conviction, their lives "ceased being their own from the moment of the [wrongful] conviction" – everything becomes about the case, and they feel like they have been incarcerated alongside their family member (Jenkins, 2013, p. 123). A mother of an exoneree in this study echoed this sentiment, saying, *It [her*

DOI: 10.4324/9781003121251-9

*son's incarceration] changed my life totally. It totally consumed my life.* This same individual also identified how isolating the experience can be, as she spent a lot of time working on the case, leaving her with little time for family or friends. In fact, her remaining friends told her to move on and, in her words, it was the loneliest battle she ever fought. She described the process as "having to disappear" for a while because she wanted to stay on top of the case and did not have time for much else.

## Trauma

The psychological and emotional trauma experienced by the wrongly convicted as articulated by Grounds (2004) can also reasonably be extended to the family of the wrongfully convicted (Jenkins, 2013). These secondary victims find themselves juggling complex emotions such as helplessness of the situation as well as hope that it may someday be remedied, while at the same time they are left to help in exonerating their loved one and deal with their own emotional struggles. The loss of a child, partner, or family member through incarceration by itself can lead to difficult emotional struggles, yet the wrongful conviction adds an additional layer of trauma, grief, and injustice.

In addition, the family is learning how to navigate an adversarial criminal justice system. Participation in the criminal justice proceedings can add to feelings of anxiety, fear, frustration, confusion, and anger that many families feel in the aftermath of their loved one being suspected of committing a crime. Involvement in the criminal justice system has been identified as a process of revictimization for original crime victims (Garvin & LeClair, 2013), contributing to symptoms of emotional stress, as well as physical and mental distress. The same can be true for the family of the wrongfully accused, whose trauma is compounded by a lack of understanding of the criminal justice system, how a trial functions, and the consequences of a finding of guilt. According to Jenkins (2013), families of the wrongfully convicted found that their experience with the criminal justice system had a negative impact on their ability to recover from the experience of being a secondary victim.

## Grief and Ambiguous Loss

Many secondary victims experience grief as the wrongfully convicted are removed from their daily lives; for many, the process of seeing their child, parent, or family member go to prison is devastating. Pauline Boss, an educator and researcher in the interdisciplinary study of family stress, identified this type of loss, where the individual is alive but not present, as *ambiguous loss* (Mendoza, 2017). Ambiguous loss is particularly challenging because individuals are stuck between feelings of hope and hopelessness, which can make it impossible for them to move on with their lives. Many family members in this study clearly struggled with ambiguous loss, as the niece of an exoneree stated: *I feel like I personally was robbed. I think my life would have been completely different had he been out.*

A mother of an exoneree explained that the family experienced grief daily, to the point that they could not bear to hear other people laugh, saying:

> But one of the things that happens to you when this happens to you, you absolutely cannot bear to hear people laugh. You don't understand. You know, I know the first time that we went out and had a pizza, we just left because we could not bear to hear people laugh. It wasn't that we envied them, that our pain was too great. The grieving is absolutely ... you're in grief every day.

The secondary victims also grieve the loss of what could have been a normal relationship or normal childhood. One child described missing her wrongly convicted mother throughout her childhood, unable to engage in normal daughter–mother activities because her mother was in prison.

Additionally, in a small number of cases, the wrongfully convicted may die in custody, or may die shortly post-incarceration due to health complications directly linked to their time in prison, further exacerbating the grief. The niece of an exoneree, whose uncle passed post-exoneration, described this as her greatest challenge, saying: *The greatest challenge for me, I kind of feel like he was taken from me twice.*

The trauma experienced by the primary and secondary victims of wrongful conviction may be even more pronounced for cases involving a "victim" and defendant from the same family (i.e., a mother wrongfully convicted for the death of a child; Jenkins, 2013). This is because not only are they are grieving one loss, such as a child family member, they are also grieving the loss of the family member suspected and wrongfully convicted of committing the crime. One child of an exoneree in this study lost both parents at the same time, one to death (alleged homicide) and one to incarceration, creating compounded grief and a dilemma over allegiance to the parent who would later be exonerated due to a determination that a crime never took place.

## Sense of Injustice

Children and partners often struggle with other emotional burdens, such as dealing with the strain of knowing a family member was being pressured to accept blame for a crime while maintaining their innocence (Jenkins, 2013) or attempting to fight for their innocence on the outside. One mother said:

> My son is the most important thing; he knows I'm going to fight for him. I won't give up; there is nothing like a mother fighting for her son. I didn't know I had that kind of fight. It took everything from me; no one can imagine the suffering we go through – no one cares.

Even when hearing of their parents' stories from others, children identify it as hurtful to know what their parent had to go through when wrongfully convicted. Additionally, one mother said that the hardest part of the ordeal was struggling with anger because she knew her son was innocent, yet he had to go through a trial and was wrongly incarcerated. She knew there was nothing she could do while her child, with whom she was close, was suffering. A niece described the pain of seeing how her uncle was treated in prison; the family had to carry on knowing he was being beaten and raped in prison for being labeled a child molester, even though he was innocent. He would often show up to visitation with bruises and black eyes.

## Stigma

Based upon research on the experiences of relatives of those who have committed serious offenses, more can be understood about the lived experience of the secondary victims in their community, as they suffer as a consequence of being the relative of someone so labeled (Condry, 2007). While stigmatized in their communities, this can also contribute to feelings of helplessness, loneliness, anxiety, and depression.

The secondary victims of wrongful conviction often experience "family blaming" and cannot change others' negative perceptions of their relative's guilt or of the family they come from (Condry, 2007; Jenkins, 2013). Family members become inexplicably woven into the narrative and are seen as "bad" themselves. Children may experience bullying; adult family members may experience cold shoulders at work or in the community. The niece of an exoneree described dealing with bullying, saying:

> *You keep your mouth closed. You learn how to take verbal abuse. You learn how to just let things roll off your back when you hear them [talk] about somebody that you love because you can't fight everybody all the time.*

In other cases, some described how friends would hide from them when out in public, not because they blamed the family but because they didn't know what to say.

Family members may receive greater societal stigma and shaming if the exoneree has been wrongfully convicted for a sexual offense, such as a niece whose uncle was falsely accused at the start of the "day-care sex-abuse hysteria" scandal that became prevalent during the 1990s. Although the alleged crime(s) was completely fabricated and can fall into the category of "no-crime" cases as discussed in previous chapters, during the initial investigation, conviction, and incarceration the community may still be prejudiced against a family related to an alleged child molester. The niece also described violence directed toward her family throughout the trial, as well as memories of her grandmother moving from town to town, losing all of her friends, to get away from the gossip and to live a quiet life. Jenkins (2013) also found that to avoid stigma, family and friends give up old friend groups or places in exchange for a place where they were not known.

Sometimes the stigma is lessened once the courts consider an appeal (Jenkins, 2013). However, several individuals interviewed for this project described stigma even post-release. One partner spoke about her family's doubts and apprehension when she began a relationship with the wrongfully convicted post-release, worried about whether the relationship would jeopardize her job or others' opinions of her, particularly given that the wrongfully convicted was charged with a sexual offense involving children. One wife of an exoneree shared that her former husband tried to use the relationship with the exoneree against her in court for the custody of their children, claiming she was married to a convicted murderer. Because the wrongfully convicted receive so much media attention, post-release, their business becomes more widely known, and small run-ins with the police can become sensationalized headlines, as happened for a partner of an exoneree. In this case, the wife described the reaction of the police who showed up for a misunderstood domestic call:

> *This is what irritated me the most. A cop came into my home while xxx is out in the car and looked and said, "You're married to xxx right?" And I said, "Yeah." And he goes, "I suggest you go into the courthouse tomorrow and file for a divorce, because once a murderer, always a murderer."*

Even post-release families and exonerees will still continue to live with the stigma from the original wrongful conviction.

## Psychological Effects of Incarceration on Children

Research on the psychological effects of incarceration on children can show parallels in the experiences of the children of the wrongfully incarcerated. Many aspects of a child's life change when a parent is incarcerated. When asking children how the wrongful conviction affected them, one said: *I would say that it greatly impacted the way I lived. You know, the way I was raised.* The limited research in this area has found that parental imprisonment can be directly related to adverse outcomes for children, likely caused by the trauma of separation, financial strain in the family, stigma, stress among the remaining caregivers, and challenges in visitation (Murray & Farrington, 2008). Many children report prolonged issues with depression and anxiety when their parent is incarcerated (La Vigne et al., 2008). Children may struggle with aggression, sleeping disorders, regressive behaviors, behavioral problems, poor school performance, eating disorders, withdrawal, and low self-esteem. The child of an exoneree in this study said that she spent a lot of her childhood angry because of her mother's incarceration, blaming herself, her mother, and God. She also believes the incarceration led to emotional problems for her as an adult and she doubted whether she would have needed special education classes if her mother had been around.

The effects of imprisonment vary among children based on the circumstances of their parent's incarceration. For example, the effects may be more pronounced if the mother is incarcerated and if the parent experiences harsh treatment while incarcerated (Murray & Farrington, 2008). The effects also vary based upon the child's circumstances; children will have a more positive experience if they have stable caregivers, social and economic support, and sympathetic attitudes toward crime and punishment from others (Murray & Farrington, 2008).

Moreover, children may be greatly affected by the stigma surrounding the incarceration of a parent in general (La Vigne at al., 2008). The stigma denies the child the normal outlets for grieving this ambiguous loss of their parent. La Vigne et al. (2008) noted that "regardless of the nature of a child's response to such stigma, it represents one of the most damaging results and heaviest burdens of parental incarceration, lasting for many children long after the parent is released" (p. 9). Like their parents, children of wrongly convicted persons face the burden of their friends' belief that their parent is guilty. All of the children interviewed for this study reported that they did not share their belief in their parent's innocence with their classmates as they felt they would have been ridiculed. They also reported that they were lonely as they did not have friends during childhood. Some believed that classmates' parents kept their children away from them. One child described the stigma associated with having a parent incarcerated, saying:

> *Growing up with the stigma of, you know, your mom's a murderer. She's in prison for murdering your dad. That was a big thing as a child. It's not that it was really broadcast from the mountaintops. But as soon as someone would find out or it got brought up, you know, kids will just be kids and try to, you know, torment and bully and just get under your skin a little bit. The biggest stigma was just her being incarcerated.*

Parental imprisonment has been found to be a risk factor for delinquency among boys (Murray & Farrington, 2005). This appeared true for one male child of an exoneree interviewed in this study. He turned to drugs and alcohol at 12 or 13 years old, had felony drug charges at 15, and had felony drug trafficking charges by 16. He reported that he, along with his siblings, was placed in foster care; however, he was not placed with any of his siblings, and he was moved five times in the first year. In his case, one parent had been wrongly accused of murdering the other; thus, he was coping with both the death of one parent and the loss of the other parent to incarceration. Years after exoneration, he reported that his siblings still will not speak with the exonerated parent. Additionally, it took years for him to believe in their innocence. Today, he lives near his parent but still does not see them often.

## Hardships of an Incarcerated Loved One

### *Financial Strain*

Families of the wrongly incarcerated often suffer extreme financial difficulties for many different reasons. A major source of financial strain is the loss of income, particularly if the wrongfully convicted individual contributed significantly to the household income (Jenkins, 2013). Financial hardship may also arise for other reasons, such as legal costs associated with the case and costs associated with funding campaigns against the wrongful conviction (Jenkins, 2013). While incarcerated, families also bear the burden of costs for phone calls and care packages. McKay and colleagues (2016) called these the "hidden costs of family contact during incarceration" (p. 532). One mother of an exoneree described her frustration with the legal costs, saying: *They're [the lawyers] not putting up a good fight for you and you've paid out thousands of dollars and you're going broke.*

She also described the financial burdens of visitations and phone calls, saying her phone bill increased from $40 per month to $120, and every time she visited her son she struggled with the costs of gas and vending machine lunches; to this day she still carries a large debt. For her, "going totally broke" was one of the greatest challenges she experienced with her son's wrongful conviction.

Moreover, while they attempt to cope with the injustice or fight the wrongful conviction, some family members find it difficult to maintain their jobs and businesses, creating further financial difficulties. One mother described a unique financial challenge; her husband was transferred to a different county to work, yet she remained in the county where her son was wrongfully convicted so she could be part of the legal process and file paperwork as she did not trust the attorneys. The family paid for two homes during the process so she could stay close to the case and struggled to keep up with the many associated bills.

### *Visiting the Incarcerated*

Visitation of an incarcerated loved one is a mutually beneficial process, having positive impacts for both the incarcerated and the family outside (Lockwood & Lewis, 2019). For those incarcerated for crimes they committed, visitation can lower the risk of reoffending once an inmate is released from prison (Mitchell et al., 2016). Mitchell and colleagues (2016) analyzed data across 16 different studies on the effects of visitation on the incarcerated and found an overall 26% reduction in reoffending post-release. Visitation likely impacts reoffending because it allows for the continued development of healthy social bonds with family and friends, which may be protective against engagement in criminality upon release. While exonerees may not struggle with "re-offending" post-release as they have been incarcerated wrongfully in the first place, the benefits of visitation likely extend to them as a population. The maintenance of social bonds while in prison will assist the exoneree in the challenging transition out of prison. Several interviewees described visits as generally happy because their loved one was grateful for the connection with family.

Unfortunately, research has shown that less than half of all inmates actually receive visitation from family or friends (Bales & Mears, 2008). This may be due to the fact that many family members describe the process as time-consuming, stressful, and often humiliating (Lockwood & Lewis, 2019). For the wrongly convicted, on top of these "normal" visitation stressors, there is the added injustice that many family members *know* their loved one should not be incarcerated, and visitation becomes an even more stressful event that is repeated weekly or monthly over years of incarceration. Their belief that the family member is innocent may make family members feel as though visitation is even more necessary, adding pressure, guilt, and more stress to the process.

## Barriers to Visitation

One major barrier to visitation is that prisons are often in rural areas that may be located far from family members' homes, making visitations difficult and costly. According to the Prison Policy Initiative, distance is the number one barrier to maintaining in-person contact with families as reported by the incarcerated (Rabuy & Kopf, 2015). In fact, the majority of inmates are located in prisons over 100 miles away from their family. Given that prisons are typically located in rural areas, public transportation is often not available (Lockwood & Lewis, 2019). When family members do have the resources to travel, they may spend hours or days just arriving for short visits. Two individuals in this study, the son and the niece of exonerees, explained they traveled 3 to 4 hours to visit their loved one in prison. Another, the mother of an exoneree, said she couldn't visit her son as often as she would like because of the distance. Additionally, prisons often have visitation policies that create further barriers for family. According to Rabuy and Kopf (2015), "The only constant in prison rules between states is their differences" (para. 3). The mother of an exoneree described a visitation policy that required an appointment. The process of reserving an appointment for visitation was incredibly frustrating, sometimes causing her to spend hours on the phone every day just to reserve her twice-monthly visits with her son.

## Emotional Strain of Visitation

In addition to the physical barriers to visitation, prison visits carry many emotional challenges as well. According to Jenkins (2013), visiting an incarcerated parent can be emotionally draining, sometimes lasting for several days post-visit. The sister of an exoneree in this study shared this experience, saying the visits would drain her physically: *I feel like I was in jail with my brother. There's so much evil in there, and all the evil in that place is, like, pulling at you as a person because you're from the outside.*

Moreover, families may also be made aware of abuses their loved ones are facing during visitation, such as the niece who described visiting her uncle in prison when he had recently been beaten, suffered concussions, and wore sunglasses throughout the visit, while also being unable to speak properly. This experience was traumatic, and she remembers crying with her grandmother the entire ride home from this visit, as well as on other visits. Crying on the way home was common among individuals. The mother of one exoneree stated:

> It was very hard. It was not hard going to visit, but it was hard coming back. … We went, uh, happy to see her. But, coming back, it was very hard because we had to leave her there. And, uh, so in the beginning, it was extremely hard. We came home in tears. And, uh, as time went on, you know, and we got kind of, like, got used to it. It was … it got a little bit better, you know?

Visits also revealed to one mother the harshness of the conditions her daughter was living in, with exposure to the elements in a barracks-style facility, where the sun would beat down all summer and there was improper heat in the winter. She described the conditions, saying:

*I was worried about her ... the conditions there were terrible. They didn't have any protection from the sun. And there was, of course, the winter, where the winter was terrible. Also, because now they were freezing. You know, they only got, like, one blanket, and they kept their clothes on. They get their clothes on, they put on the extra jacket, extra whatever they have. And they were still cold. You know, that was, this was during the winter, and she was near a vent where she was very – there was cold air coming down right on her ear, she said it was worse for her. ...*

### Visiting an Incarcerated Parent

Visiting a parent in prison may present its own unique challenges, and some children may not want to visit at all. One individual stated that visits felt like school – just a bunch of questions about what he was doing, without ever discussing the case. Another, whose mother was incarcerated for the alleged murder of his father, said that his older siblings stopped visiting because they thought their mother was guilty; he followed suit at age 10 or 11. Another shared that she stopped visiting her parent as a teenager because her grandfather became ill and could not take her as regularly. She also grew tired of visiting as she aged, saying: *Because I'm a teenager, and then who wants to go see their mom in prison?*

While some children may choose not to visit their parents during their incarceration, many children of exonerees in particular see the visitations as important so their parent knows they are on their side (Jenkins, 2013). This became part of life for a family member who said it was as if they "lived two lives": the one everyone saw and the one where they paid for prison phone calls twice each week, sent packages to prison, and visited almost every other Sunday. For this family member, the time with her uncle (who was like a father) was important, and he even used the visits as an opportunity to teach her about life. Another individual whose mother was incarcerated said the visits were important as a child; her mom would read books and sing to her.

Ultimately, while visits were stressful and frustrating, many found them to be an important part of maintaining a relationship with the exoneree and ensuring that the exoneree knew that people were on their side. For one brother, the visits sparked a passion for sharing his brother's story and being involved in the criminal justice system.

## Fractured Relationships

### Family Life Outside Prison

For families, while visitations, when possible, are beneficial to maintain the relationships to the incarcerated person, life must continue on the outside without them. However, coping in this situation is unique as grief, loss, and separation are present, yet the incarcerated person is not gone forever and may one day rejoin the family unit again. Families are also struggling with the obligations of having a loved one in prison while also meeting their families' needs and goals unrelated to prison life (Christian et al., 2016).

### Caring for Children

Partners may find it challenging to cope with everyday life while their loved one is incarcerated, particularly with raising children (Jenkins, 2013). Family members with children are involved in the emotional caretaking of themselves, the incarcerated, and the children as they try to help children understand why the parent is gone and provide a sense of security about the future (Christian et al., 2016). The challenges of parenting may be more difficult if the mother of the children is incarcerated, as women traditionally tend to take on more responsibility for raising children.

Wrongfully convicted incarcerated parents tend to be mothers. While there are more wrongfully convicted males in prisons, they tend to be incarcerated as young adults prior to having children. Some families have support in this arena from other people, as one child of an exoneree described her teachers as supportive, teaching her how to do her hair and makeup and providing her with clothing while her mother was incarcerated. Others may not have the ability to care for children, leading to the placement of children in foster care. The child of an exoneree said that he was young (only 4 years old) when his parent was incarcerated for a crime they did not commit. He and his siblings were raised in foster care because other family members could not care for them and, as discussed earlier, he moved around a lot while his parent was incarcerated. Placement in foster care, the removal of a birth parent, and separation from siblings are compounded traumatic experiences.

### Coping Mechanisms

Families are also coping with the fact that the exoneree will miss many milestones in life that the family has to endure without them. A sister of an exoneree in this study described how her brother had to miss their mother's funeral due to his incarceration. Family members cope with these unique losses in a number of ways. Some found solace in their religion and spirituality – two mothers of exonerees described praying daily. Others cope in unhealthy ways, through substance abuse. The brother of an exoneree described how his other siblings struggled with addiction or became completely consumed by the case, talking about little else. Some are grateful to have support from those around them; one mother described her other grown children coming together to support their wrongfully convicted sibling, working overtime to send money and packages and always checking on the case, describing how her family became closer because of the experience. The partner of an exoneree believed a support group would be helpful for those who have a loved one spending time in prison, to help cope with the "loss" of a loved one and the separation. In researching families of incarcerated individuals, Christian and colleagues (2016) found that hope and looking ahead to the future relationship post-release are "important anchors" for family members as they cope with incarceration.

### Belief in Innocence

Family members may struggle with their belief in the exoneree's innocence and split allegiances between the exoneree and other immediate or secondary family members (Jenkins, 2013). This is likely to be more evident in cases where the exoneree and the victim are from the same family. For these secondary victims, talking to others about the wrongfully convicted individual's innocence might be difficult to do as others may not share those beliefs. And yet, others, such as a child of an exoneree in this study, struggled with their belief in the innocence of the wrongfully convicted. In the case involving his parent, his siblings testified in court against their own parent who was accused of murdering their other parent, yet he continued to support the incarcerated parent.

For many secondary victims, the firm belief in their family member's innocence made the entire process much more difficult because they knew their loved one was locked up, suffering for something they did not do. This was also the greatest challenge identified by an exoneree's brother: that of convincing others of his brother's innocence. The intuitive instinct or factual knowledge that their family member is innocent makes many want to "fight more and help more," in the words of an exoneree's domestic partner. For her, the wrongful conviction opened her eyes to the issues of innocence. She said:

> When you watch the news and you see somebody get arrested, you might think that they got the right person to be arrested and coming up with evidence. But nobody really puts too much thought to it until you actually know someone … to reach someone … that you know is innocent.

### Working Toward Innocence

A mother of an exoneree described all of the work she did to prove her son's innocence: sleepless nights spent making notes on legal files, pouring over court transcripts, writing down questions she needed answered, and detailing the differences between her son's appearance and the description given by the witnesses. The process was very draining for her, as she felt no one was really fighting for her son, not even his lawyers. Family members may aid in a campaign for the wrongfully convicted, which can lead to empowerment and community. Even years post-release, family members may continue to try to bring awareness to the case, such as an exoneree's girlfriend who was promoting his book among family and friends and researching other cases because her knowledge of her boyfriend's wrongful conviction brought awareness to the issue.

Others had hope: one mother said, *Today they know him as a convicted rapist, but one day the world will know who he really is.*

Others may have the support of someone else rallying for justice for the innocent; one exoneree's brother said the real perpetrator wrote a letter confessing to the crime for which his brother had been serving time. In addition, the support of family and friends can have a significant impact; one mother of an exoneree stated that she received a lot of support from her boss and co-workers, which made visits to see the exoneree possible.

For some families, it may be years before anyone ever acknowledges that their family member is actually innocent. For the niece of an exoneree, 15 years after his exoneration a former worker from the day care where her uncle worked when he was accused of molesting a child came forward and said she believed in his innocence. Growing up, no one had ever said that, but his family believed in him. Once her uncle was released and the news of his innocence hit the media, the community rallied around them, raising over $330,000 for the legal costs of his defense. His network of supporters also helped him get a job, as he still had a record upon release. A mother of an exoneree described how former prisoners who had served time with her son came to her home and spent time with her, telling her they knew her son was innocent. This same mother had a prison guard tell her once that she knew her son should not be in prison. She also had the support of her son's friends on the outside who believed he was innocent. They would drive her to court and speaking events, and helped with difficult paperwork.

### Adjusting to Life Post-Release

Many family members looked forward to the day of release throughout their loved one's incarceration (Christian et al., 2016). However, the return of a family member is often not as straightforward as it seems: they need to adapt to change, reconnect emotionally, and understand the "new" person. As described by the wife of an exoneree, it involved "many wild roller coasters, from extreme highs to extreme lows."

## Changes in Familial Relationships

The process of wrongful conviction and incarceration can change the landscape of an intimate or familial relationship. Relationships may suffer greatly if the wrongfully convicted serves a lengthy sentence prior to exoneration. Most released individuals are divorced or estranged from their partners within 2 years post-release (Jenkins, 2013). Navigating relationships post-release also becomes particularly challenging if the victim of the original crime and the exoneree are from the same family, due to divisions created as families took sides or continued doubting their innocence.

It may be especially difficult to reconnect with children, as the exoneree is coming home to young adults who have lived a life without them (Jenkins, 2013). In addition, children may have expectations that things will go "back to normal" post-release, as one child of an exoneree described. She was unaware that her mother needed to get herself "steady" and begin to deal with the trauma of the wrongful conviction before she could live with her; the first few years post-release were difficult for both of them. For parents of exonerees, difficulties may arise in cases where the exoneree goes into prison as a teenager or young adult and is released as a middle-aged person. This can lead to unmet, unrealistic expectations if the parent wants the now middle-aged adult to live with them but the exoneree is ready to live on their own as any adult would want.

## Connecting Emotionally

The wrongfully convicted may have dealt with their emotions in prison by blocking off painful feelings and may continue to be withdrawn post-release, losing the emotional intimacy that was there prior to the wrongful conviction (Grounds, 2004). This can lead to estrangements in previously close relationships. Men and women also tend to cope with traumatic experiences differently. Martin and Doka (2000) described these differences between genders dealing with trauma; they believe men tend to stay busy (as instrumental grievers), whereas women to want to discuss the tragedy (as intuitive grievers). Tensions can arise in the newly re-formed relationship when it is assumed that an instrumental griever is indifferent to the situation.

## Understanding the "New" Person

As previously discussed, it is beneficial in most cases for families to maintain relationships with the incarcerated family member through visits and other means. Visits allow families to see the changes in the individual over time and help them to understand that the person will have different needs upon release than they did upon entering. The sister of an exoneree said that one of the greatest challenges about her brother's incarceration was that she had to come outside of her bubble and realize he was not her little brother who would sing and dance in the living room anymore; it was difficult for her to get to know her brother as a grown person.

## Supporting the Exoneree Upon Release

The exoneree often relies upon the family for support in many areas, which can be burdensome in some cases (Christian et al., 2016; National Public Radio, 2013). Many families are also not equipped to help an exoneree process the psychological consequences of the wrongful conviction, and the effects of prison will vary for each exoneree. The partner of an exoneree found that post-exoneration their partner shut down, saying:

> She shut down really bad when she was exonerated, and that was hard for me because I was trying to console her or see what's wrong. And she just needed some time. And then about four or five hours went by and she just said, "You know, I've had to for 20 something years, all I ever knew to do was to fight for my innocence, and, I don't know what to do now. I'm 40 something years old, and what do I do now?" Yeah, she was decompressing very, very hard, and I couldn't reach her at that point.

Another mentioned extreme reactions from her son post-release; she never went into his room because in prison somebody was always in his room, and he would scream because his sister bought him clothing and he wanted to buy his own. A husband of an exoneree described her nightmares and constant paranoia, how she was always afraid of getting in trouble because of what happened. A child of an exoneree described his mother's anxiety and fear post-release, saying:

> She was, you know, totally dropped back out to the point where, you know, we'd even be at the beach and she'd be worried that we were playing the radio too loud and be looking around, paranoid. She was afraid, you know, … she's gonna get in trouble for that. It took a lot of … hugging and calming her down. I would say, "You know you're not there anymore. You're here." She would say, "Thank you."

The partner of an exoneree described the adjustment to a new "outside" relationship with the exoneree as the exoneree was used to relationships on the "inside" for 13½ years, as these relationships had different parameters that the exoneree and the new partner had to work around. A mother concluded: You do not have a script on how to deal with these guys when they come back.

This is a sentiment that many families likely share as they navigate the traumatic effects of prison post-release. Several also expressed feeling as if they were alone in the care of the exoneree, unsure what the exoneree would do without them. Post-release, some wrongfully convicted remain engrossed in bitterness and resentment and may even become obsessed with campaigning their case and fighting the system (Jenkins, 2013). Families may feel that the bitterness hinders their ability to process, recover, and heal as a family. Additionally, given that most exonerees' records are not expunged immediately upon release, family members may have to support them as this makes it almost impossible to get a job or adequate housing. When asked about the greatest challenge of the wrongful conviction, the niece of an exoneree said post-release was difficult and services for her uncle would have been helpful, particularly housing, a safe place to go, and a job.

## Physical Restrictions for the Exoneree and Family

Family may also have to adjust to physical restrictions still placed upon the exoneree, such as needing to continue to register as a sex offender, parole officer visits (depending on whether they have been released via parole before an exoneration takes place), or bureaucratic red tape that remains even after an official exoneration. One partner described how her life was drastically changed once the wrongfully convicted was released; they had to be mindful of avoiding places where children might be gathered, she could not have alcohol in her home, and her once vibrant social life was limited as her partner was banned from doing many things in a social setting for fear of breaking sex offender registry laws. Even more difficult, family gatherings with young children were restricted as the nature of the charge against the wrongfully convicted restricted with whom they could interact.

## Continued Involvement With the System

Families have also experienced continued involvement with the system post-release, in the form of either seeking compensation or filing a civil lawsuit. Several family members described the process of settling a civil suit out of court as a means for courts to minimize the publicity of the suit, while others were able to receive compensation from the state. This became a tricky course to navigate, as when news spreads about compensation, according to one partner of an exoneree, everyone comes out of the woodwork telling the exoneree and the family how the money should be spent. The niece of an exoneree even discussed the fact that the exoneree and the family were unable to keep the entire compensation award, as lawyers' fees and other legal fees were paid before the family received the money. While nothing can provide the exoneree and the family the years lost, financial assistance can help everyone adjust to life post-release. Some exonerees are not fully exonerated upon release, and families may have to continue to work through parole visits and registration with the sex offender registry.

## Trust in the Criminal Justice System

Wrongful convictions have a significant impact on individuals' trust in police and the criminal justice system as a whole.[2] Several family members identified that their experience decreased their trust in the system. The niece of an exoneree said she learned from her uncle's wrongful conviction that people are not good, that even the people in power act immorally. Another said one of the greatest challenges of the wrongful conviction was the lies told by the police detective, who changed the description of the perpetrator given by the female victims to more closely fit her son, something that she could prove through the original hand-written descriptions given by the victims. A child of an exoneree said she still feels anxious around police to this day because she has a decreased trust that they will "get it right."

For some families, the distrust extended to others, such as the media, who used them for a story, making them believe the media was on their side and then exploiting them. Several exonerees' families also struggled with the fact that eyewitnesses had misidentified their loved one and they felt it was unfair, affecting their trust of people in general. The partner of one exoneree used her boyfriend's story as a teaching lesson to her own children to be careful not to get caught up in the system. She also mentioned that she struggles with believing that criminal justice actors are honest people.

## The Importance of Restored Relationships

Familial relationships are often deeply affected by incarceration, with family interactions and emotional support declining significantly between pre- and post-incarceration (McKay et al., 2016). To address this, McKay and colleagues (2016) recommended that programs and policies be put in place to support healthy family relationships for families of the incarcerated. For the wrongfully convicted, this pattern may differ as many are often immediately released upon exoneration, without community supports. The trauma of incarceration for the wrongfully convicted and their family is very real, regardless of the release process. However, policies aimed at reunification are not typically offered to this population, so they do not currently benefit from any re-entry services and are often released with nothing.

Despite the lack of resources upon re-entry, several individuals described positive reunions with family. One child described how his mom apologized to him for everything, but he said he was the one who needed forgiveness for doubting her unwavering story for 22 years. Post-release, the exoneree was able to meet her grandchildren for the first time. He said that he ultimately came to the point where he knew it was his decision to either hold on to the past or move forward.

Limited research has explored the benefits of programs for families upon release to support healthy family reunification for those wrongfully convicted. Some recommendations include programs during and after incarceration, such as increasing parent and child contact, parenting classes, and involving families in the re-entry process (La Vigne et al., 2008; McKay et al., 2016). Family re-entry planning is typically offered prior to re-entry and focuses on shared expectations for release, including expectations for parenting, housing, transportation, and finances (McKay et al., 2016). Another recommendation is providing support groups for caregivers on the outside to allow them the opportunity to hear from others about the best way to navigate the restoration of family relationships when the incarcerated is released.

As stated, the dearth of re-entry programs for the wrongfully incarcerated is problematic. One individual from this study identified the lack of resources post-release as the greatest challenge she experienced. She believed there should be counseling services provided for the trauma experienced by the exoneree and the family, as well as support groups to share and hear from others who have lived through the injustice and the trauma. In an interview with the Innocence Project (2015), exoneree Mark Schand expressed the frustration that many exonerees face post-release, saying,

> *I don't deserve to be where I am right now financially. I don't deserve to be away from my family as long as I was away from my family. They can't make that whole again no matter what, you know? But I think they deserve to try. (para. 11)*

Exonerees like Schand find support through nonprofit organizations rather than the state.

Centurion (2020) is the nonprofit organization that assisted Mark Schand. The organization's mission is to free the wrongfully convicted, focusing mainly on non-DNA cases and supporting exonerees and their families post-release. Post-release support includes connection to local resources for the exoneree such as employment, housing, and medical/psychological care, as well as support for the exonerees' families, such as mentoring them in their assistance of the exoneree and connecting them with a support group of individuals with their shared experience. Another organization that focuses on post-release support is the nonprofit After Innocence (n.d.), whose mission is to assist exonerees and their families in accessing local support and social services, including health care and public benefits, pro bono legal representation, and mentorship opportunities.

Another area of restoration that has proven to be effective for some traditionally incarcerated populations post-release is addressing the relationship between victim and offender. Restorative justice is a process, where appropriate, that allows for a victim and offender to interact through restorative discussions to repair the harm caused by the criminal act (Lloyd &

Borrill, 2020). First introduced in North America in the 1970s, restorative justice is an alternative to traditional criminal sentencing, with the goal of the offender repairing the violated relationship between them and the victim, thereby "restoring" the relationship and/or the community to its prior status. Where appropriate, restorative justice programs can be beneficial for victims because they are given a central role in the process, as opposed to traditional adversarial justice. Victim–offender mediation can provide an opportunity for both parties to come together, discuss their feelings about the incident and the harm that followed, and plan for reparation, such as community service or financial restitution.

The restorative justice[3] approach can also be applied to the exoneree and the original crime victim, with a recognition that both were victims of a system that allowed the injustice of wrongful conviction to take place. When appropriate and agreed upon by both parties, it may be mutually beneficial to be supported in a discussion about the incident and the factors leading to the wrongful conviction. While a significant amount of trauma is experienced by the original crime victim in a wrongful conviction, a restorative justice approach may allow both the victim and exoneree to begin the process of healing from the trauma associated when the wrong person is identified, convicted, and incarcerated. Discussing the case, offering forgiveness, and speaking out about wrongful conviction together can be an important part of the healing process. The brother of an exoneree in this study described the importance of a restored relationship with the original crime victim in his brother's case. The day that their first meeting took place, the mother of the wrongly convicted person and the original crime victim met on the front steps of the mother's home. Upon arrival, the victim began crying, begging for forgiveness because she had misidentified this woman's son as her rapist. He described his mother's response: *And my mother grabbed her under her chin and held her face up. And she said, xxx, stop crying. You were a victim, just as my son was. I have nothing to forgive you for.*

In this case, sadly, the wrongfully convicted person had died while in prison, so the original crime victim could not seek forgiveness directly from him, but she did start an ongoing relationship the day she asked the family for forgiveness. The original crime victim and the wrongfully convicted individual's mother also went on to do speaking engagements together to discuss the many traumatic experiences of those impacted by wrongful convictions.

## Conclusion

Research on the impact of incarceration for families and children of the wrongly convicted sheds light on how wrongful convictions may affect these secondary victims as they cope with grief, trauma, fractured relationships, and hardship. Yet, the experiences of the secondary victims of wrongful conviction are unique as, in addition to the challenges of ambiguous loss, their experiences are all the more tragic due to the injustice of the wrongful nature of the conviction and incarceration. The family of the wrongfully convicted vacillate between feelings of hopefulness and helplessness as they struggle against the system and often work toward proving their loved one's innocence. As literature on wrongful convictions continues to expand to include the voices of the exonerees, it is necessary to also include the voices of the secondary victims: the parents, children, partners, and other family members affected by the wrongful conviction. They are victims, too.

## Notes

1  All of the children interviewed were underage when their parent (mother/father) was wrongly incarcerated but were adults when interviewed for this study.

2 These issues will be discussed in greater detail in Chapter 9.
3 Westervelt and Cook (2012) also advocated for restorative justice networks to develop between the wrongly convicted and communities upon their release. In their view, these networks would be similar to "circles of support" for released sex offenders and also include assistance from ex-exonerees and/or death row survivors as mentors to help new exonerees meet the demands of release. They would provide opportunities for exonerees to participate in community reintegration forums, where they could publicly share their experiences and thereby "shed negative stigma" and "... participants in this forum would include those who are responsible for the injury so they could hear, firsthand, how the harm has affected the person injured and his or her companions" (Westervelt & Cook, 2012, pp. 234–235).

# 8

# REVICTIMIZATION OF THE ORIGINAL VICTIM

*Margaret Pate*

"The day I learned of the exoneration was worse than the day I was assaulted. I really fought back when my attacker grabbed me. I scratched him, I kicked him. I did not go gently. After the DNA results came back, I just felt powerless. I can't un-ring this bell. I can't give Steve back the years that he's lost. ... And my testimony sent an innocent person to prison. His kids have grown up without him. I absolutely wanted the earth to swallow me."

*Penny Beerntsen (cited in C. Thompson, 2016)*

## Introduction

In this volume thus far it has been established that the impact and consequences of a wrongful conviction are most strongly experienced by the wrongly convicted person themselves. At the same time, it is clear that the secondary or indirect victims of a wrongful conviction, in the form of family and friends, are also affected and suffer short- and long-term consequences of these miscarriages of justice. Important, and sometimes overlooked at exoneration, are the consequences of a wrongful conviction on the actual crime victim, the person and family members who were victimized by the "true" perpetrator of the "original" crime. There have been some recent efforts to support these victims, who are ultimately revictimized a second time, as well as academic efforts to understand how they experience the trauma. Jennifer Thompson, a victim of rape in 1984, misidentified the perpetrator, and Ronald Cotton spent 11 years incarcerated for a crime he did not commit. Later exonerated by DNA, Cotton and Thompson have written about their experiences (Thompson-Cannino & Cotton, 2010), and now Thompson heads Healing Justice, an organization that supports those who have experienced trauma and inequity in the criminal justice system. Moreover, the work of Cook (2022) and Irazola et al. (2013, 2014) drew attention to the experiences of the "original" crime victims and how they navigate through the process of a wrongful conviction and exoneration. The objective of this chapter will be to situate the experiences of original crime victims, through the court and trial process, as well as how they experience an exoneration, focusing specifically on addressing their unique needs and challenges.

DOI: 10.4324/9781003121251-10

## Victims and the Criminal Justice System

Victims (and witnesses) of crimes are often required to participate in the criminal justice process, regardless of whether they willingly reported the crime. Participation in the criminal justice proceedings can add to the feelings of anxiety, fear, frustration, confusion, and anger that victims feel in the aftermath of victimization. According to Herman (2003), "For victims of violent crime, who may suffer from psychological trauma as the result of their victimization, involvement in the justice system may compound the original injury" (p. 159). Additionally, victims may feel that their experience is being dragged out for an unnecessary length of time as months or years pass between the time the crime occurred and when an individual is convicted and sentenced for the crime.

For some victims, participation in criminal justice proceedings can provide closure and healing, whereas for others, the successful prosecution of a suspect may not. For Trisha Meili, the victim of a brutal attack and rape in Central Park in 1989, "it was not the prosecution that gave her comfort, but rather her own psychological and spiritual journey toward understanding what happened the night she was brutally raped" (Mills, 2006, p. 458). At the same time, the psychological needs of victims are often in direct contradiction to the needs of the legal system. Victims need support, the ability to establish power and control, and opportunities to tell their story, yet the system requires they participate in a procedure designed to test their credibility, limit their control, and respond to yes-or-no questions with rules and processes that are difficult to understand (Herman, 2003). Moreover, victim satisfaction with the criminal justice system appears to be affected by the victim's characteristics (Kilpatrick et al., 1998). Victims who identify as female and White and have a higher income tend to be more satisfied than those who identify as male, African American, or lower income. In addition, victims were more satisfied with the criminal justice system if they lived in states that recognized more legal rights for victims, if they were informed of these rights, and if they believed their participation had an effect on the case (Kilpatrick et al., 1998). Despite the shortcomings of the system, victims can provide information that may prove vital in the apprehension and conviction of perpetrators.

## Investigation and Arrest

Victims assist in multiple stages of the criminal justice process, the first being the investigation and arrest stage. A victim's first point of contact with the system is typically contact from a law enforcement officer either when the victim reports the crime, an officer responds to the scene, or an officer reaches out to the victim to gain details about the crime. Law enforcement interaction with the victim has a significant impact on the continued post-traumatic stress symptoms experienced by victims (Parsons & Bergin, 2010). First contact with law enforcement would also be a critical opportunity to inform victims of their rights, which, as discussed, can have an impact on their overall satisfaction with the criminal justice system (Kilpatrick et al., 1998).

During the investigation stage, if the perpetrator is unknown to the victim, victims are often asked to assist in procedures used to identify the culprit. The first step of this process may include the victim providing a written description of the perpetrator and helping with the development of a composite image. Once a suspect is identified, the victim may then take part in an identification via a photo or live lineup, a procedure where the suspect is placed among other people (called *fillers*) and shown to the victim (or other eyewitnesses) to determine whether the victim can identify the suspect as the actual perpetrator (Wells &

Olson, 2003). In an attempt to develop strong evidence in support of the successful prosecution of a suspect, a victim-witness may be asked to participate in multiple lineup procedures. As discussed in Chapter 3, however, identification procedures should follow strict guidelines and best practices as established by over 30 years of research into eyewitness reliability in order to reduce the likelihood of a misidentification (Wells & Olson, 2003).

## Trial Procedures

Within 48 hours of an arrest, the suspected perpetrator will be brought forward in front of a judge for the initial appearance (also called *first appearance*). At this stage, a judge will set release conditions, including pretrial release; however, not all suspects are released, and some may be detained until the trial if the crime was particularly severe or if the suspect is determined to be a flight risk. Pretrial release may be difficult for victims as they may struggle with fear for their safety and confusion over the system that would allow their offender to "go free" for a time. Fear of retaliation is a valid concern as there are few witness protection measures available and little the criminal justice system can do to enforce them (Herman, 2003). Additionally, while the state may require that victims be notified of pretrial release, many victims never receive this notification (Kilpatrick et al., 1998).

Following the initial appearance, if the prosecutor files charges against the individual, the victim may be required to testify before a grand jury. The grand jury proceedings are where a decision is made as to whether there is enough evidence to provide probable cause that the suspected perpetrator committed the crime. Despite their potential reluctance, victims may be subpoenaed and compelled by the state to testify. From the prosecution's point of view, a successful grand jury will lead to an indictment against the accused. After indictment, an arraignment will take place. The suspect is now considered a defendant and goes before a judge to enter a plea; victims may choose to be present at the arraignment. Resolution of a case by way of a guilty plea may result in more positive psychological outcomes for victims as opposed to cases that go through to trial (Herman, 2003), because they can avoid living through detailed and contested facts about the crime. However, victims whose cases go to trial are afforded the opportunity to share their experience (as witnesses), increasing feelings of control and the perception that they had an impact, which may in turn lead to more positive mental health outcomes (Parsons & Bergin, 2010). While a majority of cases (97%) in the United States end with a plea deal where the defendant pleads guilty, only 11% of DNA exoneration cases tracked by the Innocence Project involved a guilty plea, indicating that in cases where the defendant is innocent, the likelihood of a trial is greater (Cooper et al., 2019).

The victim typically plays a critical role in the trial itself, offering testimony on behalf of the state. Victim testimony may be given voluntarily or involuntarily, as they can be subpoenaed to testify during the trial. Victim-witnesses may also be called upon to give an eyewitness identification in court or recount the process by which they identified the defendant during the investigation. Victims may see the trial as an opportunity to acknowledge the pain they have suffered, yet in an adversarial system this rarely happens, and it is more likely that their credibility, character, and sexual history will be questioned and publicly challenged (Parsons & Bergin, 2010). In addition, victims are often required to provide harrowing details of an assault or sit by as graphic images are shown to the court, often as a strategy by the prosecution to pull on the emotional strings of the jurors. Victims may expect support from the prosecution, viewing their relationship as akin to a defendant and their defense attorney. Most of the time, prosecutors are focused on successful prosecutions – on "winning" – which may not always represent the wishes of the victim. Victims may walk away from the trial feeling disappointed and disillusioned, like a pawn in a chess match, rather than empowered and in control. In some cases, at the end of the long, arduous trial, crime victims may find comfort in the conviction and ultimate sentencing or incarceration of the convicted offender, believing that their attacker is behind bars, never to hurt them or another victim again.

Victims face considerable challenges through their participation in the criminal justice system. Over the last several decades, due to the Victims' Rights Movement, major reforms have taken place in an effort to empower victims and legally protect their rights. The Victims' Rights Movement (discussed in Chapter 2) was born from the perception that the system was more concerned with the rights of criminal offenders than with the rights of the crime victims (Kilpatrick et al., 1998). Since the 1990s, all 50 states have passed a statutory crime victims' bill of rights, a majority of the states have amended their constitutions to include a victims' rights amendment, and a proposed change to the U.S. Constitution allowing for a victims' rights amendment has come before congress several times in recent years but is yet to be enacted. Basic rights established for crime victims at the federal level by the Crime Victims' Rights Act of 2004 include the right to reasonable protection from the accused; notification (reasonable, accurate, and timely) of public court proceedings or parole proceedings involving the crime or the release/escape of the accused; be present at public court proceedings; be heard at any public proceedings involving release, plea, sentencing, or parole; confer with the attorney for the government in the case; full and timely restitution (if applicable); proceedings free from unreasonable delay; and fairness, respect, dignity, and privacy. In addition to these rights, the Victims' Rights and Restitution Act of 1990 requires that law enforcement agencies provide victims with information on victim assistance programs to support crime victims' emotional and physical needs.

The federal victims' rights amendment has received opposition from several groups that advocate for victims and other oppressed groups, including the American Civil Liberties Union (ACLU, n.d.), because of the unintended consequences and restrictions to the rights of the accused that such a proposed constitutional amendment could bring. A few of the fundamental objections raised by the ACLU include arguments around the notion of being "innocent until proven guilty," due process, and obstruction of justice. According to the ACLU (n.d.), "Identifying victims and allowing their interests to be heard before a jury returns a verdict contaminates the deliberation process and runs counter to the idea that all Americans are 'innocent until proven guilty'" (para. 4). In addition, they argued that due process protections are in place to protect the innocent accused from a wrongful arrest and conviction, yet allowing a victim to request a guilty verdict from the jury or rushing the trial process curtails these protections. Finally, if victims have the ability to greatly impact legal proceedings, such as influencing a plea agreement, this may lead to the obstruction of justice as defendants accept plea agreements in exchange for testimony against other offenders. It is important that crime victims be afforded basic rights and services following the trauma they have experienced in order to encourage recovery and participation in the system. However, it is also important that this be balanced with a defendant's right to only be convicted in a fair and unbiased trial process.

## Victims and Exonerations

As discussed in previous chapters, according to the National Registry of Exonerations (2021), over 2,800 individuals have been exonerated in the United States since 1989. A majority of the exonerations did not include DNA, since most crimes do not produce the biological evidence necessary for DNA testing. The most common crime for which exonerees were wrongfully convicted was murder (38%), followed by drug crimes (14%), sexual assault (12%), child sexual abuse (10%), robbery (6%), and other violent and nonviolent crimes such as assault, burglary, weapons possession, and bribery. Since the late 1980s, researchers have developed extensive information on the case characteristics and causes of wrongful convictions, as well as demographic information about the exonerees themselves. More recently, exoneree experiences have also been analyzed in order to understand more about their victimization. A majority of wrongful convictions involve either a primary or secondary crime victim, yet until 2011 no empirical research had been conducted on the original crime victim's experience, including the exoneration process, the impact of the wrongful conviction, and victim support. Most of what was known came from anecdotal evidence told through individual stories.

To date, only two empirical studies have been conducted in the United States on original victims' experiences. Most recent is a publication by Cook (2022) of 21 in-depth interviews with original crime victims, including homicide victims' family members and rape survivors. The first, however, was a study conducted by a group of researchers (Irazola et al., 2013, 2014) from ICF International and funded by the National Institute of Justice, which provides information about the crime victims that is not often reported in statistics on wrongful conviction and exoneration. The researchers conducted case studies and interviewed primary and secondary original crime victims (immediate family in cases of murder), prosecutors, victim service providers, law enforcement officers, family members of the original crime victims, victim attorneys who provided legal advice, and innocence commission members.

In their review of the cases, they found that approximately half (52%) of the victims knew the wrongfully convicted individual before the crime took place (Irazola et al., 2013). Of the victims who knew the wrongfully convicted individual, a majority of the relationships were as romantic partners (64%), followed by family members (18%) and friends (9%). Many of the victims were also involved in the criminal justice process, either participating in the trial (90%), providing eyewitness identification (74%), or providing a victim impact statement at sentencing (62%).

## The Exoneration Process

While crime victims may believe their participation in the criminal justice process ends at sentencing, in cases of wrongful conviction they may be called upon to participate in the exoneration process as well. Victims may be required, or even volunteer, to provide DNA samples, testify for the prosecution, or testify for the defense (Irazola et al., 2013). The process by which a victim is notified of the *potential* for wrongful conviction is important as it is this first step that "catapults them back into a system they thought was long behind them" (Levey, 2004, p. 697). It is important for officials to consider that every time a victim is contacted with new information about the case, they relive the crime. Sensitivity to the victim's experience and the impact that the wrongful conviction has on them is important.

The process by which victims are notified about a wrongful conviction varies from case to case, with some victims never formally receiving notification at all. The timing of an official notification is largely dependent on the victim's role in the exoneration process. For instance, if an individual is exonerated through an executive pardon, the victim will likely not have a role and may be notified later than a victim who is called upon to testify in a retrial. In cases of DNA exoneration, prosecutors' offices have flexibility in the timing of their contact with the victim; they can choose to notify the victim when the offender requests testing, testing is agreed to by the state, a date for testing is set, or after the testing (Jenkins, 2009). If a victim is never officially notified of the proceedings leading to an exoneration, they may discover that the individual they believed to be their perpetrator has been released via the media or an automated message from the Department of Justice (Irazola et al., 2013). In their review of cases, Irazola and colleagues (2013) found that most victims were notified before the individual was exonerated (88%) and they were most often notified by victim service providers (58%). Initial notification was also made by law enforcement (16%), media (such as hearing about it on the news or being contacted by a reporter; 11%), automated notification (5%), or another source (11%). Later in the chapter (see Notification and Information section), victims' perceptions of best practices for being notified of the potential wrongful conviction and exoneration will be discussed.

## Impact of Wrongful Conviction

As Irazola et al. (2014) noted, "For some victims, the impact of the wrongful conviction may be comparable to — or even worse than — that of their original victimization" (p. 35). The knowledge that a wrongful conviction has taken place disrupts the lives of victims and their healing process. The exoneration process can feel like a revictimization, and initial feelings of disbelief, anger, fear, and confusion arise (Levey, 2004). While each victim experience is unique, the impact of the wrongful conviction also varies based on family and friends' knowledge of the crime, the victim's involvement in the conviction as an eyewitness, support they received from victim services following their original victimization, and the media and legal actors' public response to the exoneration.

### Guilt

It makes sense that original crime victims may experience a flood of emotions when they learn about the exoneration of the individual they believed was the perpetrator of the crime against them. Many experience shock when first told about the exoneration, followed by intense feelings of guilt (Irazola et al., 2014). In Irazola and colleagues' (2013, 2014) interviews with 11 victims of crimes that resulted in a wrongful conviction (including immediate family members in the cases of homicide), they found that guilt was especially persistent for those who identified their perpetrator via eyewitness identification, as they believed they may have contributed to the conviction. Penny Beerntsen, the original victim who wrongly identified Steven Avery as her attacker in Avery's case of wrongful conviction (popularized by Netflix's *Making a Murderer*), described extreme feelings of guilt in her personal essay about her experience (Thompson, 2016). Ultimately, she felt responsible for someone else's suffering, even though she herself was subjected to a flawed process as an eyewitness. Jennifer Thompson, mentioned earlier, who misidentified her offender in the wrongful conviction of Ronald Cotton, described guilt and shame that were paralyzing (National Public Radio [NPR], 2013). Jennifer recalled feeling as though she were now an offender; her feelings of guilt were amplified because she and Ronald were the same age at the time of the attack and subsequent wrongful conviction, and she knew firsthand the types of experiences Ronald was missing out on over those 11 years that she herself was able to experience.

### Fear

In addition to feelings of guilt, original crime victims have reported feeling fear post-exoneration, including a fear of retaliation from the individual who was wrongfully convicted and fear of the actual perpetrators (Irazola et al., 2013). In an interview with NPR (2013), Jennifer Thompson explained the fear she felt, saying,

> *I mean, fear set in, and it just took a hold of me, and, you know, terrified that at any minute he [exoneree] was going to spring up behind any dark corner and want to set the record straight and, you know, hurt me or take something away from me.*

Victims may also fear the media scrutiny that comes with the case resurfacing (Levey, 2004). In addition, victims fear reliving the uncertainty of each day as they had to at the time of their original victimization. Feelings of fear lead to isolation, helplessness, depression, and even suicidal ideation for some crime victims (Irazola et al., 2014).

## Public Scrutiny

Most cases of wrongful conviction receive intense media attention, placing both the exonerees and crime victims in the spotlight. And while this coverage draws attention to the issue of wrongful conviction, many victims receive backlash from the public as a consequence (Irazola et al., 2014). Media coverage also tends to focus more on the perspective of the wrongfully convicted person, leaving victims to feel misrepresented as the media may claim that they intentionally misidentified the exoneree (Irazola et al., 2013). In Penny Beerntsen's case, the post-exoneration period involved a lot of publicity and media attention. According to Penny,

> *Steve was made out to be a hero, and I went from having sympathy to being this horrible person who made a mistake and is responsible for someone else's suffering. The first time I went out in public, an acquaintance of mine said, "I can't believe you're brave enough to show your face.".*
> (C. Thompson, 2016, para. 7).

Yet another original victim said the media and public comments were incredibly harmful, such as, "this person [original victim] should go to prison, someone should kill them, this person should commit suicide" (National Institute of Justice, 2016, p. 9). Victims often wish they were protected from such media intrusions.

## Anger

Original crime victims in cases of wrongful conviction and exoneration may experience feelings of anger and frustration, often directed at the system itself, for a number of reasons. Once DNA has been used to exonerate an individual, it is possible that this biological evidence can affirm the guilt of the true perpetrator. However, in cases of sexual assault in particular, a statute of limitations may prevent the prosecution of the true perpetrator (Jenkins, 2009), no doubt frustrating victims seeking closure. Similarly, victims may become frustrated if DNA cannot identify the true perpetrator and their case becomes a cold case. Victims may also experience anger with the system – a system that allowed a wrongful conviction to happen and victimized both the wrongfully convicted and the original crime victim (Levey, 2004). Furthermore, in many cases the true perpetrator is able to hurt others because they were not behind bars while an innocent individual was (NPR, 2013). Finally, the crime victims may experience anger at the system as more information is revealed to them, through news stories or Internet searches, about the lack of evidence in the initial investigation that led to all of this unnecessary hurt for themselves, the exoneree, and families impacted by the wrongful conviction (Irazola et al., 2013).

## Confusion and Denial

After an exoneration, victims may experience confusion with the legal system all over again, and they may ask, "What now?" According to Post-Conviction Survivor Resources (n.d.), the original crime victims are usually the last to know about an exoneration and have nowhere to find information. Victims have identified the lack of information about the process and a desire to know the next steps as something they needed most and did not receive (National Institute of Justice, 2016). Of the 23 service providers interviewed by Irazola and colleagues (2013), only one represented an agency that had established guidelines for working with and communicating information to original crime victims in cases of exoneration. Another group that struggles with questions and need for support are the family and friends of homicide victims, who fall "outside the reach of traditional victim services" (Post-Conviction Survivor Resources, n.d.).

The victims may also have specific questions about DNA testing and whether the lack of a DNA match really means the accused was not part of the crime (Levey, 2004). For a victim, a wrongful conviction may not mean innocence but that instead something went wrong with the system to allow a guilty offender to walk free. It is possible that some crime victims will never come to terms with the fact that the wrong individual was convicted and the person they knew as their offender is factually innocent, regardless of the new evidence in support of the conviction being in error (Irazola et al., 2013; Jenkins, 2009). This may be especially true in cases where DNA evidence is not available to conclusively show the victim that the convicted offender is innocent (Irazola et al., 2013). Confusion about guilt and innocence can be exacerbated by law enforcement if they continue to collect evidence against the wrongfully convicted post-exoneration, as some victims have reported.

## Emotional Burden of Others

Through their interviews with the original crime victims, Irazola and colleagues (2013) found that many were carrying the emotional and psychological consequences of the wrongful conviction for their family members, in addition to their own. One victim expressed their struggle with this, saying,

> People don't realize it's not about them. This is not about them. It's about what do I need? And that … is what needs to be kept in the forefront. It's about what do I need. I shouldn't be the one having to take care of somebody else because, I'm really in no capacity to do that. (Irazola et al., 2013, p. 46)

## Physical and Financial Struggles

In addition to the emotional and psychological burdens crime victims or families may face in the aftermath of an exoneration, many struggle with physical and financial consequences. The physical struggle can mimic the physical reactions they may have experienced to their original victimization, including difficulty sleeping (exhaustion, nightmares, sleeplessness), stomachaches, trouble eating, and muscle weakness (Irazola et al., 2013). The manifestation of physical consequences can take a financial toll as victims seek medical treatment or stay home from work. This could also include the cost of counseling for the original victim who finds themselves with fresh trauma they thought was buried long ago.

## Victim Support

Enhanced media and popular attention to cases of wrongful conviction and exoneration has revealed that there is little support for exonerees post-incarceration. While there have been some small efforts to mitigate the challenges faced by exonerees (see Chapter 5), original crime victims are often ignored in the post-exoneration process. At the same time, research has discovered that crime victims also have unique needs following the exoneration of the individual they believed had committed a crime against them. As discussed, through interviews with crime victims, prosecutors, service providers, and law enforcement officers, researchers have uncovered several areas of service needs of the original crime victims (Irazola et al., 2014).

### *Notification and Information*

According to victim service providers and victims, the sharing of information about the case in person, rather than via email or phone, is helpful for victims (Irazola et al., 2014; Levey, 2004). One director of victim services in Texas recommended that a team including a police officer, prosecutor, and victim advocate, all familiar with the case, deliver messages to the victim personally (Levey, 2004). When notification is provided by officials involved in the original case, this is beneficial to the victim as a form of support (Irazola et al., 2013). However, it can be difficult to establish the appropriate time for notification, as time varies (weeks, months, or even years) from case to case between the confirmation of the wrongful conviction and release of the individual (Irazola et al., 2014). Law enforcement and prosecutors are hesitant to reach out to victims every time a convicted offender claims innocence, yet all parties agreed that notification should come before the wrongfully convicted person is at the point of release. In addition, service providers recommended that when post-conviction DNA testing is involved and leads to an exoneration, victims should be given the opportunity to speak with the DNA expert and the prosecutor so they can answer any questions the victim has about the process (Irazola et al., 2013; Levey, 2004).

After initial notification, it is recommended that service providers give victims printed materials to process and go to for questions (Irazola et al., 2014). Some crime victims may also want to receive frequent case updates and information about the exoneration process as this may help them feel in control and like they are part of the process, whereas others may not want ongoing updates. Victims do recommend that the information shared about the process be expressed in a neutral manner, without expectation that they take a position for or against the exoneration. Ultimately, victims should be able to participate in the process, and at initial notification they should be asked by service providers the type of information they want to receive and how they would like to receive it. It is also important for law enforcement and victim advocates to have protocols in place for proper notification and dissemination of case information to minimize the harm done to the victim (Irazola et al., 2013). Some states have also begun addressing the issue of notification via legislation. States such as Hawaii and Maine have legislation requiring victim notification of post-conviction DNA testing, and Colorado requires the victim be notified if post-conviction DNA testing leads to a vacated sentence. The only state with victim notification legislation that incorporates both DNA and non-DNA cases is North Carolina (North Carolina Innocence Inquiry Commission, 2016). Their legislation requires victim notification when any formal inquiry into factual innocence is granted. Model legislation would include language specific to wrongful convictions and the requirement of manual rather than automated notification and represent both DNA and non-DNA cases.

## Privacy

It is likely that as time passes, victims may recover from the initial trauma of their victimization. They may have moved to a new area, started a family, and developed a community of friends; some likely never share their victimization experience with others. It is important for legal actors and service providers to consider victims' needs for confidentiality throughout the exoneration process. Jenkins (2009) shared a story of a young woman who moved away from the area where she was sexually assaulted and did not tell her family about the crime. Nearly 20 years after the crime, the individual convicted for the crime requested DNA testing, requiring a swab from the original victim. The investigator for the prosecution's office flew to meet her, in the airport security office, took her swab, and flew back, all without her family or her employer knowing, in order to maintain her privacy. In addition, victims should have privacy in the media coverage of the case.

## Safety and Security Planning

As discussed, many crime victims struggle with fear post-exoneration, including fear of retaliation from the wrongfully convicted or harm from the true perpetrator. However, very few victims feel as though their safety concerns are supported by law enforcement or other criminal justice officials (Irazola et al., 2013). Regardless of officials' perceptions of the validity of a victim's fears, safety and security planning can help a victim feel supported and in control. These plans can include additional locks on the victim's home, being provided recent pictures of the exoneree, and increased patrol of the victim's neighborhood around the time of the exoneration (Irazola et al., 2014).

## Counseling and Victim Services

Post-exoneration, victims may require assistance in many forms, including information/referrals, legal advocacy, or court accompaniment (Irazola et al., 2013). However, many victims express a greater need for counseling and psychological support. In their interviews with victims, Irazola and colleagues (2013) found that counseling was the most common service need identified. Counseling services offered by professionals trained in working with victims of trauma may help victims process and cope with the wrongful conviction (Irazola et al., 2014). Victims who have received counseling during and after the exoneration process found that it was an important step that helped them understand, accept, and process the wrongful conviction (Irazola et al., 2013). Counseling services may also be beneficial to the family members of the victims to help them cope without adding an emotional burden to the victim.

Victim compensation, another victim service need, is not currently widely offered in cases involving wrongful conviction (Irazola et al., 2013). New Hampshire legislation provides victims access to compensation and services when a convicted offender's request for post-conviction DNA testing has been filed (New Hampshire Victims' Bill of Rights, 2019). However, this legislation is restricted to cases where DNA evidence is available. Most jurisdictions only allow compensation for the original victimization, even though the reopening of the case and knowledge of a wrongful conviction have been described as more traumatic for victims than the original victimization. The process by which victims apply for and receive compensation in original cases is also confusing and limiting, as victims must file paperwork by strict deadlines and meet narrow eligibility requirements.

## Peers and Victim Advocacy Group

Victims have expressed a desire for peer support during and post-exoneration (Irazola et al., 2014). One specific recommendation from victims is that a neutral victim-centered organization develop a national network of original victims in cases of wrongful conviction, in order to facilitate peer support. As mentioned earlier, Healing Justice (2022), founded by Jennifer Thompson, is the only national nonprofit organization that works with all individuals affected by a wrongful conviction and provides peer support for the many victims of wrongful convictions. Peer support is beneficial as it allows victims to identify with others going through a unique, traumatic, and potentially isolating experience. Peer support meetings, in a group or one-on-one, are a place where victims can talk about their struggles, receive advice, and process their experience (Irazola et al., 2013).

## Access to Legal Counsel

Once it has been established that a wrongful conviction has taken place, it is recommended that victims receive access to independent legal counsel (Irazola et al., 2013). Attorneys do not recommend that victims continue to be represented in court by the state or a victim advocate who is typically based in the prosecutor's office, as this creates a conflict of interest. The state is no longer "on the victim's side" and may attempt to protect themselves by portraying the victim in a bad light. Victims will need legal counsel in cases where there is civil or criminal litigation post-exoneration and in cases where they provided eyewitness testimony against the wrongly accused as there are risks of being charged criminally for perjury or obstruction of justice. It is recommended that legal counsel retained by victims possess unique qualifications, such as expertise in criminal defense and experience working with victims of trauma.

## Opportunities for Restorative Justice

One important step in the process of coping with a wrongful conviction identified by victims and other service providers is the opportunity for the victim and the wrongfully convicted individual to eventually meet (Irazola et al., 2013). The opportunity for victim–offender mediation is a restorative justice practice, discussed in Chapter 7, and is often used in the criminal justice system, in businesses, with families, and in other communities where harm has been created (Zack, 2019). These practices are often victim-initiated, allowing the victim to choose when and whether they are ready to meet with the offender or, in this case, the wrongfully convicted individual. While research has yet to explore the benefits of restorative justice practices with original crime victims and wrongfully convicted individuals, anecdotal evidence suggests that the process can be positive and cathartic. Victims who were stuck feeling guilty and believing the wrongfully convicted hated them were able to receive forgiveness from the individual, which led to healing (Irazola et al., 2013). One victim in Irazola and colleagues' (2013) study stated that meeting the wrongfully convicted person changed everything: they were no longer fearful and no longer viewed the wrongfully convicted person as a monster.

Healing Justice provides opportunities for restorative justice, for exonerees, victims, and victims' families, (sometimes not from the same case) to come together and share their experiences (Zack, 2019). According to Jennifer Thompson, "Using restorative justice principles, we [Healing Justice] seek to create individual and collective healing for all those harmed by wrongful convictions—the original crime victims and their families, the exoner-ated and their families, jurors, law enforcement, attorneys and judges" (Zack, 2019, para. 20). Since January 2016, Healing Justice has hosted retreats for people affected by wrongful con-victions to join together to engage in therapeutic activities that are directed at helping them recover from the traumatic experience. Healing Justice also hosts listening sessions for those affected by wrongful convictions to share their experience and discuss reforms to be made; the "listeners" are criminal justice officials and policymakers (Zack, 2019).

### Training for Criminal Justice Personnel

The criminal justice system may be better equipped to serve victims in cases of wrongful conviction if law enforcement, service providers, and prosecutors received training on the unique issues that can arise in wrongful conviction cases. Irazola and colleagues (2013) recommended that criminal justice personnel be trained in the following areas: (1) victims' right to notification and information, (2) engaging victims without unduly influencing them, (3) the impact of trauma, and (4) the impact of a wrongful conviction. According to victims, personnel should also be trained in sensitivity regarding the victims' needs and directing vic-tims to appropriate services (National Institute of Justice, 2016). This training should also involve the voice of the victims, inviting them to share their experiences in the same way that Healing Justice conducts their listening sessions. Training can also address the secondary trauma that a wrongful conviction has on those in the system who participated in the original investigation and prosecution, as they may also be emotionally affected. The incorporation of such training into existing academies would allow access for all criminal justice professionals.

### Conclusion

There is a robust body of research that has examined the experiences of victims of crime. There is no debating that being a crime victim causes great suffering and most victims require some form of support. In the realm of wrongful convictions, the consequences of the original victimization are often noticed and validated by the criminal justice system, service providers, and the community. Victims may receive a sympathetic ear, media sound bite, or assistance from others. Yet, once it is known that a wrongful conviction has taken place, the original crime victim is often forgotten as the focus shifts to another important victim, the wrongfully convicted: "You see exoneration cases. You see the media's flash when they're walking out of the courthouse. Everybody is excited, and yet quietly sitting at home by themselves is the victim" (Irazola et al., 2013, p. 48). Through organizations like Healing Justice and research such as Cook's (2022) and that undertaken by Irazola et al. (2013, 2014), crime victims are being given the opportunity to tell their story and talk about the impact the wrongful con-viction and exoneration had on them. Hearing stories of the original victims does not take away from or discount stories of the exonerees; instead, it helps in better understanding a more holistic picture of the damage done to all victims of a wrongful conviction. Under-standing the retraumatization of the original crime victims allows the system to better address their needs during and post-exoneration and minimize further harm.[1]

### Note

1  To learn more about supporting crime victims through an exoneration, see a panel hosted by the Institute for Innovation in Prosecution at John Jay College (2021).

# 9

# SOCIETY AS A VICTIM OF A WRONGFUL CONVICTION

*Kathryn M. Campbell*

## Introduction

This chapter will explore how mistakes made in the criminal justice system that result in wrongful convictions can also victimize society.[1] These errors not only result in misery for the wrongly convicted, their families, and victims of the actual crimes but also raise larger questions about the legitimacy of the state itself, given that the state derives its legitimacy from the people (Forst, 2004). In this way society, becomes a "victim" of a miscarriage of justice, although in a qualitatively different way than the other victims described in the earlier chapters of this book. In order to understand how this occurs, this chapter will consider questions of legitimacy, the impact of crime victim revictimization on society, the issue of compensation by the state for an exoneration from a wrongful conviction, wrongful conviction as a state crime, the costs associated with a wrongful conviction, and how society itself, through the action of a wrongful conviction, ultimately becomes victimized.

## Questions of Legitimacy

In any democracy, the functioning of governmental bodies is largely dependent on the level of faith that citizens hold in that system. This is especially true of the criminal justice system, given the fact that involvement in it can have an impact on the most fundamental of all freedoms – liberty. Faith in the criminal justice system is based on societal perceptions about the actions of a number of individual actors (police, prosecutors, defense counsel, judges) and a number of systems (courts, prisons, parole). When the system errs to the extent that the wrong person is incarcerated for a crime they did not commit, the criminal justice system has failed, and hence its legitimacy can be called into question. As Zalman et al. (2012) noted, "Perhaps no problem challenges the legitimacy of the criminal justice system more than the conviction of factually innocent individuals" (p. 51).

In this way, *legitimacy* is considered to be the acceptance of a state government and a belief in its ability to govern. It also relates to public perceptions about the system itself. For social scientists, the idea of a legitimate society is tied to a population that accepts and defers to the power holders in society, whether government, politicians, or others in positions of authority. For that matter, for a society and its power holders to be considered legitimate depends on a

DOI: 10.4324/9781003121251-11

number of things. This includes public perceptions that the system is just and effective and also concepts of racial justice, access to justice, political obligation, accountability, and the existence of a system without corruption and public misconduct (Forst, 2004). Moreover, the earliest theorizing of legitimacy in this way can be traced to Packer (1968), who speculated about the opposing views of the purpose of the criminal justice system or, rather, "the limits of the criminal sanction." When applying this to ideas about the legitimacy of the system, Packer described a conflict between two differing types of legitimacy: due process and crime control legitimacy. Due process legitimacy centers around the legitimacy that the system creates when it protects the rights of individuals against the coercive practices of the state. When the actors within the system perform their duties while respecting the rights of individuals who are caught in that system, this is described as due process legitimacy. On the other hand, crime control legitimacy results from the legitimacy or authority the state obtains through the function of law enforcement when it acts to control and prevent crime (Campbell, 2019). Thus, there is said to be crime control legitimacy when states undertake the control of crime through law enforcement. With respect to the problem of wrongful convictions, these divergent models emphasize a conflict that can occur between, on the one hand, society's interest in convicting the guilty (due process legitimacy) and, on the other, the rights of criminal defendants (crime control legitimacy; Packer, 1968).

Moreover, it is important to note that when there are diminished perceptions of the legitimacy of the criminal justice system in a society, this in turn can have an impact on whether or not citizens decide that the laws apply to them. When state or system legitimacy is called into question, the resultant lack of trust has a larger impact than just simply on perceptions; in fact, this also may affect individuals' willingness to collaborate with the social contract, to obey laws in place for societal protection, and to respect others.

## Legitimacy Through Procedural Justice

Recent theorizing in criminology around legitimacy has focused on it as a result of what has been described as *procedural justice* (Tyler, 1990). Procedural justice is said to occur when citizens feel they have been treated fairly by law enforcement authorities and when law enforcement authorities treat citizens with proper respect. This also involves perceptions on the part of citizens about the legitimacy of criminal justice actors and institutions. For Tyler (1990) it is procedural justice that serves as a measure of state legitimacy. Procedural justice, in this sense, translates into perceptions about procedural *fairness*, particularly around decision making; that is, whether the practices employed by the police in arresting and charging a suspect and the steps undertaken by prosecutors in pursuing a suspect are ultimately fair, unbiased, and impartial. The importance of fair treatment by the actors in the criminal justice system has been underscored by others, in particular Beetham (2013). A functional, legitimate criminal justice system plays a significant role in a democratic society. For Beetham (2013), procedural justice can be understood as

> the idea that the behaviour of those subject to authority, whether it be cooperation of the public with the police or obedience of prisoners to prison staff, depends on their being treated fairly and with dignity to their interactions with power-holders. It is the quality of these interactions that determines how far those exercising authority are regarded as legitimate, and the extent to which those subject to authority are prepared to cooperate in turn. (p. 23)

In this context, then, legitimacy runs both ways: the criminal justice system is considered to be legitimate when it treats those contained within it fairly, while, in turn, those subjected to its authority respond to it favorably when they perceive those in authority as treating them respectfully.

## Wrongful Convictions and Legitimacy

The concept of legitimacy within the context of the study of miscarriages of justice has been addressed, to a limited degree, in previous studies (cf. Campbell, 2019; Forst, 2004; Huff et al., 1996). Societal expectations are that when a crime occurs, police will seek out evidence that factually supports a charge, the prosecution will attempt to ascertain the truth, and if a conviction results, the suspect will have been found guilty beyond a reasonable doubt. Campbell (2019) has argued, however, that the existence of a wrongful conviction is evidence of a legitimacy deficit, and the fact that it occurs raises questions about the legitimacy of the criminal justice process. As noted in Chapter 3, the failings of the criminal justice system have been well documented, and innocence scholarship over the past 30 years has repeatedly demonstrated that the wrong people are frequently convicted for crimes they did not commit due to a number of clearly evident contributing factors. As outlined, the types of errors include those made by eyewitnesses who fail to identify the correct suspect or were pressured in some manner by the police to identify the accused; the courts' use of confession evidence regarding the commission of a crime that is false, often in response to the psychological pressures involved in a coercive police interrogation; when convictions are obtained through the use of perjured testimony from a jailhouse informant who receives a benefit; and the use of expert testimony that may be based on faulty forensic science that is then used to convince a jury of the defendant's guilt (Campbell, 2019). To consider how society can, in fact, be victimized through a wrongful conviction, first I conceptualize a wrongful conviction as a state crime.

## Wrongful Conviction: A State Crime?

Understanding a wrongful conviction as a state crime is an interesting and rather unusual position, as the central actors involved in this context are not normally viewed as criminal (Stratton, 2015). Moreover, when a wrongful conviction occurs, it is sometimes difficult to pinpoint an individual who is directly responsible for the action or inaction that resulted in the miscarriages of justice. In some cases, therefore, the responsibility for the error is systemic, wherein no individual in the process is entirely to blame (Stratton, 2015).

When a wrongful conviction occurs as the result of state action or inaction, it in turn perpetuates the legitimacy deficit; members of society lose faith in a government or state actor who effectively commits a crime through the conviction of an innocent person. As discussed earlier in the book (see Chapter 5), the term "state crime" itself is difficult to define, as it is often applied to a wide range of state sponsored egregious acts of torture, war, or genocide. At the same time, it can be understood as referring to state-induced harm that occurs through acts of commission and omission. As described by Stratton (2015):

> At their barest form, crimes of commission and omission are a method of distinguishing between different levels of complicity the state may have in relationship with a crime. Commission is regarded as those acts that involve active and conscious state involvement, whereas omission is defined by the absence of state involvement or negligence where a state role should have been present. As a wrongful conviction occurs within a criminal justice system run by the state, it serves to follow that many errors could be placed within such a framework. (p. 27)

Stratton further defined crimes of commission as those acts that result in injury, and while the state may be an indirect actor in such instances, its involvement in the harms incurred are still regarded as criminal. On the other hand, crimes of omission are less clearly defined and take place when the state disregards its obligations to protect the community from unsafe or unfair conditions.

When the state is involved in a wrongful conviction, it has the responsibility to compensate the wrongly convicted, as in some cases it plays a direct role in systemic error that resulted in the wrongful conviction in the first instance. Justice Peter Cory (2001) articulated this responsibility in the inquiry examining the wrongful conviction of Thomas Sophonow for murder in 1985:

> In the case of wrongful conviction, it is the State which has brought all its weight to bear against the individual. It is the State which has conducted the investigation and prosecution on the individual that resulted in the wrongful conviction. It is the State which wrongfully subjected the individual to imprisonment. (p. 169)

As discussed in Chapter 5, Westervelt and Cook (2010) also advocated that the wrongly convicted are victims of state crime, that the harms they suffer through a wrongful conviction are state produced:

> Exonerees are victims of the state. They have been wrongly convicted and incarcerated for crimes they did not commit as a result of explicit illegal state action or the misapplication of state power. Whether the result of willful, illegal conduct by state officials, implicit public pressure on and tunnel vision by the police, an imbalance of resources in favour of the state, or sheer carelessness by investigators and prosecutors, wrongful convictions cause harm and produce victims. (p. 261)

The state crime perspective also focuses on the notion of *social harms*, or harms that occur as a consequence of state action or inaction. Naughton (2004, 2007) examined miscarriages of justice from this perspective, which includes wrongful convictions, among other injustices, and described the many resultant deprivations that occur through a wrongful conviction as actual forms of social harm, including physical, emotional, psychological, and financial. While some might argue that viewing wrongful convictions as resulting from state crime may represent an extreme position, nonetheless it is the employees of the state (police, prosecutors, and judges) who at times directly contribute to wrongful convictions through their role in the criminal justice system, who are in turn protected by the state through qualified immunity from being pursued by citizens for their errors. If one accepts that a wrongful conviction is indeed a state crime, one way to regain legitimacy – to rectify an error and to affect societal perceptions – is to provide compensation for that error.

## Compensation and Legitimacy

In cases where there is an *exoneration*, a finding for innocence or some other form of liberation from a conviction, it would follow that the state is responsible for compensating the individual for their ordeal. Individuals who are victims of state harm are deserving of governmental assistance in making their recovery, and the wrongly convicted fit into this category, similar to actions in civil law. For example, when the state fails to clear snow from a public sidewalk and an individual slips and breaks their arm, the state has an obligation to compensate that person due to their negligence – this obligation is grounded in tort law, which is the private law of civil wrongs. For the wrongly convicted it is essentially the same: in most cases, they are victimized by the state through some form of systemic error and, as a result, the state has both a moral and a legal obligation to compensate them. The moral obligation that is fundamentally tied to compensation in these instances concerns the nature of the state and its obligations to and relationships with individuals and with the law itself (Campbell, 2005; Cohen, 1986). Legal obligations, however, are more dependent on geography and whether a given state or country has a statute in place that mandates compensation. A study by Norris (2012) demonstrated that just more than half of American jurisdictions currently have compensation statutes in place and no uniform template exists for such policies. The statutes vary widely across many dimensions, including monetary and other assistance, limitations, and disqualifications.

The act of compensation itself reflects a kind of "taking of responsibility" for state action that resulted in the errors behind the wrongful conviction. While less clear, the types of damages that individuals suffer through a wrongful conviction are difficult to articulate. However, in an inquiry examining the wrongful conviction of Thomas Sophonow in Winnipeg, Manitoba, in 2001, Justice Peter Cory (2001), a former Canadian Supreme Court justice, attempted to enumerate the effects of a wrongful conviction, and they included

- a host of deprivations, such as liberty, civil rights, reputation, enjoyment of life, and potential normal experiences, and intercourse with friends, neighbors, and family;
- other foregone developmental experiences, such as education and social learning in the workplace;
- humiliation and disgrace, as well as pain and suffering;
- physical assaults while in prison by fellow inmates and staff;
- accepting and adjusting to prison life, knowing that it was unjustly imposed;
- prison discipline, including extraordinary punishments imposed legally;
- prison visitation and diet;
- effects on the claimant's future, specifically the prospects of marriage, social status, physical and mental health, and social relations generally; and
- effects of postacquittal statements made by public figures, police officers, and the media.

In most cases it is neither automatic nor certain that an exonerated individual will in fact receive compensation for the damages caused to them by a wrongful conviction, which Kaiser (1989) referred to as the "compensatory obstacle course."

Compensation, however, can play a role with respect to not only perceptions of state legitimacy but also to victimization. Given that in many cases it is state error that causes a wrongful conviction – through inadvertence or misconduct – as mentioned, the state ultimately has a responsibility to "make things right" for the individual who was harmed. Causation must be proved in most cases, which may be based on the "but for" test in negligence law, roughly translated as a plaintiff must prove on a balance of probabilities that "but for" the defendant's breach the loss would not have occurred and thus the causation element has been met (Nash & Moore, 2019). In fact, the essence of "but for" is stated in the following manner from a high court judgment: "The essential purpose of tort law, [which] is to restore the plaintiff to the position he or she would have enjoyed but for the negligence of the defendant" (*Athey v. Leonetti*, 1996). For the wrongly convicted, the individual would have carried on with life on the outside *but for* the state's actions that led to a wrongful conviction and incarceration. Financial compensation, while always welcomed, cannot restore other, more intangible losses, including lost time with families and children, lost opportunities for work and education, and the loss of those many things that cannot hold a dollar value. Regardless, compensation may ultimately bring a small sense of satisfaction in that the balance has been restored to a degree and responsibility has been taken by the state for the suffering and victimization it caused through its actions.

## Revictimization and Legitimacy

While the impact of victimization and revictimization on the "original" crime victim was discussed in greater detail in Chapter 8, a further discussion is necessary in a chapter on societal victimization, given the impact that such revictimization can have on perceptions about legitimacy. When a wrongful conviction is overturned, the processes involved can in turn revictimize crime victims. In many cases, in a retributive sense, victim's families are seeking some form of justice and may have participated in the entire arrest, trial, conviction, and sentencing of an alleged perpetrator. Such families are often hoping to find some type of solace in knowing that the individual who harmed them or their family member(s) is ultimately convicted of the crime. However, when the wrong person[2] is in turn victimized – in other words, when the wrong person is convicted for a crime they did not commit – it can serve to shatter the crime victim's family's faith that the criminal justice system operates as it should.

A further issue that results from these errors is that while the wrongly convicted person is incarcerated for something they did not do and suffers the indignities inherent to imprisonment, the "true" perpetrator is often at large and, in many cases, creates further victims by committing other crimes. In a recent study of 375 DNA exonerations from the Innocence Project in New York City, it was found that in 165 of those cases (less than half), the actual assailants were identified. Furthermore, these actual perpetrators had gone on to be convicted of 154 additional violent crimes, including 83 sexual assaults, 36 murders, and 35 other violent crimes, while those who were innocent of the earlier crimes were incarcerated (Innocence Project, n.d.). These background tragedies that occur through wrongly convicting someone else underscore the impact that these other crimes, which were entirely preventable, have on societal perceptions about procedural justice.

Unless investigative procedures have identified another perpetrator, as occurred in the Innocence Project data stated in the previous paragraph, the crime may remain unsolved. In such instances, the criminal justice system has not operated in a fair manner, it has convicted the wrong person, and ultimately no one is held accountable for the crime. As Kent and Carmichael (2015) note, "The public's confidence in the criminal justice system is shaken as they grapple with both the public safety concern that the actual perpetrator is among them, as well as the disappointment in the system's concern with individual justice" (p. 148). In fact, research indicates that victims' families – as members of society – are revictimized regardless of the outcome: when the "true" perpetrator is found the second time around, they may have to go through another investigation, trial, and sentencing for the original crime, and in those instances when no other perpetrator is found, when the crime remains unsolved,[3] they must live with the consequences of no resolution (Gould & Leo, 2015).

An example of the impact of a wrongful conviction in this sense comes from the notorious Canadian case of David Milgaard. Milgaard was convicted for the rape and murder of Gail Miller in Saskatchewan, Canada, in 1969. He served over 22 years in prison for this crime and had his conviction set aside in 1992; however, he was only truly exonerated in 1997 when DNA evidence (which was in its infancy in the 1990s as an investigative tool) proved that he could not have murdered Gail Miller. Later it was revealed that not only was Larry Fisher the actual perpetrator but he had committed at least seven other violent sexual assaults, both before and after the murder of Gail Miller, between the fall of 1968 and 1980 (Boyd & Rossmo, 2008). Fisher was effectively a serial rapist, and had he been identified earlier on, Gail Miller may have lived and several other women have been spared the trauma of a sexual assault.

While it is important for victims' family members and society as a whole to ultimately charge the "true" perpetrator in these cases when they are able to be identified, most of the time it is not possible. In some instances, too much time has passed, evidence has disappeared, and/or witnesses have died. In those rare cases where there is physical evidence and it has been preserved, finding the true perpetrator also requires that that person's DNA be in a data bank somewhere, that the person can be found, and that they are still living. Where possible, these actions serve to maintain public safety and have a discernible further impact – facilitating re-entry for the wrongfully convicted (Weintraub & Bernstein, 2020). At the same time, this may also restore a sense of legitimacy and faith in the criminal justice system itself. For the wrongly convicted, despite an exoneration, if the true perpetrator is never found, in some cases there may still be lingering questions in the minds of community members as to whether or not the individual is, in fact, innocent. For some, an exoneration without a charge and/or conviction of the actual perpetrator is not enough to convey innocence.

## Societal Costs and Mass Incarceration

A further way of understanding how society is ultimately victimized through a wrongful conviction is by examining the financial costs associated with rectifying these errors. As Jeffery Deskovic stated in the preface of this book, not only was he awarded over $21,000,000 in compensation for his 17-year wrongful conviction by the counties and municipalities involved in this case but they also absorbed associated legal fees. His case took almost 10 years to be completed, and he is just one of thousands of wrongly convicted persons who are awarded compensation by the state for its egregious errors in these miscarriages of justice. All of that money could have been saved if his and other wrongful convictions had not happened in the first place.

There are often unpredictable and unexpected repercussions when compensation is awarded in this manner. Also problematic for various state governments is funding the compensation awards. With limited tax dollars at the best of times, such governments have to dig deep to pay out these large compensatory awards. What happened to the "Beatrice Six" – a cohort of six defendants who were wrongly convicted for a rape and murder they did not commit in Beatrice, Nebraska, in 1985, illustrates the fallout from these awards. It took them 10 years following their exoneration in 2009 to obtain a $28.1 million jury award in compensation. However, as a result of this award, property taxes in their county were increased to the maximum amount 2 years later. Not surprising, many residents were and continue to be resentful over this payout (Prison Legal News, 2019).

The National Registry of Exonerations has tracked compensation paid out to exonerees, which has now totaled over $2.2 billion, a shocking amount to pay for state error. Aside from these direct costs paid out in compensation, there are many other accompanying costs that occur from investigating, prosecuting, and incarcerating tens of thousands of innocent people, costs that are impossible to calculate but have an enormous impact on taxpayer dollars. Moreover, prosecuting, convicting, and jailing the innocent has likely had a nonnegligible impact on the phenomenon of mass incarceration, a sad indictment on the American criminal justice system, discussed earlier in this book. If even half of 1% of the over 2.3 million Americans who are behind bars today are innocent, then almost 50,000 of those people are wrongly convicted. If most states pay an average of $25,000 to $30,000 per incarcerated person annually (Stephens, 2021), that translates to approximately $1,250,000,000 to incarcerate people who may not be guilty. Moreover, those who are arrested and prosecuted but released before any conviction – that is, those found not guilty – also cost the system.[4] The overall amounts for these errors are staggering, and besides the financial costs, this book has underscored the many other psychological, emotional, and social costs of a wrongful conviction and exoneration.

## Society as Victim

As many noted innocence scholars have pointed out (Garrett, 2011; Gross, 2008; Leo, 2005), the belief that the criminal justice system can err to the extent of convicting the innocent is a relatively recent one. The DNA revolution that occurred during the 1990s, and since, has provided almost irrefutable proof that the wrong people are sometimes convicted for things they did not do. Concomitant to that is not only the undeniable harms caused to the wrongfully convicted and their families but also other consequences in terms of societal perceptions around the legitimacy of the criminal justice system itself. If the system can get it so terribly wrong, then who is to say that everyone is immune from such errors? There has not been a great deal of research, however, that has examined public perceptions about the occurrence of wrongful convictions (Clow & Ricciardelli, 2014). What little research that does exist points out that the public is actually quite supportive of exonerees, although many believe a wrongful conviction is a very infrequent occurrence (Blandisi, 2012). Regardless, there appears to be a dearth of systematic studies that have explored the extent to which these state errors affect public perceptions regarding the efficacy of state actors.

One study that examined public perceptions about the appropriateness of compensating the wrongly convicted found that many believed in the importance of not only compensation for losses but also the need for a public apology. People interviewed believed that "… public apologies would positively impact the Criminal Justice System, as well as benefit the wider community" (Clow et al., 2011, pp. 1415–1416). An apology represents the taking of responsibility and sends a public message that the state erred and is now attempting to rectify its error.

An earlier study found that on those rare instances when a random criminal justice official took responsibility for the errors that resulted in a wrongful conviction, the wrongly convicted underlined how significant that can be (Campbell & Denov, 2004). Other researchers have noted, however, that while an apology is significant, it occurs rather infrequently[5] (Penzell, 2007). An apology represents a public admission of wrongdoing that also may have an impact on how the criminal justice system is perceived, but it can also eliminate any ongoing suspicions about an exoneree's guilt upon release (Penzell, 2007; Westervelt & Cook, 2010). More often than not, however, the wrongly convicted are left with very little support, financial or otherwise, upon their exoneration.

## Conclusion

What this chapter has attempted to do is to illustrate how a wrongful conviction can have an impact on perceptions about the legitimacy of the criminal justice system and whether it is functioning as it should. These errors can be viewed as victimizing society, whereby its citizens can no longer have faith that justice officials will convict only the guilty. As Campbell

(2019) has argued, a wrongful conviction ultimately creates a legitimacy deficit and, at times, criminal justice and governmental procedures in place can serve to overcome that deficit through exonerating and compensating the wrongly convicted. It is only when a system is perceived to be just, where citizens feel that their treatment at the hands of law enforcement is deemed to be fair, and when the authorities treat citizens with proper respect that a system can be considered legitimate. By examining a wrongful conviction as a state crime and studying the role of compensation and the costs associated with rectifying a wrongful conviction, it is contended that when that legitimacy deficit is not addressed, society as a whole becomes victimized.

## Notes

1 Some of the ideas in this chapter have been previously discussed in Campbell (2019).
2 It should be noted that wrongful convictions can occur in a number of ways. The "wrong person" wrongful conviction is likely the type that most think about in this way, where the person who in fact did not commit the crime is nonetheless convicted. Less well known are those cases of "no-crime" wrongful convictions. In these instances, a crime has not in fact occurred, but death may have taken place but resulted instead from a suicide or accident. Women are more likely to fall victim to these types of no-crime wrongful convictions, as discussed in Chapter 6, as they often occur in sexual assault cases, where the case itself may rest on faulty evidence or questions of consent. For the purposes of this chapter, the wrong person wrongful convictions are the focus of this discussion.
3 The Innocence Project, which only deals with DNA exonerations, has found that only half of identified true perpetrators in DNA exoneration cases have been charged with the original wrongful conviction crime.
4 For example, each year approximately 37,000 Californians are arrested and prosecuted but released before any conviction. If each of them spends only 17 days in custody, Californians are paying $70 million a year for their incarceration (Silbert et al., 2015).
5 Jeff Deskovic, in the foreword to this book, explained the importance of an apology to the wrongly convicted regardless of whether it was proffered from original criminal justice system actors who caused his wrongful conviction or not.

# 10

# POST-RELEASE VICTIMIZATION

## "Freedom Is Never Free"

*Nicky Ali Jackson*

### The Kick in the Pants on Your Way Out the Door!

Given all of the obstacles that wrongly convicted people have already endured from their arrest to incarceration, unfortunately, their difficulties are not left behind in prison (Chinn & Ratliff, 2009; Chunias & Aufgang, 2008). Upon release, a new type of victim is created by the criminal justice system; the label of "convict" transformed to that of "exoneree" brings forth a new set of challenges. As shared by one male exoneree:

> I was living a simple life. In a blink of an eye, I was given a sixty-year prison sentence. I went from living a normal life to living an abnormal life. Prison is a structured environment similar to that of a country run by a dictator. Leaving prison brought new challenges. I equate it to being dropped in the middle of China and you don't know the language or culture. Technology has made the world a lot smaller, and I had to make the proper adjustments. I knew this new world would not wait on me. I had to adjust to it. There were no other options. Luckily, family and friends were able to help me make those adjustments. I could not do it alone.

The focus of this chapter will be on highlighting the difficulties that the wrongly convicted encounter once they have been exonerated and released into the community. Given that there is a dearth of literature that examines these post-conviction experiences, this chapter will enhance an understanding of the challenges faced by exonerees through the use of the extant literature, excerpts, and examples from the interviews of exonerees undertaken for this volume.

Most of the existing research on incarceration effects does not discriminate between a guilty or innocent inmate. Released prisoners face many struggles post-incarceration regardless of their actual guilt or innocence. However, exonerees face different burdens than their ex-offender counterparts upon release. These additional burdens will be addressed throughout this chapter. Drawing from both post-incarceration and exoneration literature, the myriad of challenges exonerees encounter post-release will highlight their continued systemic victimization. Their struggles continue as they try to rebuild their fractured lives (Weigand, 2009).

The initial challenge exonerees address occurs on their first day of release. Particular concerns include, where will they go? How will they get there? Where will they live? How will they

DOI: 10.4324/9781003121251-12

get food? (Shlosberg et al., 2020). These are a sample of the myriad of questions exonerees face as they leave prison for the first time after years of imprisonment. In general, two immediate survival concerns include financial insecurity and housing. Additional forms of victimization present in a variety of forms, such as psychological effects, mental health concerns, physical health effects, re-entry challenges, and compensation relief struggles.

## Financial Insecurity

A short- and long-term struggle among exonerees is gainful employment. Upon release from prison, they may be left to survive with only the clothes on their back and what little money they have in their prison accounts. As such, the need to secure a job is paramount. Many barriers to employment exist, such as a lack of credit, a lack of skills, or transportation issues. Like their ex-offender counterparts, exonerees experience hiring discrimination, although, in fact, exonerees have greater difficulties finding employment when compared to ex-offenders (Clow & Leach, 2015). Parolees receive job placement assistance, whereas an exoneree – not qualifying for services because they are innocent – is provided no public assistance upon release. Some have family members to help, but this is often a short-term solution. The cruel reality is that employers, even with the knowledge that the applicant was wrongly convicted, are reluctant to hire exonerees due to their criminal record, lack of skills, and the number of years they spent in prison (Giguere & Dundes, 2002; Scott, 2010). Moreover, crafting a solid resumé is challenging as exonerees must frame an explanation for their large work history gap. In addition to resumé struggles, lack of credit, transportation difficulties, and lack of skills or education, exonerees may struggle with authority figures resulting in difficulty finding or maintaining employment. Asked whether he currently works, an exoneree replied:

> No. Huh-uh. No. I have trouble … I have a problem with people telling me what to do. Now I have a big problem with that. I've been fortunate that the Innocence Project had me speaking. You know I've spoken all over the world. I have been to five countries speaking. So I got lucky there for a while. COVID killed that, so I was eligible for Social Security. I get a little bit. …

The 24 exonerees interviewed for this study had been out of prison for an average of 12 years. Two exonerees had been released from prison within the previous year and two exonerees had been out of prison for 2 years. As the most recent exonerees in the study, their employment opportunities highlight the immediate challenges exonerees experience. One exoneree reported that he was fortunate to have earned a paralegal certificate in prison, which provided him work opportunities upon release:

> Well, I paid to go to paralegal … I have to get my paralegal certificate. I also took up an accounting degree. I have I have associates … in business, … you know. Well, I worked as a paralegal for several months. My situation is a little bit different than some of the typical guys who normally get out … because I had a paralegal certificate. I was fortunate to where I did some work on my own. So when I came home, a few places were like, yeah, we'll hire him. But it took some time for me to get that. You know, it took like a few weeks. Within a month I had a job. I've worked as a paralegal for a little [non] profit organization.

In the current study, 50% of male exonerees reported working in construction, whereas 50% of female exonerees reported not working (see Figure 10.1). Of the four female unemployed exonerees, three were full-time mothers and one was at retirement age with health concerns (see Figure 10.2).

One male exoneree reported he had avoided applying for jobs post-release due to the high-profile nature of his case:

> *I didn't even try because of the notoriety of my name and the notoriety of my case. I knew good and well that I wasn't gonna be able to get employed. I was unemployable, and anybody who did employ me was going to be highly scrutinized.*

Finding gainful employment is one of several financial concerns among exonerees. Due to their incarceration, they may have lost pension funds and have little, if any, savings for

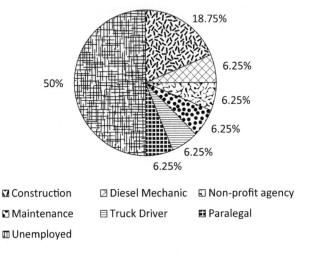

**FIGURE 10.1** Male Exonerees' Employment Status

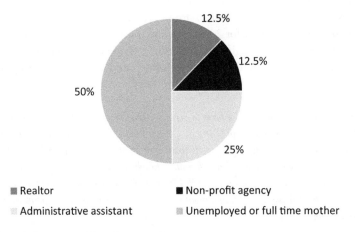

**FIGURE 10.2** Female Exonerees' Employment Status

retirement. Any monies that they may have previously had was most likely spent on legal fees. Additionally, having been incarcerated for much of the formative years due to a wrongful conviction which likely prohibited financial maturation, exonerees may be unequipped to handle financial matters such as creating budgets, overspending, and difficulties saving for retirement (Page, 2013). As one male exoneree shared:

> *I didn't know how to write a check or use a credit card. I didn't know how to budget. I was just a kid when I was locked up so when I got out, I had to learn these things and that was not easy. They don't teach you how to budget money in prison or how to write checks.*

One male exoneree described another exoneree's naiveté with money:

> *My buddy won $7 million in a lawsuit. He lost it all. Spent it on women. One woman blackmailed him and said she would go to the police and report that he had sex with her daughter. He was so afraid that he bought her a house and a car. Then his next girlfriend threatened to go to the police that he committed a crime so he paid her off. Now, he is broke and working temporary jobs.*

This is a stark reminder of exoneree vulnerabilities and how they can fall prey to others. Lacking financial understanding and fear of retaliation place exonerees at a high risk of financial strain and re-entry into the criminal justice system.

## Housing Discrimination

Generally, housing is a constant struggle for people with criminal records. Paradoxically, wrongly convicted persons do not qualify for reintegration programs as they are not classified as parolees or ex-offenders. Thus, housing assistance efforts do not exist for exonerees. Research on housing discrimination is very limited and mainly focuses on ex-offenders rather than specifically addressing the exoneree population (Visher et al., 2004). The exonerees in this study were varied in their feelings about housing. Even those who had a place to live immediately after release still felt housing insecurity. They recognized that this may be a temporary solution to a long-term problem. On release, exonerees experienced a range of emotions: some felt lucky to have had a bed waiting for them, while others reported not knowing where they would land after release. One exoneree shared how fortunate she was but understood that this may be a short-term solution to a long-term problem. She shared the following:

> *I was lucky. [A famous person] heard about my case and offered to help. I was able to live with her elderly mother and help care for her. It isn't easy, and I don't know how long this will last.*

A male exoneree shared not wanting to tell his family about his release; therefore, he had to sleep on a park bench for several months:

> *I didn't want to be a burden on my mom. I didn't tell my children, either. I didn't even know these people anymore. How could I ask them to take me in? It wasn't fair to ask them, do you think? I ended up sleeping on a park bench for several months until I found a shelter that would take me in. They were all full. I got lucky because the weather wasn't bad. I didn't even tell my*

*family I was out of prison until I got a bit settled. When I saw my kids, it was like seeing strangers. They didn't know me. I didn't know them. It was easier to be alone than to move in with complete strangers who were my kids and my mom.*

Taken together, employment difficulties and the absence of a credit history create a barrier to stable housing. Even those who have financial resources to pay rent encounter housing discrimination as landlords typically do not want to rent to those with criminal records (Kirshenbaum et al., 2020). Landlords perceive exonerees similarly to other offenders. Zannella et al. (2020) found that landlords were significantly less likely to respond to lease requests from exonerees than from the general public. Implicitly or explicitly, they do not recognize them as innocent victims of an unjust system; rather, they identify them simply as ex-offenders. Likewise, exonerees face discrimination from the community; most citizens do not believe that wrongful convictions exist (Zalman et al., 2012), which affects perceptions of exonerees post-release (Faison & Smalarz, 2019; Shlosberg et al., 2020). Negative stigma attached to an exoneree affects the public's willingness to embrace them in their communities. In the likely event that an exoneree experiences housing discrimination, there is possible recourse under Title VIII of the Civil Rights Act of 1968 to file a discrimination claim (Kirshenbaum et al., 2020). While these are viable options, the processes are arduous, lengthy, and costly and leave immediate housing concerns unaddressed.

## Short- and Long-Term Effects of a Wrongful Conviction Post-Release

### Psychological Impact

Research has shown that some prisoners on release may experience a unique set of mental health symptoms that bear some resemblance to post-traumatic stress disorder (PTSD) (Liem & Kunst, 2013). Through their research on released life sentence prisoners who had served lengthy sentences, Liem and Kunst (2013) found evidence for what they and others term *post-incarceration syndrome* (PICS), overlapping with or a subtype of PTSD but also capturing the unique effects of incarceration on mental health. A term originally coined by Gorski (2001), PICS[1] is thought to be evident through a number of symptoms, including institutionalized personality traits, evidence of PTSD, social–sensory deprivation syndrome, and social–temporal alienation.

### Institutionalized Personality Traits Resulting From Incarceration

A common personality trait following incarceration described by participants in the Liem and Kunst (2013) study was paranoia, as well as an inability to make decisions and engage in relationships. These personality traits are likely the result of the prison total institution culture. Specifically, inmates live in an oppressive environment that demands complete obedience. Inmates are not allowed to think or move freely: every action is controlled and monitored. Thus, when they are released from prison, they have difficulty adjusting as they lack the appropriate skills for independent thinking. As one exoneree shared:

*When I got out, I had no clue on how to do anything. I didn't even know how to pick food. In prison, meals were set, so I didn't get to choose. Once I got out, I had no clue what I wanted to eat because prison never allowed me to make my own decisions. For xx years, I was told when to shower, when to eat, what to eat, when to sleep, so I had no clue on how to make my own decisions when I left.*

## Post-traumatic Stress Disorder From Pre-incarceration Trauma

PTSD is a recognized psychiatric disorder, as contained in the *Diagnostic and Statistical Manual of Mental Disorders*, Fifth Edition (DSM-5; American Psychiatric Association [APA], 2013), that normally follows the witnessing of a traumatic event that is then persistently reexperienced in a number of ways. For prisoners, it may also be the result of preexisting trauma that may have been experienced pre-incarceration, during incarceration, or both. Gorski (2001) described six PTSD symptoms often found in the backgrounds of prisoners: (1) flashbacks of severe institutional abuse; (2) intense psychological distress and physiological reactivity when exposed to cues triggering memories of the institutional abuse; (3) episodes of dissociation, emotional numbing, and restricted affect; (4) chronic problems with mental functioning that include irritability, outbursts of anger, difficulty concentrating, sleep disturbances, and an exaggerated startle response; (5) persistent avoidance of anything that would trigger memories of the traumatic events; (6) hypervigilance, generalized paranoia, and reduced capacity to trust caused by constant fear of abuse from both correctional staff and other inmates that can be generalized to others after release.

Exonerees in this study reported numerous effects of PTSD, including flashbacks, nightmares, anxiety, loss of interest in hobbies, avoidance of people or places that bring on traumatic feelings, and difficulty sleeping (APA, 2013). Given that the symptoms of PTSD significantly disrupt an individual's life, these effects also hinder an exoneree's ability to successfully reintegrate into society (Wildeman et al., 2011). Many exonerees learn coping skills; however, the effects of PTSD continue throughout their post-exoneration lives. As stated by a male exoneree:

> *We all come out with PTSD. That's what we all come out with. Effects from depression and memory loss. And we struggle mentally and emotionally still. Uh, that's the reason, you know, that all of us exonerees have these social issues that still haunt us. Because no matter what, we will never fit back into society.*

## Antisocial Personality Traits

Antisocial personality traits are developed from preexisting symptoms and can also surface during incarceration as an institutional coping skill and psychological defense mechanism. K. A. Fisher and Hany (2021) reported that antisocial personality disorder[2] presents in a variety of ways, including disregard for others, social irresponsibility, and criminal behavior with no remorse. Other manifestations include failure to conform to the law, challenging authority, manipulation, and inability to form stable relationships (Black, 2015). Many exonerees who struggle upon release learned how to be compliant in prison, where they would follow the rules when in front of guards yet engage in aggressive behavior behind their backs. Exonerees in this sample did not report perpetrating any predatory crimes[3] but did report having to engage in self-defense mechanisms to survive.

## Social–Sensory Deprivation Syndrome

Social–sensory deprivation syndrome is the result of the effects of prolonged confinement, which imposes both social isolation and sensory deprivation. This is not restricted to only those who were kept in solitary confinement but is also true of any prison experience (Liem & Kunst, 2013). Inmates who experienced extended periods of time in solitary isolation incur a wide range of post-incarceration effects such as headaches, impaired impulse control, disassociation, inability to concentrate, spatial disorientation (Liem & Kunst, 2013), and repressed rage (Gorski, 2001). There are also numerous health consequences of solitary confinement, including skin irritations, musculoskeletal pain, and extreme fluctuation in weight (Strong et al., 2020). An exoneree described the impact that social–sensory deprivation had on him.

> I got thrown in the hole – that's what you people call it – many times. We call it "the box." Not 'cause I was doing bad things but because guards liked seeing me suffer. I spent months at a time in a tiny cell with nothing but a blanket, toilet, sink, and mattress. I made noise just to hear others. They fed me two pieces of bread a day and some water – they didn't care. How could I tell anyone? Who would listen to me? And if I told when I got out, then the punishment was worse. I was constantly starving. … Then one day, they let me out of prison because they figured out I was innocent. No apology, no nothing. Just out the door. I felt like a freak as no one could figure me out. I would scream in the middle of the night, I get angry at little things, and I always have a headache or body ache from all those years cramped in a tiny prison cell. …

Other features that have been reported to be related to PICS include social–temporal alienation and reactive substance abuse disorders. *Social–temporal alienation* reflects feelings of not belonging in social settings, accompanying the belief that "good things can be taken away at any moment" (Liem & Kunst, 2013, p. 336). In addition, Gorski (2001) argued that many prisoners who experience PICS upon release suffer from substance abuse and alcohol addiction. Researchers have found a strong connection between pre-incarceration drug use and post-incarceration substance abuse (Visher et al., 2004; Western & Simes, 2019). Chamberlain et al. (2019) also found that unstable housing had in impact on post-incarceration drug use. Particularly, persons who lived with friends or family members were at higher risk of post-release substance abuse than those who lived in other housing situations. It is difficult to assess the extent of post-release substance abuse with pre-incarceration substance use among exonerees, although there are likely some parallels with other prisoners.

In terms of success upon release, Gorski (2001) found a number of factors that affect a prisoner's successful re-entry into society. Those who were incarcerated for more than 1 year, endured extended periods of solitary confinement, and experienced severe institutional abuse were the most vulnerable to experiencing PICS (Liem & Kunst, 2013). Gorski suggested that inmates who are afforded educational and rehabilitation opportunities while incarcerated are least vulnerable to PICS. Based on his assertions, exonerees would be at a high risk for PICS due to the fact that post-release rehabilitation programs are not designed for them, nor do they receive this support.

## The Psychological Impact of a Wrongful Conviction

In addition to the mental health concerns discussed above, exonerees face further mental health challenges upon release. In fact, Grounds (2005) argued that the most significant obstacles to successful reintegration for exonerees from a wrongful conviction are mental health concerns. Evidence has been found for depression, anxiety, self-stigma and guilt, distrust and fear of the criminal justice system, and change in strained relationships.

## Depression and Anxiety

Studies of post-exoneration experiences report depression and anxiety as harmful effects of a wrongful incarceration (Alexander-Bloch et al., 2020; Burnett et al., 2017; Grounds, 2005; Konvisser, 2015). Depression and anxiety will often emerge during incarceration and continue post-release; however, the lack of appropriate therapy during and following incarceration leaves depression and anxiety untreated. A study conducted by Alexander-Bloch et al. (2020) found that there was an inverse relationship between the period of time post-release with depression and anxiety. That is, the greater the number of years since release from prison, the lower levels of depression and anxiety that were experienced.

## Self-stigma and Guilt

*Self-stigma* can be defined as a perception that develops when individuals become aware of the public's negative perceptions toward them and identifies with that label. Self-stigma involves three components: awareness of the stereotype, agreement with it, and applying it to oneself. Those experiencing self-stigma suffer low self-esteem and low self-efficacy (Corrigan et al., 2009). The exonerated simultaneously wear "ex-convict" and "exoneree" hats. Moreover, perceived societal stigma affects how an exoneree reintegrates into society (A. M. Thompson et al., 2012).

One exoneree described the self-stigma of being an ex-offender:

> *No matter what I do, no matter where I go, I am always going to be seen as a convict. People don't look at me and think a man was wrongfully convicted; what they see is a man who spent over two decades in prison. They believe that I must have done something to be in prison and that I got out on some crazy technicality. They don't care to figure out why I was locked up and how I was a victim just like the victim they accused me of murdering. Now that I'm out, I get it. I will always be an ex-con. I am an ex-con. I am a convict even though I'm exonerated. Weird, huh? An exoneree is forever an ex-con, so we better face that reality. It will haunt us 'til we die. …*

Self-stigma may also occur among individuals who are convicted of a crime that they did not commit but are unable to prove themselves innocent (Burnett et al., 2017). This produces feelings of guilt as some believe that their wrongful conviction is, in part, their fault as they must not have fought their case hard enough (Brooks & Greenberg, 2021). These feelings are further exacerbated when an individual has contributed to their wrongful conviction by falsely confessing to a crime.

Many exonerees experience another type of guilt. Given that many exonerees only learn of their release mere hours before they leave prison, some are said to experience survivor guilt (Clow et al., 2011). *Survivor guilt* reflects guilt associated with surviving a traumatic event when others did not. This does not give an individual the opportunity to say goodbye to the friends they are leaving behind. Moreover, it does not give them time to process what this new freedom means. Exonerees are now burdened with the same question they asked themselves when they were wrongly convicted. They may ask, "Why me?," but the conceptual framework of the question is different. Upon exoneration, they find themselves questioning why they were the "lucky" ones to leave prison while their friends are left behind. One exoneree described the feeling of survivor guilt:

*I am not sure why I was picked to get out as there were other innocent guys left in prison. Even those who were guilty shouldn't still be in prison. They done (sic) their time and should have gotten out. ... I didn't even know I was getting released. I was taken to the county jail thinking there was another hearing taking place. I didn't like going to the jail because I had to sleep on a concrete floor with no pillows, blankets, or anything. It was torture. I wanted to go back to prison. Then, my lawyer came and told me I was going home. I couldn't believe it. I didn't get to say goodbye to my friends in the prison. ...*

Similar to the moment when the system plucked an innocent man from society and locked him away from his family and friends for more than 20 years, it plucked the same innocent man from prison and took him away from his prison environment, friends, and small comforts. In fact, the exoneree above had spent more time in prison than he had in the free world, so those friendships were longer than the ones he had known prior to incarceration. In order to deal with survivor guilt, some exonerees, once released, pursue the fight for innocence for those individuals they left behind who they believe are wrongly convicted.

## Distrust and Fear of the Criminal Justice System

Understandably, exonerees have little faith in the criminal justice system, and many were quite cynical about it (Burnett et al., 2017; Campbell & Denov, 2004). As the National Registry of Exonerations (2020a) reported, official misconduct is a leading factor of wrongful convictions. The fact that innocent men and women were removed from society and wrongly convicted as a result of police or prosecutorial misconduct best explains the distrust exonerees have about these criminal justice actors. As a male exoneree shared:

*The police detective wanted to make a name for himself. He bullied me and the lady victim. ... He even had my DNA and knew that if it was sampled, I would be let go. So, he let me rot in prison until my attorney got the DNA tested, which proved I couldn't have done the rape. Nothing happened to that officer. In fact, I think they even gave him a promotion after my conviction. He has a pension and I got nothing. He doesn't have to go to prison for lying and forcing the victim to identify me. It's horrible what the system allows these officers to get away with. And don't get me started with the prosecutor, because he allowed the lies to be told and did not have my DNA tested.*

Worse still, upon release, given how they were wrongly convicted with no real evidence, exonerees continually struggle with the fear of retaliation. They have little to no trust in the system and believe that if they do something to aggravate the police, such as pursue a lawsuit or discuss official misconduct with the media, they could be thrown back into prison. A male exoneree shared his fear of the police:

*I drive the speed limit. I don't want them [police] to know where I work. If they do, they will harass me. I have a pending lawsuit against them, so I am scared that they will pin something on me that I didn't do. ... I make sure I stand in front of cameras wherever I go so people will know where I am. I also save all my receipts in case something happens.*

Recently, there was a bank robbery and the security guard was murdered in the same town where this exoneree resides *and* banks. He was terrified that the police would blame him for the robbery and murder, as those were the two offenses for which he had been wrongly convicted. Due to his fear of being suspected of these crimes, he took a picture of a fast food receipt showing where he had been at the time of the crime. Given that exonerees cannot rely on the truth to set them free, self-preservation becomes a way of life. Thus, they may document all activities that may absolve them of any suggestions of future criminal involvement.

## Fractured Relationships

Incarceration creates wounds to relationships that may never be repaired. Relationships become fractured and, for many, take years to heal. Even in cases where family members believed in their innocence and maintained a relationship with them throughout incarceration, upon release, for many exonerees their relationships have a new landscape. Some are fortunate to be able to rebuild strong relationships with those they love, while others are not as fortunate.

Exonerees experience myriad strains in their family relationships, such as divorce, loss of custody of children, and death of a loved one (Brooks & Greenberg, 2021). Some exonerees report no prison visits during the entire length of their incarceration, while others report fewer visits over the course of incarceration. The desire to go home with family was unbearable for some, so many chose to avoid prison visits (Scott, 2010). Other reasons prison visits did not occur included the fragility of a parent's health and the transportation and financial costs associated with the travel. As parents aged, health issues made visits more physically challenging. In addition, older family members were forced to rely on others to drive them to the prison. Some exonerees were incarcerated in another part of the state, which also restricted prison visits. Travel included gas and lodging, which made it cost-prohibitive for some family members to visit. One male exoneree shared that he did not want any of his family members to see him in prison:

> I never let Mom come to prison. I was ashamed. She was a proper lady and should not have been searched and humiliated, so there was no way I was going to let her come visit me. I talked to her on the phone, which was hard, but it would have been horrible to see her treated the way they treat visitors. They [guards] have no respect for our friends and family. Mom was already an outcast because her son was locked up. No way was I going to have her mistreated. ... So, when I got out of prison, she barely knew who I was. I barely knew who she was.

One female described the pain she felt when her kids were taken away from her:

> The hardest part of prison was having my kids away from me. They were being punished just like me. I didn't get to make decisions that moms get to make for their kids or do things with their kids, like I didn't get to go dress shopping for prom with my daughter. ... I didn't get to meet any of my kids' teachers. ... I didn't get to help give them baths. ... I didn't get to do anything. I was still their mother but in name only. Their grandmother took over being their mom. I missed out on so much. ... Then, they let me out of prison and my babies were now adults. They didn't need me anymore. They didn't even really know me. It wasn't like they were rude to me or anything, but I was their birth mom and not their everyday mom. That still hurts. ...

One male exoneree explained why he asked his wife for a divorce once he was sent to prison:

> *I knew I wasn't coming home for a long time, if ever. It wasn't fair to leave her alone. Let's be honest, how could anyone stay married to a person in prison? She has needs. There is no way she is gonna wait for me. I never wanted to hear that she was cheating on me. So, I told her that I wanted a divorce. I never told her why. I just told her I did. She begged me to not file the papers, but I did. I have followed her for years and know she remarried. I am glad she found some love. I will always love her, and that is why I had to let her go. I thought about reaching out to her now that I'm out, but it would hurt too much. Best to remember the good times … when life was so different.*

## The Physical Impact of a Wrongful Incarceration

Regardless of guilt or innocence, prison inmates endure similar physical pains of imprisonment, many of which extend upon release. Although there is little research on the physical health consequences of post-incarceration, limited research does exist addressing the physical ailments suffered by inmates (N. A. Jackson et al., 2021; Schnittker & John, 2007). One study found former inmates to be at high risk for premature death (Binswanger et al., 2007). Drawing on the interviews from exonerees in the current study and a former study conducted by N. A. Jackson et al. (2021), exonerees reported suffering sleep disturbances as well as health and dental issues. In both studies, exonerees reported interrupted sleep during incarceration and post-release. During incarceration, inmates begin their days predawn, and upon release it was difficult to break that early morning cycle (N. A. Jackson et al., 2021; Shlosberg et al., 2020; Westervelt & Cook, 2008). As with many aspects of their daily lives, the exonerees must relearn how to sleep (Iannozzi, 2015). One exoneree described sleep problems:

> *Sleep is something that prison took from me. I didn't sleep well in prison and I don't sleep well now. Getting out of prison doesn't change how you sleep. I wasn't comfortable on my prison cot and I'm not comfortable on my bed now. I don't think I will ever be comfortable again. … When I got out of prison, I came to my mom's house. She had my bedroom ready for me. What she didn't know was that I was not ready for my bedroom. I was used to being in a small cell with a tiny steel slab with a flimsy mattress. While it wasn't comfortable, it was what I knew. I couldn't sleep on my new bed [on release], so I slept in the corner of my room on the floor. That must sound weird, but that is how it was. Today, I am sleeping on a bed, but it took a long time to be able to do that. …*

Exonerees also report medical concerns upon release. Prisoners, in general, experience higher rates of disease than the general public (Cloud et al., 2014; Schnittker & John, 2007). Infectious diseases that surfaced during incarceration often persist, and the inadequate prison medical care received impacts lingering health problems (Greifinger, 2007). As exonerees do not have immediate health care accessible either due to lack of health insurance or inadequate transportation, their health problems go untreated.

Oral health is often highly neglected in incarceration and exoneration literature. Although scholars have failed to study the impact of imprisonment on dental health, every exoneree in this study reported oral health concerns. Some reported having excruciating tooth pain. Others reported rotted teeth, which resulted in having them removed. As they did not have access to dental insurance, many were forced to have the teeth removed rather than repaired. As one exoneree reported:

*My tooth was hurting so bad but I didn't have no (sic) money to get it fixed. I waited and waited just to make enough to have a dentist pull the tooth. In prison, the dentist pulled teeth. They do the same thing on the outside because I don't have insurance. I am so glad that the tooth was in the back, but I know some guys have no front teeth. It isn't fair. … Every exoneree should be given insurance.*

## Financial Reparations: A New Source of Revictimization

Just as their lives were abruptly stolen from them years earlier, the system continues to treat exonerees unfairly by creating obstacles that affect their ability to access financial reparations. Paradoxically, although the wrongly convicted are victims of state harm (Westervelt & Cook, 2010), as exonerees they are not afforded reintegration assistance from the very system that caused their victimization. A new battle emerges, and while they may have spent years fighting to clear their name from a wrongful conviction, exonerees now have to fight another battle, namely, for compensation. In general, there are three financial remedies available to exonerees. These include filing civil rights lawsuits (tort claims), presenting a private bill to the legislature for their case, or recovery under a compensation statute (Trivelli, 2016). It is important to note that exonerees, for the most part, must choose one avenue for redress, as most states prohibit exonerees from "dipping in all the cookie jars."

Exonerees have a right to pursue a civil rights violation under 42 U.S.C. § 1983, Civil Action for Deprivation of Rights (Civil Rights Act of 1871, 2006), which allows them to sue the government for their wrongful incarceration. While common sense would suggest that exonerees should prevail in civil litigation after a wrongful conviction and false imprisonment, these lawsuits are often unsuccessful, for a variety of reasons. Regardless of the circumstances surrounding the wrongful conviction, exonerees must prove a constitutional violation took place in order to prevail in such a lawsuit (Mandery et al., 2013). Despite the fact that the primary contributing factors to a wrongful conviction include mistaken eyewitness identification, false confession, incentivized witnesses, and junk science (S. R. Gross, 2008), these errors alone are insufficient claims for civil redress. What is required is a specific constitutional violation that permits an exoneree to recover damages in a tort claim. For example, a plaintiff who was wrongly convicted as a result of police or prosecution withholding exculpatory evidence – evidence that would have been favorable to their case – may pursue civil litigation as this represents a *Brady* violation and violates a defendant's constitutional right to due process.

As challenging as it is to recover monies through a civil lawsuit, an even more daunting option is to present a private bill to the legislature. This requires a great deal of effort and has little chance of success. In order to pursue a private bill, a campaign manager and a lobbyist are required (Mandery et al., 2013). Private bills also require financial resources and political mobilization, which may not be accessible to most exonerees (Norris et al., 2018). As such, this is the least popular option among exonerees.

The third option for financial reparation is through compensation statutes. Currently, only half of the states have a compensation bill available for exonerees (Norris, 2012), and they vary significantly in their provisions and eligibility criteria. For example, in some states compensation is not available to those who somehow contributed to their own wrongful conviction, and those who falsely confessed – even when under duress – would therefore not be eligible (Mandery et al., 2013). Some states offer a fixed monetary amount regardless of the number of years falsely imprisoned, while other states offer a payout based on the number of years. In addition, eligibility requirements are extremely restrictive. Although exonerees do not have to prove official misconduct in their wrongful conviction (Shlosberg et al., 2020), for the most part, they are required to prove "factual innocence." In essence, they must prove they were innocent of the crimes for which they were wrongly convicted. While our judicial system places the burden on the state to prove a defendant guilty beyond a reasonable doubt, the compensation bill now shifts the burden on the defendant to prove their innocence, and for many exonerees this is virtually impossible. Lacking in financial resources to test DNA, recover court documents, or hire an investigator, applying for compensation is a challenging task for exonerees. For these reasons, attorneys and other advocates may be needed to help the exoneree pursue compensation.

Many states do not allow exonerees to recover monies through civil litigation and compensation simultaneously. Thus, exonerees are faced with the painful choice of suing those who victimized them or attempting to access compensation through statute. In essence, this can be viewed as a form of lawful extortion. That is, the state will pay an exoneree for a wrongful conviction but the individual actors who intentionally contributed to the wrongful conviction are protected from civil liability. For example, in Indiana, exonerees must withdraw their civil lawsuits if they are awarded compensation. This is a dilemma one exoneree described:

> If I take the compensation money, the police who did this to me will get away with it. That's how they keep getting away with what they are doing. They are not held accountable. If I stick with my lawsuit and win, then I have to wait and see if the city even has money to pay me. …

His case is emblematic of many exonerees. Moreover, compensation statutes have timelines for application; most are typically within 2 years of exoneration. However, there are no timelines for the agency reviewing the applications. For example, in Indiana, exonerees are required to complete their application process within 2 years of exoneration but there is no set deadline for the Indiana Criminal Justice Institute, the body reviewing compensation applications, to initiate or complete their investigation. This is another example of how the criminal justice system retains control over the exoneree, even after their release. Essentially, they are forced to gamble their futures, as in some cases they have to choose one avenue for monetary recovery and ignore the other. At the same time, the process and outcomes for each avenue of redress differ. Pursuing a civil lawsuit is important to those who suffered a wrongful incarceration as this is the avenue that holds a criminal justice agency culpable for their wrongdoing. Even so, it is not the individual actors who contributed to the wrongful conviction who will be held liable for their own errors but the agency for whom they work. Thus, there may be no closure to the exoneree even when a lawsuit is successful, which is also a gamble. Pursing a remedy through statute, on the other hand, while more likely to be successful, holds no one accountable, and the amounts provided as remedies are usually lower.

## Conclusion

This chapter has underlined the many ways in which exonerees continue to be victimized post-release. While it is impossible to capture all of the forms of victimization perpetrated against these innocent individuals, the findings revealed here underline the importance of supports being available post-release. While exonerees experience many similar challenges that affect other released prisoners, their struggles are exacerbated as they are not provided programs to assist them once in the community. Interestingly, while there is a growing movement toward addressing the mistakes that contribute to wrongful convictions, there remains very little attention paid to the harmful effects of these miscarriage of justice following an exoneration. It is egregious that exonerees, who are ultimately victims of state harm, receive little attention from the state for their victimization. Conversely, what tends to happen is the wrongly convicted continue to struggle upon release, albeit in a different manner. Freedom itself has its own costs.

## Notes

1  Post-incarceration syndrome is not recognized by the DSM-5 (APA, 2013) as a syndrome per se, but researchers are attempting to establish that it constitutes a separate cluster of symptoms (cf. Liem & Kunst, 2013).
2  Antisocial personality disorder is a personality disorder also found in the DSM-5 (APA, 2013); however, the existence of traits alone does not constitute the disorder.
3  It is impossible to ascertain whether this is true, and it is likely that those who agreed to be interviewed would convey themselves in a favorable light.

# 11

# FINAL THOUGHTS AND FUTURE CONSIDERATIONS

*Kathryn M. Campbell and Nicky Ali Jackson*

"Thanks for telling our stories. Our voices need to be heard."

*Male exoneree*

## Overview

This book has attempted to develop a new approach to the study of wrongful convictions, specifically by positioning wrongly convicted persons, their family and friends, original crime victims, and society as *victims* of a miscarriage of justice. Unlike other wrongful conviction scholarly works that examine contributing factors and consequences of wrongful convictions (Campbell, 2018; S. R. Gross, 2008; Haney, 2002; Leo, 2009; Norris et al., 2018), this monograph illustrates how innocent people are victimized either directly or indirectly by a wrongful conviction. Through a qualitative analysis, exonerees' and their family members' voices depicted the harms they have suffered individually and collectively. Their voices, along with scholarly literature, have explained not only how these egregious errors occurred but also the impact that these errors have had on them, essentially illustrating how they were victimized.

In this book, what has been established is that, through their ordeal, the wrongfully convicted suffer a victimization. Given that injury is a key element in understanding the process of victimization, what has been established is that they suffer a myriad of injuries: physical, psychological, emotional, social, and financial (Burgess et al., 2013). Their victimization begins when they are first suspected of involvement in a crime, continues through arrest, and extends beyond release, in those cases where they are fortunate enough to be released. Moreover, what is likewise significant is that their family members are also victimized by their loved one's wrongful conviction; they suffer alongside them. Their victimization differs as it is vicarious but nonetheless causes pain, misery, and grief. Other victims of a wrongful conviction discussed in this book include the "original" crime victim, who is revictimized through an exoneration, and society itself, whereby faith is lost in the criminal justice system as it no longer functions as it should: to convict only the guilty and free the innocent. Finally, the post-conviction and release experiences of the wrongly convicted illustrate once again how their victimization experiences follow them through their exoneration.

DOI: 10.4324/9781003121251-13

## The Victimology of a Wrongful Conviction

In the first part of the book, the groundwork was laid for understanding how a wrongfully convicted person can be considered as a victim and how the social science discipline of victimology can be useful for framing these miscarriages of justice. By outlining the tragic story of Willie T. Donald, the first chapter presents an overview of how he was victimized by the criminal justice system, despite clear evidence of his innocence. Mr. Donald's nightmare is not unique; it is emblematic of all those falsely arrested, wrongly convicted, and falsely imprisoned. While the facts illustrate his story, the human aspects of what happened to him further illustrate his victimization: he missed out on important life events (births and deaths of family members), technological advancements passed him by, and he suffered the painful deprivations of prison life for over 24 years. Upon release, he faced financial difficulties and health issues due to years of neglect. Other, intangible costs Mr. Donald suffered were just as harmful, including a continued fear of police, interrupted sleep, difficulty rebuilding trust in others, and the stigma attached to his conviction. Mr. Donald's experiences put a human face on what a victim of a wrongful conviction goes through.

Chapter 1 further outlines the methodology for the book and provides demographic information on the 24 exonerees who were interviewed for this study: their convictions, the years lost, and the time they served. In presenting a theoretical overview from within which to understand the experience of the wrongly convicted as victims, Chapter 2 situates how their suffering, through arrest, trial, conviction, sentencing, and finally exoneration and release, is similar to that of other victims. A number of well researched, "canonical" factors have been clearly established that contribute to a wrongful conviction and are discussed in Chapter 3. These individual and systemic factors include eyewitness misidentification, false confessions, misused forensic science (and expert testimony), unreliable and incentivized informants, and government misconduct, illustrating how, through inadvertence or misconduct, a wrongful conviction can occur. Chapter 4, contributed by guest authors Professors Hattery and Smith, underscores the way in which the criminal justice system (called *legal system* by these authors as notions of *justice* are absent for them) victimizes innocent Black men, the most likely of all to be wrongly convicted. This occurs through racist and disturbing police practices that ensnare innocent Black Americans, and especially Black men, including stop and frisk, fishing expeditions, pretrial detention, police killings of unarmed Black people, and a legal system that values punishment over innocence.

The second half of the book expands on the experiences of the many victims of a wrongful conviction. Chapter 5 outlines how the wrongly convicted are victimized from the moment they become a suspect and how the different actors in the system (police, prosecutors, and judges) contribute to their victimization. It also focuses on the differing consequences of a wrongful conviction and their impacts on innocent inmates, illustrated through the voices of the interviewees. Chapter 6 examines the experiences of the women exonerees who participated in our study. Given that research has demonstrated that women's experiences in the criminal justice system more generally differ from those of men, the experiences of wrongly convicted women are also qualitatively different. It is harder for women to be exonerated due to the fact DNA is not often involved in their cases, they are often convicted in "no-crime" cases (where no crime occurred at all), and sexist and stereotypic motives are often ascribed to them, which are difficult to counter.

The victimization experiences of the families of the wrongly convicted are examined in Chapter 7, gleaned from interviews undertaken with 13 family members for this book. As secondary victims of crime, these family members conveyed how they are also left to struggle with the psychological consequences of a wrongful conviction, including financial hardships, fractured relations, difficulties surrounding their beliefs in their loved one's innocence, and practical constraints of life with an incarcerated family member. The revictimization of the "original" crime victims is discussed in Chapter 8, and it is clear that by revisiting another possible arrest, trial, and conviction for the "true" perpetrator, they are once again victimized. This chapter situates their experiences through the court and trial process, as well as how they experience an exoneration, focusing specifically on addressing their unique needs and challenges. Chapter 9 takes a unique approach by exploring the possibility that society as a whole is also victimized by a wrongful conviction. What occurs is that the criminal justice system itself is no longer considered legitimate due to the wrongful conviction itself, as well as a lack of compensation for the state crime committed, which often occurs. Moreover, the costs associated with incarceration are further increased when compensation amounts are added and, in an indirect way, wrongful convictions contribute the ongoing problem of mass incarceration in American society.

Chapter 10 illustrates how innocent inmates such as Mr. Donald face an additional burden that is not required of guilty inmates; that is, to prove their innocence in hopes of exoneration (N. A. Jackson et al., 2021). The "lucky" ones will be exonerated, but they then face a new burden: to clear their names and recover financial damages. They are now tasked with proving factual innocence in order to win a civil judgment or receive state compensation. Given the many roadblocks to establishing innocence, due mainly to the passage of time and the intransigence of criminal justice system actors, the system continues to victimize innocent men and women. The irony of this should not be taken lightly – they are required to fight to receive monies that are owed to them, yet they do not have access to the funding needed in their pursuit.

This research has established that exonerees continue to be victimized upon release from prison. They face many of the same problems that ex-prisoners face, including, but not limited to, health issues, mental health challenges, financial strains, difficulties in employment and housing, as well as connecting to family/friends and keeping up with changes that occurred while they were incarcerated. However, these problems are exacerbated for the wrongly convicted due to the lack of re-entry assistance. In addition, their financial strain is often higher as many continue to fight to overturn their conviction and for the expungement of their criminal records.

## Future Considerations

As the canonical list of contributing factors, discussed in Chapter 3 and first established by Gross (2008), point to how a wrongful conviction happens, in the past 30 years of the innocence movement there have also been a number of concerted policy changes to prevent those same difficulties from re-occurring (Medwed, 2017). While this does not mean that wrongful convictions are no longer happening, it does mean that state governments and officials have a much greater awareness as to *why* they happen and are in a better position to institute policy changes to *prevent* them from happening in the future. Some very promising changes that have occurred include, but are not limited to, changes in how police lineups are administered to enhance correct identifications, recording of all police interviews to deter police misconduct and false confessions, the establishment of conviction integrity units in some district attorneys' offices to function as post-conviction review programs to secure exonerations, establishing policies around limiting the use of jailhouse informant testimony and insisting on corroboration, and establishing national standards for forensic science disciplines so that there is less ambivalence about the scientific strength of previously questionable "pseudo-scientific" evidence (Campbell, 2018).

In this volume, and through the interviewees conducted, some important directions for change also emerged that can be added to this list. For one, given that the exonerees are clearly victims themselves, they should benefit from the resources legislated and provided to other crime victims. That would include recognition under the Crime Victims' Rights Act under the Justice for All Act of 2004. While the exonerees' needs are unique, the provisions under the act would not apply in the same way; however, they should be extended and centered around their distinct experiences. Another important consideration pertains to the need for re-entry services for exonerees, similar to those that are given to parolees. Exonerees are often seeking to clear their names and obtain compensation on release. Given these concerns, there is a need to recognize that re-entry poses very specific challenges to them, for which they currently receive no support.

What this study also revealed is the unmet needs of secondary victims of a wrongful conviction: the family members of the wrongfully convicted. Family members have disclosed that they, too, face challenges. Family members also suffered as victims, emotionally and financially; thus, programs directed toward their needs need to be created. This should include mental health supports and financial reparations. These secondary victims are often forgotten in the storm of a wrongful conviction; thus, further research must be conducted to establish ways in which to better to assist them.

While efforts to help the wrongly convicted are laudable, they are just small steps and point to the need for larger social and structural changes to occur in order to have a true impact on the occurrence of these types of miscarriages of justice. In a society that is rife with racism, sexism, and classism, only greater efforts at addressing the differences that result from race, class, and gender will have any sort of real or sustained impact on wrongful convictions.

## Conclusion

In a recent talk given at the Purdue University Northwest Sinai Forum on December 5, 2021, Bryan Stevenson, noted American lawyer, social justice activist, and founder/executive director of the Equal Justice Initiative, spoke about the importance of being uncomfortable, calling on everyone to make a conscious decision to be willing to do uncomfortable things (Watkins, 2021). What he was referring to was the need, as a society, to not accept the status quo, to be uncomfortable in order to confront injustices, as ultimately it is the only way to advance justice. He explained that this involves not turning away from injustice but in fact turning toward it, increasing our proximity to it, as there is power in proximity. Proximity, in terms of wrongful convictions, occurs when people position themselves near those who have been wrongly convicted or their family members to best understand their ordeal. In fact, for Stevenson, it is the only way for any societal change to happen. This message clearly resonates in this book dedicated to examining how victimization occurs through a wrongful conviction, as it underlines the important obligation, as a society, to address why such miscarriages of justice occur, attempt to rectify them, and prevent them in the future. Not only will these actions help to address the *victimization* of the wrongly convicted themselves and that of their families but it will also signify a society that values justice and fairness, one that is proximate to the suffering that a wrongful conviction evokes.

This book has illustrated the myriad victims borne from a wrongful conviction – the wrongly convicted, their families, "original" crime victims, and society itself. By listening to the voices of the exonerees and their families, the consequences of their victimization were laid bare; they suffer in many ways, and this suffering continues to follow them upon release, upon exoneration, and, for some, even after being compensated. It is hoped that the messages they have revealed will resonate for those who are working in or plan to work in the criminal justice system. These stories have underlined the importance of getting it right the first time – that the consequences of error are enormous and far-reaching and can last a lifetime. Greater vigilance is required on behalf of all those who have the potential of contributing to a wrongful conviction and creating further victims, which includes the police, district attorneys, defense counsel, and judges. It is only through a greater awareness of how this type of victimization occurs that it ultimately can be prevented.

# APPENDIX

## Exoneree Interview Questions

### Demographic Questions

1. Current age:
2. Age of arrest for wrongful conviction:
3. Race:
4. Gender:
5. Current marital status (i.e., married, single, widowed, separated, divorced):
6. Education/training (pre/post prison; in prison):
7. Are you currently working? Yes _____ No _____ If yes, what type of work? Did you have trouble finding a job?

### Wrongful Conviction Questions

8. Do you feel that your prison experience was different as an innocent person than someone who was guilty? Yes ___ No _____ Please explain.
9. What were the greatest challenges you faced in prison?
10. How did you become exonerated?
11. Were you given any compensation by the state or did you receive a payout from a lawsuit after your exoneration?
12. What challenges have you faced since your release?
13. How have your relationships been since your release (with previous and/or new family members)?
14. What kind of supports do you think would have helped you upon your release that were not available to you?

### Family of the Exoneree Interview Questions

1. Can you please start by describing your relationship and the nature of your relationship to the exoneree?

2. Did you know the exoneree prior to incarceration? Yes ____ No ____
3. In what way has the exoneree's incarceration affected your life?
4. Were you able to visit him/her while they were incarcerated? What was that like?
5. If you knew the exoneree prior to incarceration, did you always believe in their innocence?
6. Do you ever talk to friends or family about how you feel about the exoneree's incarceration and their release?

    a. If not, why not?

    b. If yes, has talking to others been helpful to you?
7. If you knew the exoneree prior to incarceration, did your relationship with the exoneree change once they were released? In what way?
8. What do you think would have been helpful for you and the exoneree to help in adjusting to release back into the community?
9. What has been the greatest challenge for you regarding the exoneree's wrongful conviction, incarceration, and/or release?

# REFERENCES AND FURTHER READING

After Innocence. (n.d.). Connecting exonerees to the support they are eligible for. https://www. after-innocence.org/coordinating.

Akers, R. L., Sellers, C. S., & Jennings, W. G. (2020). *Criminological theories: Introduction, evaluation, and application* (8th ed.). Oxford University Press.

Alexander, M. (2010). *The new Jim Crow: Mass incarceration in the age of colorblindness.* New Press.

Alexander-Bloch, B., Miller, M. A., Zeringue, M. M., & Rubens, S. L. (2020). Mental health characteristics of exonerees: A preliminary exploration. *Psychology, Crime & Law, 26*(8), 768–775. https://doi.org/ 10.1080/1068316X.2020.1733571.

American Civil Liberties Union. (n.d.). ACLU fact sheet on the proposed victims' rights amendment. https://www.aclu.org/other/aclu-fact-sheet-proposed-victims-rights-amendment.

American Psychiatric Association. (2013). *Diagnostic and statistical manual of mental disorders* (5th ed.).

Anderson, C. (2016). *White rage: The unspoken truth of our racial divide.* Bloomsbury.

Anyaso, H. H. (2011, June 20). *The high cost of wrongful convictions in Illinois: Dollars wasted, lives lost & ruined, justice run amok: A landmark investigation.* Northwestern. https://www.northwestern.edu/ newscenter/stories/2011/06/wrongful-conviction-cost.html.

*Athey v. Leonetti,* 3 S.C.R. 458 (1996).

Baldus, D., Pulaski, C., & Woodworth, G. (1983). Comparative review of death sentences: An empirical study of the Georgia experience. *Journal of Criminal Law and Criminology, 74*(3), 661–753.

Bales, W. D., & Mears, D. P. (2008). Inmate social ties and the transition to society: Does visitation reduce recidivism? *Journal of Research in Crime & Delinquency, 45*(3), 287–321. https://doi.org/ 10.1177/0022427808317574.

Bard, M., & Sangrey, D. (1986). *The crime victim's book* (2nd ed.). Brunner/Mazel.

Baum, D. (2016, April). Legalize it all: How to win the war on drugs. *Harper's Magazine.* http://harpers. org/archive/2016/04/legalize-it-all.

Beck, A. J., & Harrison, P. M. (2007). *Sexual victimization in state and federal prisons reported by inmates, 2007* (Report No. NCJ 2194414). U.S. Department of Justice. https://bjs.ojp.gov/content/pub/pdf/ svsfpri07.pdf.

Beetham, D. (2013). Revisiting legitimacy, twenty years on. In J. Tankebe & A. Liebling (Eds.), *Legitimacy and criminal justice: An international exploration* (pp. 19–36). Oxford University Press.

Bellin, J. (2019). The power of prosecutors. *New York University Law Review, 94*(2), 171–212. https:// scholarship.law.wm.edu/facpubs/1907.

*Berger v. United States,* 295 U.S. 78, 55 S. Ct. 629, 79 L. Ed. 1314 (1935).

Binswanger, I. A., Stern, M. F., Deyo, R. A., Heagerty, P. J., Cheadle, A., Elmore, J. G., & Koepsell, T. D. (2007). Release from prison—A high risk of death for former inmates. *New England Journal of Medicine, 356*, 157–165. https://doi.org/10.1056/NEJMsa064115.

Black, D. W. (2015). The natural history of antisocial personality disorder. *The Canadian Journal of Psychiatry, 60*(7), 309–314. https://doi.org/10.1177/070674371506000703.

Blandisi, I. M. (2012). *Societal perceptions of wrongful convictions* [dissertation]. University of Ontario Institute of Technology (Canada). Proquest Dissertation Publishing. http://hdl.handle.net/10155/257

Bonilla-Silva, E. (1997). Rethinking racism: Toward a structural interpretation. *American Sociological Review, 62*(3), 465–480. https://doi.org/10.2307/2657316.

Boyd, N., & Rossmo, D. K. (2008). *Milgaard v. The Queen*: Understanding a wrongful conviction for sexual assault. In D. K. Rossmo (Ed.), *Criminal investigative failures* (pp. 179–204). CRC Press.

*Brady v. Maryland*, 373 U.S. 83, 83 S. Ct. 1194, 10 L. Ed. 2d 215, 1963 (1963).

Britton, D. (2000). Feminist criminology: Engendering the outlaw. *The Annals of the American Academy of Political and Social Science, 571*(1), 57–76.

Brooks, S. K., & Greenberg, N. (2021). Psychological impact of being wrongfully accused of criminal offences: A systematic literature review. *Medicine, Science, and the Law, 61*(1), 44–54. https://doi.org/10.1177/0025802420949069.

Broyles, R., & Lynn, T. J. (2018). Prosecutorial misconduct: Typologies and need for policy reform. *Academic Leadership Journal in Student Research, 5*(1), 1–22.

Bruckert, C., & Law, T. (2018). *Women and gendered violence in Canada: An intersectional approach.* University of Toronto Press.

Bruinsma, G. (2014). History of criminological theories: Causes of crime. In G. Bruinsma & D. Weisburd (Eds.), *Encyclopedia of criminology and criminal justice* (pp. 2137–2148). Springer. https://doi.org/10.1007/978-1-4614-5690-2_547.

Burgess, A. W., Regehr, C., & Roberts, A. R. (2013). *Victimology: Theories and applications* (2nd ed.). Jones and Bartlett Learning.

Burnett, R., Hoyle, C., & Speechley, N. (2017). The context and impact of being wrongly accused of abuse in occupations of trust. *Howard Journal of Crime and Justice, 56*(4), 176–197. https://doi.org/10.1111/hojo.12199.

Buser, M. E. (2015). *Lockdown on Rikers: Shocking stories of abuse and injustices at New York's most notorious jail.* St. Martin's Press.

Calamur, K. (2014, November 25). Ferguson documents: Officer Darren Wilson's testimony. NPR. https://www.npr.org/sections/thetwo-wa/2014/11/25/366519644/ferguson-docs-officer-darren-wilsons-testimony.

Caldero, M. A., Dailey, J. D., & Withrow, B. L. (2018). *Police ethics: The Corruption of noble cause* (4th ed.). Routledge.

California Innocence Project. (n.d.). Prosecutorial misconduct. https://californiainnocenceproject.org/issues-we-face/prosecutorial-misconduct/.

Campbell, K. M. (2005). Policy responses to wrongful conviction in Canada: The role of conviction review, public inquiries and compensation. *Criminal Law Bulletin, 41*(2), 145–168.

Campbell, K. M. (2018). *Miscarriages of justice in Canada: Causes, responses, remedies.* University of Toronto Press.

Campbell, K. M. (2019). Exoneration and compensation for the wrongly convicted: Enhancing procedural justice? *Manitoba Law Journal, 42*(3), 249–273.

Campbell, K. M., & Denov, M. (2004). The burden of innocence: Coping with a wrongful imprisonment. *Canadian Journal of Criminology and Criminal Justice, 46*(2), 139–163. https://doi.org/10.3138/cjccj.46.2.139.

Carson, E. A. (2020). Prisoners in 2018. U.S. Department of Justice Office of Justice Programs Bureau of Justice Statistics. https://bjs.ojp.gov/content/pub/pdf/p18.pdf.

Cassell, P. (2018). Overstating America's wrongful conviction rate? Reassessing the conventional wisdom about the prevalence of wrongful convictions. *Arizona Law Review, 60*, 815–863.

Castelle, G., & Loftus, E. (2001). Misinformation and wrongful convictions. In S. Westervelt & J. Humphrey (Eds.), *Wrongly convicted: Perspectives on failed justice* (pp. 17–35). Rutgers University Press.

*Cavazos v. Smith*, 132 S. Ct. 2 (2011).

Centurion. (2020). Our work. https://centurion.org/our-work/.

Chamberlain, A., Nyamu, S., Aminawung, J., Wang, E. A., Shavit, S., & Fox, A. D. (2019). Illicit substance use after release from prison among formerly incarcerated primary care patients: A cross-sectional study. *Addiction Science & Clinical Practice, 14*(7), 1–8. https://doi.org/10.1186/s13722-019-0136-6.

Chinn, J., & Ratliff, A. (2009). "I was put out the door with nothing" – Addressing the needs of the exonerated under a refugee model. *California Western Law Review, 45*(2), 405–444.

Christian, J., Martinez, D. J., & Martinez, D. (2016). Beyond the shadows of the prison: Agency and resilience among prisoners' family members. In J. A. Arditti & T. le Roux (Eds.), *And justice for all: Families & the criminal justice system* (Vol. 4, pp. 59–84). Michigan Publishing. http://dx.doi.org/10.3998/groves.9453087.0004.001.

Christie, N. (1986). The ideal victim. In E. A. Fattah (Ed.), *From crime policy to victim policy: Reorienting the justice system* (pp. 17–30). The Macmillan Press.

Chunias, J. L., & Aufgang, Y. D. (2008). Beyond monetary compensation: The need for comprehensive services for the wrongfully convicted. *Boston College Third World Law Journal, 28*(1), 105–128.

Chunn, D., & Lacombe, D. (2000). *Law as a gendering practice.* Oxford University Press.

Cicchini, M. D. (2018). Combating prosecutorial misconduct in closing arguments. *Oklahoma Law Review, 70*(4), 887–941.

Civil Rights Act of 1871, 42 U.S.C. § 1983 (2006).

Cloud, D. H., Parsons, J., & Delany-Brumsey, A. (2014). Addressing mass incarceration: A clarion call for public health. *American Journal of Public Health, 104*(3), 389–391. https://doi.org/10.2105/AJPH.2013.301741.

Clow, K. A., Blandisi, I. M., Ricciardelli, R., & Schuller, R. A. (2011). Public perception of wrongful conviction: Support for compensation and apologies. *Albany Law Review, 75*, 1415–1438.

Clow, K. A, & Leach, A.-M. (2015). After innocence: Perceptions of the wrongfully convicted. *Legal and Criminological Psychology, 20*(1), 147–164. https://doi.org/10.1111/lcrp.12018.

Clow, K. A., & Ricciardelli, R. (2014). Public perceptions of wrongful convictions. *Canadian Criminal Law Review, 18*(2), 183–198.

Cobbina, J. E., Huebner, B. M., & Berg, M. T. (2012). Men, women, and post-release offending: An examination of the nature of the link between relational ties and recidivism. *Crime and Delinquency, 58*(3), 331–361. https://doi.org/10.1177/0011128710382348.

Cochran, J. C., & Mears, D. P. (2013). Social isolation and inmate behavior: A conceptual framework for theorizing prison visitation and guiding and assessing research. *Journal of Criminal Justice, 41*(4), 252–261. https://doi.org/10.1016/j.jcrimjus.2013.05.001.

Cohen, L., & Felson, M. (1979). Social change and crime rate trends: A routine activity approach. *American Sociological Review, 44*(4), 588–608. https://doi.org/10.2307/2094589.

Cohen, S. (1986). *Visions of social control: Crime, punishment and classification.* Polity Press.

Coleman, J. (2021, January 1). Police release video of woman tackling Black teen after falsely accusing him of stealing her phone. The Hill. https://thehill.com/blogs/blog-briefing-room/news/532329-police-release-video-of-woman-tackling-black-teen-after-falsely.

Comack, E., & Balfour, G. (2004). *The power to criminalize: Violence, inequality and the law.* Fernwood.

Comack, E., & Balfour, G. (2014). *Criminalizing women: Gender and (in)justice in neo-liberal times* (2nd ed.). Fernwood.

Condry, R. (2007). *Families shamed: The consequences of crime for relatives of serious offenders.* Willan Publishing.

Cook, K. (2022). *Shattered justice: Crime victims' experiences with wrongful convictions and exonerations.* Rutgers University Press.

Cooper, G. S., Meterko, V., & Gadtaula, P. (2019). Innocents who plead guilty: An analysis of patterns in DNA exoneration cases. Innocence Project. https://www.innocenceproject.org/wp-content/uploads/2019/09/FSR3104-5_04_Final-Publication-Innocents-Who-Plead-Guilty-April-June-2019-1.pdf.

Corrigan, P. W., Larson, J. E., & Rüsch, N. (2009). Self-stigma and the "why try" effect: impact on life goals and evidence-based practices. *World Psychiatry: Official Journal of the World Psychiatric Association, 8*(2), 75–81. https://doi.org/10.1002/j.2051-5545.2009.tb00218.

Cory, P. (2001). The inquiry regarding Thomas Sophonow. Manitoba Justice. https://websites.godaddy.com/blob/6aaa6fc2-99d9-4af2-a3b4-51e9d74ea37a/downloads/Thomas%20Sophonow%20Inquiry.pdf?2bd500cf.

Council of Economic Advisors. (2015). Fines, fees, and bail: Payments in the criminal justice system that disproportionately impact the poor. https://obamawhitehouse.archives.gov/sites/default/files/page/files/1215_cea_fine_fee_bail_issue_brief.pdf.

Crime Victims' Rights Act, 18 U.S.C. § 3771 (2004). https://www.justice.gov/usao/resources/crime-victims-rights-ombudsman/victims-rights-act.

Daly, K., & Chesney-Lind, M. (1988). Feminism and criminology. *Justice Quarterly, 5*, 497–538.

*Daubert v. Merrill Dow Pharmaceuticals, Inc.*, 113 S Ct. 2786 (1993).

Daughety, A. F., & Reinganum, J. F. (2018). Evidence suppression by prosecutors: Violations of the Brady rule. *The Journal of Law, Economics, and Organization, 34*(3), 475–510. https://doi.org/10.1093/jleo/ewy014.

Davis, A. Y. (1983). *Women, race & class*. Vintage Books.

Death Penalty Information Center. (2020). Policy issues: Innocence. https://deathpenaltyinfo.org/policy-issues/innocence.

Delgado, R., & Stefancic, J. (2017). *Critical race theory* (3rd ed.). NYU Press.

DeLisi, M., Trulson, C. R., Marquart, J. W., Drury, A. J., & Kosloski, A. E. (2011). Inside the prison black box: Toward a life course importation model of inmate behavior. *International Journal of Offender Therapy and Comparative Criminology, 55*, 1186–1207. https://doi.org/10.1177/0306624X11383956.

Deskovic, J. (2020, July 19). Looking back: The role of prosecutors and judges in perpetuating wrongful convictions. The Davis Vanguard. https://www.davisvanguard.org/2020/07/looking-back-the-role-of-prosecutors-and-judges-in-perpetuating-wrongful-convictions/.

Dodson, L., & Zincavage, R. M. (2007). "It's like a family": Caring labor, exploitation, and race in nursing homes. *Gender & Society, 21*(6), 905–928.

Drizin, S. A., & Leo, R. A. (2004). The problem of false confessions in the post-DNA world. *North Carolina Law Review, 82*(3), 891–1008.

Dror, I., & Stoel, R. D. (2014). Cognitive forensics: Human cognition, contextual information, and bias. In G. Bruinsma & D. Weisburd (Eds.), *Encyclopedia of criminology and criminal justice* (pp. 353–363). Springer. https://doi.org/10.1007/978-1-4614-5690-2_147.

Dussich, J., Underwood, T., & Petersen, D. (2003). New definitions for victimology and victim services: A theoretical note. *The Victimologist, 7*(2), 1–8.

Duwe, G., & Clark, V. A. (2013). Blessed be the social tie that binds: The effects of prison visitation on offender recidivism. *Criminal Justice Policy Review, 24*(3), 271–296. https://doi.org/10.1177/0887403411429724.

Ellis, R. (2021). Prisons as porous institutions. *Theory and Society, 50*, 175–199. https://doi-org.pnw.idm.oclc.org/10.1007/s11186-020-09426-w.

Epp, C. R., Maynard-Moody, S., & Haider-Markel, D. (2014). *Pulled over: How police stops define race and citizenship*. University of Chicago Press.

Faison, L., & Smalarz, L. (2019). Perceptions of exonerees: A review of the psychological science. *Albany Law Review, 83*, 1021–1058.

Fanon, F. (1952). *Black skin, white masks*. Grove Press.

Fazel, S., & Baillargeon, J. (2011). The health of prisoners. *Lancet, 377*(9769), 956–965. https://doi.org/10.1016/S0140-6736(10)61053–61057.

Fazio, M. (2021). Ex-prosecutor who withheld evidence in murder case gives up his law license. *The New York Times*. https://www.nytimes.com/2021/05/18/us/rick-jackson-disbarred-texas.html.

Ferguson, C., & Turvey, B. (2009). A brief history with an introduction to forensic victimology. In B. Turvey & W. Petherick (Eds.), *Forensic victimology: Examining violent crime victims in investigative and legal contexts* (pp. 1–32). Elsevier.

Findley, K., Risinger, M., Barnes, P., Mack, J., Moran, D. A., Sheck, B., & Bohan, T. (2019). Feigned consensus: Usurping the law in shaken baby syndrome/abusive head trauma prosecutions. *Wisconsin Law Review, 4*, 1211–1268.

Findley, K., & Scott, M. (2006). The multiple dimensions of tunnel vision in criminal cases. *Wisconsin Law Review, 2006*(2), 291–307.

Fine, A. D., Donley, S., Cavanagh, C., & Cauffman, E. (2020). Youth perceptions of law enforcement and worry about crime from 1976 to 2016. *Criminal Justice and Behavior, 47*(5), 564–581. https://doi.org/10.1177/0093854820903752.

Fine, M., & Carney, S. (2001). Women, gender, and the law: Toward a feminist rethinking of responsibility. In R. K. Unger (Ed.), *Handbook of the psychology of women and gender* (pp. 388–409). John Wiley & Sons.

Fisher, B. S., Reyns, B. W., & Sloan, J. J., III. (2016). *Introduction to victimology: Contemporary theory, research and practice.* Oxford University Press.

Fisher, K. A., & Hany, M. (2021). Antisocial personality disorder. In *StatPearls* [Internet]. StatPearls Publishing. https://www.ncbi.nlm.nih.gov/books/NBK546673/.

Forst, B. (2004). *Errors of justice: Nature, sources and remedies.* Cambridge University Press.

Frey, J. H., & Delaney, T. (1996). The role of leisure participation in prison. *Journal of Offender Rehabilitation, 23*(1–2), 79–89. https://doi.org/10.1300/J076v23n01_08.

*Frye v. United States,* 293 F. 1013 (D.C. Cir., 1923).

Garrett, B. (2011). *Convicting the innocent: Where criminal prosecutions go wrong.* Harvard University Press.

Garvin, M., & LeClair, S. (2013). Polyvictims: Victims' rights enforcement as a tool to mitigate "secondary victimization" in the criminal justice system. *Victim Law Bulletin.* https://law.lclark.edu/live/files/13797-ncvlipvvictims-rights-enforcement-as-a-tool-to.

Gelles, R. J. (1987). *Family violence* (2nd ed.). Sage.

Gershman, B. L. (2014). The prosecutor's contribution to wrongful convictions. In A. D. Redlich, J. R. Acker, C. L. Bonventure, & R. J. Norris (Eds.), *Examining wrongful convictions: Stepping back, moving forward* (pp. 109–122). Carolina Academic Press.

Giguere, R., & Dundes, L. (2002). Help wanted: A survey of employer concerns about hiring ex-convicts. *Criminal Justice Policy Review, 13,* 396–408. https://doi.org/10.1177/088740302237806.

Gorski, T. T. (2001). Post incarceration syndrome. *Addiction Exchange, 3*(4).

Goudge, S. T. (2008). Inquiry into pediatric forensic pathology in Ontario. http://www.attorney-general.jus.gov.on.ca/inquiries/goudge/index.html.

Gould, J. B., & Leo, R. A. (2015). The path to exoneration. *Albany Law Review, 79*(2), 325–370.

Greifinger, R. B. (2007). *Public health behind bars from prisons to communities.* Springer.

Gross, A. (2012). Ricardo Aldape Guerra. National Registry of Exonerations. http://www.law.umich.edu/special/exoneration/Pages/casedetail.aspx?caseid=3267.

Gross, A. (2018). Audrey Edmonds: Other shaken baby syndrome cases. National Registry of Exonerations. https://www.law.umich.edu/special/exoneration/Pages/casedetail.aspx?caseid=3201.

Gross, S. R. (2008). Convicting the innocent. *Annual Review of Law and Social Science, 4,* 173–192.

Gross, S. R., & O'Brien, B. (2008). Frequency and predictors of false convictions: Why we know so little and new data on capital cases. *Journal of Empirical Legal Studies, 5,* 927–962.

Gross, S. R., Possley, M. J., Roll, K. J., & Stephens, K. H. (2020). Governing misconduct and convicting the innocent: The role of prosecutors, police and other law enforcement. National Registry of Exonerations. https://www.law.umich.edu/special/exoneration/Documents/Government_Misconduct_and_Convicting_the_Innocent.pdf.

Gross, S. R., Possley, M., & Stephens, K. (2017). Race and wrongful convictions in the United States. National Registry of Exonerations. http://www.law.umich.edu/special/exoneration/Documents/Race_and_Wrongful_Convictions.pdf.

Grounds, A. T. (2004). Psychological consequences of wrongful conviction and imprisonment. *Canadian Journal of Criminology and Criminal Justice, 46*(2), 165–182. https://doi.org/10.3138/cjccj.46.2.165.

Grounds, A. T. (2005). Understanding the effects of wrongful imprisonment. *Crime and Justice, 32,* 1–58.

Gudjonsson, G. H. (2003). *The psychology of interrogations and confessions: A handbook.* John Wiley & Sons.

Gudjonsson, G. H., & Sigurdsson, J. (2004). The relationship of suggestibility and compliance with self-deception and other-deception. *Psychology, Crime and Law, 10*(4), 447–453.

Guilione, E., & Campbell, K. M. (forthcoming). Jailhouse informants in Canadian courtrooms: Problems and solutions. In K. M. Campbell, A. Horowitz, I. Cotler, & B. Ariel (Eds.), *Wrongful convictions and the criminalization of innocence: International perspectives on contributing factors, case studies and models of exoneration.* Routledge.

Gutman, J. S., & Sun. L. (2019). Why is Mississippi the best state in which to be exonerated? An empirical evaluation of state statutory and civil compensation for the wrongfully convicted. *Northeastern University Law Review, 11*(2), 694–789.

Hager, E. (2017, March 7). The seismic change in police interrogations. The Marshall Project. https://www.themarshallproject.org/2017/03/07/the-seismic-change-in-police-interrogations?utm_medium=email&utm_campaign=newsletter&utm_source=opening-statement&utm_term=newsletter-20170308–708#.OF0yiMfDd.

The Hamilton Project. (2020). Examining the Black–white wealth gap. https://www.hamiltonproject.org/blog/examining_the_black_white_wealth_gap.

Haney, C. (2002). The psychological impact of incarceration: Implications for post-prison adjustment. Urban Institute. http://webarchive.urban.org/UploadedPDF/410624_PyschologicalImpact.pdf.

Hanser, R. (2007). Feminist theory. In N. A. Jackson (Ed.), *The encyclopedia of domestic violence* (pp. 321–326). Routledge.

Harris, D. A. (1997). "Driving while Black" and all other traffic offenses: The Supreme Court and pretextual traffic stops. *Journal of Criminal Law and Criminology, 87*(2), 544–582.

Hattery, A. J., & Smith, E. (2021). *Policing Black bodies: How Black lives are surveilled and how to work for change.* Rowman and Littlefield.

Hays, S. (2003). *Flat broke with children: Women in the age of welfare reform.* Oxford University Press.

Hayes, C. (2017). *A colony in a nation.* Norton.

Healing Justice. (2022). Programs. https://healingjusticeproject.org/programs.

Henry, J. S. (2018). Smoke but no fire: When innocent people are wrongly convicted of crimes that never happen. *American Criminal Law Review, 55*, 1–45.

Henry, J. S. (2020). *Smoke but no fire: Convicting the innocent of crimes that never happened.* University of California Press.

*Henry v. Hulett*, 969 F. 3d 769, Court of Appeals, 7th Circuit (2020).

Hensley, C., Castle, T., & Tewksbury, R. (2003). Inmate-to-inmate sexual coercion in a prison for women. *Journal of Offender Rehabilitation, 37*, 77–87. https://doi.org/10.1300/J076v37n02_04.

Hensley, C., Tewksbury, R., & Castle, T. (2003). Characteristics of prison sexual assault targets in male Oklahoma correctional facilities. *Journal of Interpersonal Violence, 18*(6), 595–606. https://doi.org/10.1177/0886260503251132.

Herman, J. L. (2003). The mental health of crime victims: Impact of legal intervention. *Journal of Traumatic Stress, 16*(2), 159–166. doi:10.1023/A:1022847223135.

Hill-Collins, P. (1991). *Black feminist thought: Knowledge, consciousness, and the politics of empowerment.* Routledge.

Hill Collins, P. (2015). Intersectionality's definitional dilemmas. *Annual Review of Sociology, 41*, 1–20.

Hill-Collins, P., & Bilge, S. (2020). *Intersectionality* (2nd ed.). Wiley.

The Hill Staff. (2020). Read Philonise Floyd's statement to Congress. https://thehill.com/homenews/house/502083-read-philonise-floyds-statement-to-congress.

Hindelang, M. J., Gottfredson, M. R., & Garofalo, J. (1978). *Victims of personal crime: An empirical foundation for a theory of personal victimization.* Ballinger.

hooks, b. (2003). *We real cool: Black men and masculinity.* Routledge.

Huff, R. C., Rattner, A., & Sagarin, E. (1986). Guilty until proven innocent: Wrongful conviction and public policy. *Crime and Delinquency, 32*(4), 518–544.

Huff, R. C., Rattner, A., & Sagarin, E. (1996). *Convicted but innocent: Wrongful conviction and public policy.* Sage.

Iannozzi, C. (2015). A day in the life: The long-term effects and psychological aftermath of wrongful conviction. *SSRN Electronic Journal.* http://doi.org/10.2139/ssrn.2851150.

Inbau, F., Reid, J., Buckley, J., & Jayne, B. (2015). *Essentials of the Reid technique: Criminal interrogations and confessions* (5th ed.). Jones and Bartlett.

Innocence Project. (2009). False confessions and the integrity unit. https://innocenceproject.org/false-confessions-and-the-integrity-unit/.

Innocence Project. (2014). Mississippi and New York shaken baby convictions tossed. https://innocence-project.org/mississippi-and-new-york-shaken-baby-convictions-tossed/.

Innocence Project. (2015). Lack of post-release social services leaves exonerees high and dry. https://innocenceproject.org/lack-of-post-release-social-services-leaves-exonerees-high-and-dry/.

Innocence Project. (2019). Informing justice: The disturbing use of jailhouse informants. https://inno cenceproject.org/informing-injustice/.

Innocence Project. (2021). How racial bias contributes to wrongful conviction. https://innocencep roject.org/how-racial-bias-contributes-to-wrongful-conviction/.

Innocence Project. (n.d.a). DNA exonerations in the United States. https://innocenceproject.org/dna-exonerations-in-the-united-states/.

Innocence Project. (n.d.b). Eyewitness identification reform. https://innocenceproject.org/eye witness-identification-reform.

Innocence Project. (n.d.c). Forensic science: Problems and solutions. https://innocenceproject.org/for-ensic-science-problems-and-solutions/.

Innocence Project. (n.d.d). Key provisions in wrongful conviction compensation laws. https://www.law.umich.edu/special/exoneration/Documents/Key-Provisions-in-Wrongful-Conviction-Compen-sation-Laws.pdf.

Innocence Project. (n.d.e). Michael Morton. https://innocenceproject.org/cases/michael-morton/.

Innocence Project. (n.d.f). Steven Barnes. https://innocenceproject.org/cases/steven-barnes/.

Institute for Innovation in Prosecution at John Jay College of Criminal Justice. (2021, March 15). Supporting the original crime victim throughout an exoneration [Video file]. YouTube. https://www.youtube.com/watch?v=nCzfwJ_q5aw.

Irazola, S., Williamson, E., Stricker, J., & Niedzwiecki, E. (2013). Study of victim experiences of wrongful conviction. Office of Justice Programs. https://www.ojp.gov/pdffiles1/nij/grants/244084.pdf.

Irazola, S., Williamson, E., Stricker, J., & Niedzwiecki, E. (2014). Addressing the impact of wrongful convictions on crime victims. *NIJ Journal, 274*, 34–38.

Jackson, K., & Gross, S. (2014). Female exonerees: Trends and patterns. National Registry of Exon-erations. https://www.law.umich.edu/special/exoneration/Pages/Features.Female.Exonerees.aspx.

Jackson, K., & Gross, S. (2016). Tainted identifications. National Registry of Exonerations. http://www.law.umich.edu/special/exoneration/Pages/taintedids.aspx.

Jackson, N. A. (2007). *Encyclopedia of domestic violence.* Routledge.

Jackson, N. A., Pate, M., & Campbell, K. M. (2021). Prison and post-release experiences of innocent inmates. *Journal of Aggression, Maltreatment & Trauma, 30*(10), 1347–1365. https://doi.org/10.1080/10926771.2020.1866136.

Jackson, N. A., & Oates, G. C. (1998). *Violence in intimate relationships: Examining sociological and psycho-logical issues.* Butterworth-Heinemann.

Jenkins, C. (2009). Helping victims in DNA exoneration cases. https://www.tdcaa.com/journal/help-ing-victims-in-dna%E2%80%88exoneration-cases/.

Jenkins, S. (2013). Secondary victims and the trauma of wrongful conviction: Families and children's perspectives on imprisonment, release and adjustment. *Australian & New Zealand Journal of Criminol-ogy, 46*(1), 119–137. https://doi.org/10.1177/0004865812470384.

Kaiser, H. A. (1989). Wrongful conviction and imprisonment: Towards an end to the compensatory obstacle course. *Windsor Yearbook of Access to Justice, 9*, 96–153.

Kajstura, A. (2019). Women's mass incarceration: The whole pie 2019. Prison Policy Initiative. https://www.prisonpolicy.org/reports/pie2019women.html.

Karmen, A. (2013). *Crime victims: An introduction to victimology* (9th ed.). Cengage Learning.

Kassin, S. M. (1997). The psychology of confession evidence. *American Psychologist, 52*(3), 221–233. https://doi.org/10.1037/0003-066X.52.3.221.

Kassin, S. M. (2005). On the psychology of confessions: Does innocence put innocents at risk? *American Psychologist, 60*(3), 215–228.

Kassin, S. M. (2007). Internalized false confessions. In M. P. Toglia, J. D. Read, D. F. Ross, & R. C. L. Lindsay (Eds.), *The handbook of eyewitness psychology: Vol. 1. Memory for events* (pp. 175–192). Lawrence Erlbaum.

Kassin, S. M., Goldstein, C. C., & Savitsky, K. (2003). Behavioral confirmation in the interrogation room: On the dangers of presuming guilt. *Law and Human Behavior, 27*(2), 187–203. https://doi.org/10.1023/A:1022599230598.

Kassin, S. M., Meissner, C. A., & Norwick, R. J. (2005). "I'd know a false confession if I saw one": A comparative study of college students and police investigators. *Law and Human Behavior, 29*(2), 211–227. https://doi.org/10.1007/s10979-005-2416-9.

Kassin, S. M., & Wrightsman, L. S. (1985). Confession evidence. In S. M. Kassin & L. S. Wrightsman (Eds.), *The psychology of evidence and trial procedure* (pp. 67–94). Sage.

Kauzlarich, D., Matthews, R., & Miller, W. (2001). Toward a victimology of state crime. *Critical Criminology, 10(3)*, 173–194. https://doi.org/10.1023/A:1015744304749.

Kendi, I. X. (2020, June 1). The American nightmare: To be Black and conscious of anti-Black racism is to stare into the mirror of your own extinction. *The Atlantic.* http://bit.ly/3b6z9yD.

Kent, J. (1832). *Commentaries on American law* (Vol. 2, 1st ed.). O. Halsted.

Kent, S. L., & Carmichael, J. T. (2015). Legislative response to wrongful conviction: Do partisan principals and advocacy efforts influence state-level criminal justice policy? *Social Science Research, 52*, 147–160.

Kerner Commission. (1968). Report of the National Advisory Commission on Civil Disorders. https://www.hsdl.org/?view&did=35837.

*Khumo Tire Company Ltd v. Patrick Carmichael*, U.S.S.C. 143 L. Ed (2d) 283 (1999).

Kilpatrick, D. G., Beatty, D., & Smith Howley, S. (1998). The rights of crime victims: Does legal protection make a difference? National Institute of Justice. https://www.ojp.gov/pdffiles/173839.pdf.

Kirshenbaum, J., Cabell, J., Moody, S., & Yang, Y. (2020). Life after exoneration: An overview of factors that affect exoneree reintegration. *Advances in Psychology and Law, 5*, 179–218. https://doi.org/ 10.1007/978–973-030–54678-6_6.

Konvisser, Z. D. (2012). Psychological consequences of wrongful conviction in women and the possibility of positive change. *DePaul Journal for Social Justice, 5(2)*, 221–294.

Konvisser, Z. D. (2015). "What happened to me can happen to anybody" – Women exonerees speak out. *Texas A&M Law Review, 3(2)*, 303–366.

Kozinski, W. (2017). The Reid interrogation technique and false confessions: A time for change. *Seattle Journal for Social Justice, 16(2)*, 301–345.

Kreager, D. A., & Kruttschnitt, C. (2018). Inmate society in the era of mass incarceration. *Annual Review of Criminology, 1*, 261–283. https://doi.org/10.1146/annurev-criminol-032317–092513.

Lauritson, J. L., Laub, J. H., Samson, R. J. (1991). The link between offending and victimization among adolescents. *Criminology, 29*, 265–292.

La Vigne, N. G., Davies, E., & Brazzell, D. (2008). Broken bonds: Understanding and addressing the needs of children with incarcerated parents. Urban Institute. https://www.urban.org/sites/default/files/publication/31486/411616-Broken-Bonds-Understanding-and-Addressing-the-Needs-of-Children-with-Incarcerated-Parents.PDF.

LeFlouria, T. (2016). *Chained in silence: Black women and convict labor in the New South.* University of North Carolina Press.

Leo, R. (2005). Rethinking the study of miscarriages of justice: Developing a criminology of wrongful conviction. *Journal of Contemporary Criminal Justice, 21(3)*, 201–223.

Leo, R. (2009). False confession: Causes, consequences, and implications. *Journal of the American Academy of Psychiatry and the Law, 37(3)*, 332–343.

Levey, D. S. (2004). Wrongfully convicted: A no-win situation for the victim. *Drake Law Review, 52*, 695–701.

Lewis, A., & Sommervold, S. (2015). Death, but is it murder? The role of stereotypes and cultural perceptions in the wrongful conviction of women. *Albany Law Review, 78*, 1035–1058.

Liem, M., & Kunst, M. (2013). Is there a recognizable post-incarceration syndrome among released "lifers"? *International Journal of Law and Psychiatry, 36(3–4)*, 333–337. http://dx.doi.org/10.1016/j.ijlp.2013.04.012.

Linklaters LLP. (2016). Women who kill in response to domestic violence: How do criminal justice systems respond? Penal Reform International. https://cdn.penalreform.org/wp-content/uploads/2016/04/Women_who_kill_in_response_to_domestic_violence_Executive_summary.pdf.

Lloyd, A., & Borrill, J. (2020). Examining the effectiveness of restorative justice in reducing victims' post-traumatic stress. *Psychological Injury and Law, 13*, 77–89. https://doi.org/10.1007/s12207-019–09363-9.

Lockwood, B., & Lewis, N. (2019, December 18). The long journey to visit a family member in prison. The Marshall Project. https://www.themarshallproject.org/2019/12/18/the-long-journey-to-visit-a-family-member-in-prison.

Loeffler, C., Hyatt, J., & Ridgeway, G. (2017). Measuring self-reported wrongful convictions among prisoners. *SSRN Electronic Journal.* http://dx.doi.org/10.2139/ssrn.2862261.

Loftus, E. F., Doyle, J. M., & Dysert, J. (2008). *Eyewitness testimony: Civil & criminal* (4th ed.). Lexis Law Publishing.

Lopez, G. (2016). Nixon official: Real reason for the drug was to criminalize Black people and hippies. Vox. https://www.vox.com/2016/3/22/11278760/war-on-drugs-racism-nixon.

Lundman, R. J., & Kaufman, R. L. (2003). Driving while Black: Effects of race, ethnicity, and gender on citizen self-reports of traffic stops and police actions. *Criminology, 41(1)*, 195–220. https://doi.org/10.1111/j.1745–9125.2003.tb00986.x.

MacFarlane, B. (2008). *Wrongful convictions: The effect of tunnel vision and predisposing circumstances in the criminal justice system.* Paper prepared for the Goudge Commission of Inquiry Into Pediatric Forensic Pathology in Ontario. http://www.attorneygeneral.jus.gov.on.ca/inquiries/goudge/policy_research/pdf/Macfarlane_Wrongful-Convictions.pdf.

Mandery, E. J., Shlosberg, A., West, V., & Callaghan, B. (2013). Compensation statutes and post-exoneration offending. *Journal of Criminal Law & Criminology, 103(2)*, 553–584.

Marlow, M. A., Luna-Gierke, R. E., Griffin, P. M., & Vieira, A. R. (2017). Foodborne disease outbreaks in correctional institutions—United States, 1998–2014. *American Journal of Public Health 107(7)*, 1150–1156. https://doi.org/10.2105/ajph.2017.303816.

Martin, T. L., & Doka, K. J. (2000). *Men don't cry … women do: Transcending gender stereotypes of grief.* Brunner/Mazel.

McGlynn-Wright, A., Crutchfield, R. D., Skinner, M. L., & Haggerty, K. P. (2020). The usual, racialized, suspects: The consequence of police contacts with Black and white youth on adult arrest. *Social Problems*, spaa042. https://doi.org/10.1093/socpro/spaa042.

McKay, T., Comfort, M., Lindquist, C., & Bir, A. (2016). If family matters: Supporting family relationships during incarceration and reentry. *Criminology & Public Policy, 15(2)*, 529–542. https://doi.org/10.1111/1745–9133.12209.

Medwed, D. (Ed.). (2017). *Wrongful convictions and DNA revolution: Twenty-five years of freeing the innocent.* Cambridge University Press.

Meili, T. (2003). *I am the Central Park Jogger: A story of hope and possibility.* Thorndike Press.

Mendoza, M. (2017, September 5). Ambiguous loss: How to live with the pain of uncertainty. *Psychology Today.* https://www.psychologytoday.com/us/blog/understanding-grief/201709/ambiguous-loss.

Michaels, S. (2016). After prison, the exonerated face a different kind of hell. Mother Jones. Crime and Justice. https://www.motherjones.com/politics/2016/10/wrongfully-convicted-exonerees-ptsd-mental-health/.

Mills, A. (2020, September 10). Appeals court condemns humiliating mass strip search of women prisoners. Injustice Watch. https://www.injusticewatch.org/commentary/2020/appeals-court-condemns-humiliating-mass-strip-search-of-women-prisoners/.

Mills, L. (2006). The justice of recovery: How the state can heal the violence of crime. *Hastings Law Journal, 57(3)*, 457–508.

Mitchell, M. M., Spooner, K., Jia, D., & Zhang, Y. (2016). The effect of prison visitation on reentry success: A meta-analysis. *Journal of Criminal Justice, 45*, 74–83. https://doi.org/10.1016/j.jcrimjus.2016.07.006.

*Mooney v. Holohan*, 294 U.S. 103, 55 S. Ct. 340, 79 L. Ed. 791 (1935).

Moore, T., & Fitzsimmons, L. (2011). Justice imperilled: False confessions and the Reid technique. *Criminal Law Quarterly, 57(4)*, 509–542.

Murray, J., & Farrington, D. P. (2008). The effects of parental imprisonment on children. *Crime and Justice, 37(1)*, 133–206. https://doi.org/10.1086/520070.

Nash, K., & Moore, S. (2019). The Supreme Court of Canada and the law of causation revisited again. Blaney McMurty LLP. https://www.blaney.com/files/SupremeCourtofCanadaandLawofCausationRevisitedAgain_KNash_SMoore_RWinsor.pdf.

National Academy of Sciences. (2009, August). Strengthening forensic science in the United States: A path forward. Committee on Identifying the Needs of the Forensic Sciences Community, National Research Council. https://www.ojp.gov/pdffiles1/nij/grants/228091.pdf.

National Institute of Justice. (2016). *Exonerees and original victims of wrongful conviction: Listening sessions to inform programs and research* (Report No. NCJ 249931). https://www.ojp.gov/pdffiles1/nij/249931.pdf.

National Public Radio. (2013, April 15). Life after exoneration, for the victims on both sides. https://www.npr.org/2013/04/15/177341744/life-after-exoneration-for-the-victims-on-both-sides.

National Registry of Exonerations. (2020a). About. https://www.law.umich.edu/special/exoneration/Pages/about.aspx.

National Registry of Exonerations. (2020b). Browse cases – Detailed view. https://www.law.umich.edu/special/exoneration/.

National Registry of Exonerations. (2021). Interactive data display. https://www.law.umich.edu/special/exoneration/Pages/Exonerations-in-the-United-States-Map.aspx.

National Registry of Exonerations. (n.d.a). Glossary. https://www.law.umich.edu/special/exoneration/Pages/glossary.aspx.

National Registry of Exonerations. (n.d.b). Our mission. https://www.law.umich.edu/special/exoneration/Pages/mission.aspx.

Naughton, M. (2004). Re-orienting miscarriages of justice. In P. Hillyard, C. Pantazis, S. Tombs, & D. Gordon (Eds.), *Beyond criminology: Taking harm seriously* (pp. 101–112). Pluto Press.

Naughton, M. (2005). Redefining miscarriages of justice: A revived human rights approach to unearth subjugated discourses of wrongful criminal conviction. *British Journal of Criminology, 45*, 65–182.

Naughton, M. (2007). *Rethinking miscarriages of justice: Beyond the tip of the iceberg.* Palgrave Macmillan.

*N.C. v. Alford*, 400 U.S. 26, 91 S. Ct. 160 (1970).

Nellis, A. (2016). The color of justice: Racial and ethnic disparity in state prisons. The Sentencing Project. https://www.sentencingproject.org/wp-content/uploads/2016/06/The-Color-of-Justice-Racial-and-Ethnic-Disparity-in-State-Prisons.pdf.

New Hampshire Victims' Bill of Rights, NH Rev Stat § 21-M:8-h (2019). https://law.justia.com/codes/new-hampshire/2019/title-i/chapter-21-m/section-21-m-8-h/.

Nir, S. M. (2019). How 2 lives collided in Central Park, rattling the nation. *The New York Times.* https://www.nytimes.com/2020/06/14/nyregion/central-park-amy-cooper-christian-racism.html.

Nolan, D., & Amico, C. (2017, April 18). Solitary by the numbers. Frontline. http://apps.frontline.org/solitary-by-the-numbers/.

Norris, R. J. (2012). Assessing compensation statutes for the wrongly convicted. *Criminal Justice Policy Review, 23*(3), 352–374.

Norris, R. J., Bonventure, C. L., & Acker, J. R. (2018). *When justice fails: Causes and consequences of wrongful convictions.* Carolina Academic Press.

Norris, R. J., & Mullinex, K. J. (2020). Framing innocence: An experimental test of wrongful convictions and public opinion. *Journal of Experimental Criminology, 16*, 311–334. https://doi.org/10.1007/s11292-019-09360-7.

North Carolina Innocence Inquiry Commission. (2016). Article 92, NC § 15A (1467). https://www.ncleg.net/EnactedLegislation/Statutes/HTML/ByArticle/Chapter_15a/Article_92.html.

Novick, G. (2008). Is there a bias against telephone interviews in qualitative research? *Research in Nursing & Health, 31*, 391–398. doi:10.1002/nur.20259.

Ofshe, R., & Leo, R. (1997). The social psychology of police interrogation: The theory and classification of true and false confessions. *Studies in Law, Politics, and Society, 16*, 189–251.

Oshinsky, D. (1997). *Worse than slavery: Parchman Farm and the ordeal of Jim Crow justice.* Free Press.

Pacciocco, D. M., & Stuesser, L. (2015). *The law of evidence.* Irwin Law.

Packer, H. (1968). *The limits of the criminal sanction.* Stanford University Press.

Page, J. (2013). Financial training for exonerees awaiting compensation: A case study. *Journal of Offender Rehabilitation, 52*(2), 98–118. https://doi.org/10.1080/10509674.2012.750638.

Papendick, M., & Bohner, G. (2017). Passive victim – strong survivor? Perceived meaning of labels applied to women who were raped. *PloS One, 12*(5), e0177550. https://doi.org/10.1371/journal.pone.0177550.

Parsons, J., & Bergin, T. (2010). The impact of criminal justice involvement on victims' mental health. *Journal of Traumatic Stress, 23*(2), 182–188. https://doi.org/10.1002/jts.20505.

Patterson, O. (1982). *Slavery and social death.* Harvard University Press.

Penzell, A. (2007). Apology in the context of wrongful conviction: Why the system should say it's sorry. *Cardoza Journal of Conflict Resolution, 9*(1), 145–162.

Pereira, S. (2018). Mass incarceration: Slavery renamed. *Themis: Research Journal of Justice Studies and Forensic Science, 6*(3), 42–54. https://doi.org/10.31979/THEMIS.2018.0603.

Pierson, E., Simoiu, C., Overgoor, J., Corbett-Davies, S., Jenson, D., Shoemaker, A., Ramachandran, V., Barghouty, P., Phillips, C., Shroff, R., & Goel, S. (2020). A large-scale analysis of racial disparities in police stops across the United States. *Nature Human Behaviour, 4*, 736–745. https://doi.org/10.1038/s41562-020-0858-1.

Pollanen, M. S., Bowes, M. J., VanLaerhoven, S. J., & Wallace, J. (Eds.). (2013). *Forensic science in Canada: A report of multidisciplinary discussion.* Centre for Forensic Science & Medicine, University of Toronto. https://www.crime-scene-investigator.net/forensic-science-in-canada.pdf.

Possley, M. (2014). A. Jabir Nash. National Registry of Exonerations. https://www.law.umich.edu/special/exoneration/Pages/casedetail.aspx?caseid=4416.

Post-Conviction Survivor Resources. (n.d.). Resources for the media & public. https://www.survivorservices.org/media-and-public/.

Prison Legal News. (2019). The cost of a wrongful conviction. https://www.prisonlegalnews.org/news/2019/dec/9/cost-wrongful-convictions/.

Rabil, M. (2012). My three decades with Darryl Hunt. *Albany Law Review, 75(3)*, 1535–1577.

Rabuy, B., & Kopf, D. (2015, October 20). Separation by bars and miles: Visitation in state prisons. Prison Policy Initiative. https://www.prisonpolicy.org/reports/prisonvisits.html.

Ray, V. (2019). A theory of racialized organizations. *American Sociological Review, 84(1)*, 26–53. https://doi.org/10.1177/0003122418822335.

Redden, M. (2015, August). Why is it so hard for wrongfully convicted women to get justice? Meet the lawyers fighting to close the innocence gap. Mother Jones. https://www.motherjones.com/politics/2015/08/wrongfully-convicted-women-exonerations-innocence-project/.

Renzetti, C. (2013). *Feminist criminology.* Routledge.

Roberts, I. (2001). *Advanced leisure and recreation.* Heinemann Educational Books.

Sawyer, W. (2020). Visualizing the racial disparities in mass incarceration. Prison Policy Initiative. https://www.prisonpolicy.org/blog/2020/07/27/disparities/#slideshows/slideshow4/1.

Sawyer, W., & Wagner, P. (2020, March 24). Mass incarceration: The whole pie 2020. Prison Policy Initiative. https://www.prisonpolicy.org/reports/pie2020.html.

*Say Her Name: The Life and Death of Sandra Bland.* (2018). HBO documentary.

Schafer, S. (1967). The victim and his functional responsibility. *Criminology, 5(3)*, 25–29. https://doi.org/10.1111/j.1745–9125.1967.tb00707.x.

Schnittker, J. (2014). The psychological dimensions and the social consequences of incarceration. *The Annals of the American Academy of Political and Social Science, 651(1)*, 122–138. https://doi.org/10.1177/0002716213502922.

Schnittker, J., & John, A. (2007). Enduring stigma: The long-term effects of incarceration on health. *Journal of Health and Social Behavior, 48(2)*, 115–130. https://doi.org/10.1177/002214650704800202.

Scott, L. (2010). "It never, ever ends": The psychological impact of wrongful conviction. *American University Criminal Law Brief, 5(2)*, 10–22.

Selby, D. (2020). "I never thought this would happen": Jaythan Kendrick is exonerated in Queens after 25 years. Innocence Project. https://innocenceproject.org/jaythan-kendrick-exonerated-queens-nyc-murder/.

Selby, D. (2021). Eight facts about incarcerated and wrongfully convicted women you should know. Innocence Project. https://innocenceproject.org/women-wrongful-conviction-incarceration-facts-iwd2020/#:~:text=Nearly%2073%25%20of%20women%20exonerated,and%20crimes%20that%20were%20fabricated.

Sengstock, M. C. (1976). *The culpable victim in Mendelsohn's typology* [Paper presentation]. Annual Meeting of the Midwest Sociological Society, St. Louis, MO, April 21–24. https://files.eric.ed.gov/fulltext/ED140138.pdf.

Sherrer, H. (2003). The complicity of judges in the generation of wrongful convictions. *Northern Kentucky Law Review, 30(3)*, 539–583.

Sherrin, C. (1997). Jailhouse informants, part 1: Problems with their use. *Criminal Law Quarterly, 40*, 106–122.

Shlosberg, A., Nowotny, J., Panuccio, E., & Rajah, V. (2020). They open the door, kick you out, and say, "go": Reentry challenges after wrongful imprisonment. *The Wrongful Conviction Law Review, 1(2)*, 226–252. https://doi.org/10.29173/wclawr20.

Silbert, R., Hollway, J., & Larizadeh, D. (2015). Criminal injustice: A cost analysis of wrongful convictions, errors, and failed prosecutions in California's criminal justice system. The Chief Justice Earl Warren Institute on Law and Social Policy, University of California, Berkeley School of Law. http://static1.squarespace.com/static/55f70367e4b0974cf2b82009/t/56a95c112399a3a5c87c1a7b/1453939730318/WI_Criminal_InJustice_booklet_FINAL2.pdf.

Simon, D. (2006). *Are wrongful convictions episodic or epidemic?* [Paper presentation]. Annual Meeting of the Law and Society Association, Baltimore, MD, July 6–9.

Smart, C. (1977). *Women, crime and criminology: A feminist critique.* Routledge.

Smart, C. (1995). *Law, crime and sexuality: Essays in feminism.* Sage.

Smith, E., & Hattery, A. J. (2011). Race, wrongful conviction & exoneration. *Journal of African American Studies, 15*, 74–94. https://doi.org/10.1007/s12111-010–9130-5.

Stephens, R. (2021). Annual prison costs a huge part of state and federal budgets. Interrogating Justice. https://interrogatingjustice.org/prisons/annual-prison-costs-budgets/.

Stevenson, M. (2018). Distortion of justice: How the inability to pay bail affects case outcomes. *The Journal of Law, Economics, and Organization, 34*(4), 511–542. https://doi.org/10.1093/jleo/ewy019.

Stratton, G. (2015). Wrongfully convicting the innocent: A state crime? *Critical Criminology, 23*(1), 21–37.

Straus, M. A. (1980). *Behind closed doors: Violence in the American family* (1st ed.). Anchor Press/Doubleday.

Strong, J. D., Reiter, K., Gonzalez, G., Tublitz, R., Augustine, D., Barragan, M., Chestnut, K., Dashtgard, P., Pifer, N., & Blair, T. R. (2020). The body in isolation: The physical health impacts of incarceration in solitary confinement. *PLoS One, 15*(10), e0238510. https://doi.org/10.1371/journal.pone.0238510.

Sykes, G. M. (1958). *The society of captives.* Princeton University Press.

Thompson, A. M., Molina, O. R., & Levett, L. M. (2012). After exoneration: An investigation of stigma and wrongfully convicted persons. *Albany Law Review, 75*, 1373–1413.

Thompson, C. (2016). Penny Beerntsen, the rape victim in "Making A Murderer," speaks out. The Marshall Project. https://www.themarshallproject.org/2016/01/05/penny-beernsten-the-rape-victim-in-making-a-murderer-speaks-out#.Wb3PmLJ2H.

Thompson-Cannino, J., & Cotton, R. (with Torneo, E.). (2010). *Picking Cotton: Our memoir of injustice and redemption.* St. Martin's Press.

Trammell, R. (2012). *Enforcing the convict code: Violence and prison culture.* Lynne Rienner.

Travis, J., Western, B., & Redburn, S. (2014). *The growth of incarceration in the United States: Exploring causes and consequences.* National Academies Press.

Trivelli, A. (2016). Compensating the wrongfully convicted: A proposal to make victims of wrongful incarceration whole again. *Richmond Journal of Law and Public Interest, 19*(3), 257–282.

Tuerkheimer, D. (2011). Science-dependent prosecution and the problem of epistemic contingency: A study of shaken baby syndrome. *Alabama Law Review, 62*, 513–569.

Tyler, T. (1990). *Why people obey the law.* Yale University Press.

Tyler, T. (2016). Police discretion in the 21st century surveillance state. *University of Chicago Legal Forum, 2016*(14), 579–614.

*United States v. Garsson*, 291 F. 646, 649 (S.D.N.Y. 1923).

United States Department of Justice. (2015, March 4). Investigation of the Ferguson Police Department. https://www.justice.gov/sites/default/files/opa/press-releases/attachments/2015/03/04/ferguson_police_department_report.pdf.

*Utah v. Strieff*, No. 14–1373, 579 U.S. ___, 136 S. Ct. 2056, slip op. at 1, 6–10 (2016). https://www.supremecourt.gov/opinions/15pdf/14–1373_83i7.pdf.

Vera Institute. (2016). *Justice for all: Annual report.* https://www.vera.org/downloads/Publications/vera-annual-report-2016/legacy_downloads/Annual-Report-FINAL.pdf.

Victims of Crime Rights Act, Pub. L. No. 98–473 (1984). https://www.congress.gov/bill/98th-congress/house-bill/6403.

Victims' Rights and Restitution Act, 34 U.S.C. § 20141 (1990). https://www.law.cornell.edu/uscode/text/34/20141.

Violent Crime Control Act and Law Enforcement Act of 1994, Pub. L. 103–322 (1994).

Visher, C., LaVigne, N., & Travis, J. (2004). Returning home: Understanding the challenges of prisoner reentry. Urban Institute, Justice Policy Center. https://www.urban.org/sites/default/files/publication/42841/410974-Returning-Home-Understanding-the-Challenges-of-Prisoner-Reentry.PDF.

von Hentig, H. (1948). *The criminal and his victim: Studies in the sociobiology of crime.* Schocken Books.

Walker, L. E. (1979). *The battered woman.* Harper & Row.

Wallace, H., & Roberson, C. (2019). *Victimology: Legal, psychological, and social perspectives* (5th ed.). Pearson.

Watkins, B. (2021). Gallery: Bryan Stevenson speaks at Sinai Forum, Purdue University Northwest, Westville Campus. https://www.nwitimes.com/news/local/gallery-bryan-stevenson-speaks-at-sinai-forum/collection_c52caa50-7783-5cd4-80e3-8da3415bd9d6.html#1.

Webster, E., & Miller, J. (2015). Gendering and racing wrongful conviction: Intersectionality, "normal crimes," and women's experiences of miscarriage of justice. *Albany Law Review, 78,* 973–1033.

Wecht, C. H., & Rago, J. T. (Eds.). (2007). *Forensic science and law: Investigative applications in criminal, civil and family justice.* CRC Press.

Weigand, H. (2009). Rebuilding a life: The wrongfully convicted and exonerated. *Public Interest Law Journal, 18,* 427–437.

Weintraub, J., & Bernstein, K. (2020). Identifying and charging true perpetrators in cases of wrongful convictions. *Wrongful Conviction Law Review, 1*(2), 181–225.

Wells, G. L., & Olson, E. A. (2003). Eyewitness testimony. *Annual Review of Psychology, 54,* 277–295. https://doi.org/10.1146/annurev.psych.54.101601.145028.

Western, B., & Simes, J. T. (2019). Drug use in the year after prison. *Social Science & Medicine, 235,* 1–7. https://doi.org/10.1016/j.socscimed.2019.112357.

Westervelt, S. D., & Cook, K. J. (2008). Coping with innocence after death row. *Contexts, 7*(4), 32–37. https://doi.org/10.1525/ctx.2008.7.4.32.

Westervelt, S. D., & Cook, K. J. (2010). Framing innocents: The wrongly convicted as victims of state harm. *Crime, Law, and Social Change, 53*(3), 259–275. https://doi.org/10.1007/s10611-009-9231-z.

Westervelt, S. D., & Cook, K. J. (2012). *Life after death row: Exonerees' search for community and identity.* Rutgers University Press.

Westervelt, S. D., & Cook, K. J. (2018). Continuing trauma and aftermath for exonerated death row survivors. In H. Toch, J. R. Acker, & V. M. Bonventre (Eds.), *Living on death row: The psychology of waiting to die* (pp. 301–329). American Psychological Association. https://doi.org/10.1037/0000084–013.

Wildeman, J., Costelloe, M., & Schehr, R. (2011). Experiencing wrongful and unlawful conviction. *Journal of Offender Rehabilitation, 50*(7), 411–432. https://doi.org/10.1080/10509674.2011.603033.

Wolff, N., & Shi, J. (2009). Type, source, and patterns of physical victimization: A comparison of male and female inmates. *The Prison Journal, 89*(2), 172–191. https://doi.org/10.1177/0032885509334754.

Wolff, N., & Shi, J. (2011). Patterns of victimization and feelings of safety inside prison: The experience of male and female inmates. *Crime & Delinquency, 57*(1), 29–55. https://doi.org/10.1177/0011128708321370.

Yancy, G. (2020, May 12). Ahmaud Arbery and the ghosts of lynchings past. *New York Times.* https://www.nytimes.com/2020/05/12/opinion/ahmaud-arbery-georgia-lynching.html.

Zack, E. (2019, March 27). Healing as a crime survivor of a wrongful conviction: An interview with crime survivor and wrongful conviction advocate Jennifer Thompson. Innocence Project. https://innocenceproject.org/healing-as-a-crime-survivor-of-a-wrongful-conviction/.

Zalman, M. (2012). Qualitatively estimating the incidence of wrongful convictions. *Criminal Law Bulletin, 48*(2), 221–279.

Zalman, M., Smith, B., & Larson, M. (2012). Citizens' attitudes toward wrongful convictions. *Criminal Justice Review, 37,* 51–69. https://doi.org/10.1177/0734016811428374.

Zannella, L., Clow, K., Rempel, E., Hamovitch, L., & Hall, V. (2020). The effects of race and criminal history on landlords' (un)willingness to rent to exonerees. *Law and Human Behavior, 44,* 300–310. https://doi.org/10.1037/lhb0000419.

## Further Reading

Clow, K. A., & Leach, A.-M. (2015). Stigma and wrongful conviction: All exonerees are not perceived equal. *Psychology, Crime & Law, 21*(2), 172–185. https://doi.org/10.1080/1068316X.2014.951645.

Clow, K. A., Leach, A.-M., & Ricciardelli, R. (2012). Life after wrongful conviction. In B. L. Cutler (Ed.), *Conviction of the innocent: Lessons from psychological research* (pp. 327–341). American Psychological Association. https://doi.org/10.1037/13085–015.

Colman, S. (2014, April 14). No cost for breaking the Brady rule: Make the Brady rule on exculpatory evidence more effective by ensuring that rogue prosecutors are held accountable. *The Wall Street Journal.* https://www.wsj.com/articles/SB10001424052702303603904579494423821971900.

Costanzo, M. A., & Costanzo M. L. (2014). False confessions and police interrogation. In G. Bruinsma & D. Weisburd (Eds.), *Encyclopedia of criminology and criminal justice* (pp. 1547–1555). Springer. https://doi.org/10.1007/978–1–4614–5690–2_157.

Dror, I., Mogan, R., Rando, C., & Nakhaiezadeh, S. (2017). The bias snowball and bias cascade effects: Two distinct bias effects that may impact forensic decision making. *Journal of Forensic Sciences, 62*(3), 832–833. https://doi.org/10.1111/1556–4029.13496.

Duncan, C. (2019). Justifying justice: Six factors of wrongful convictions and their solutions. *Themis: Research Journal of Justice Studies and Forensic Science, 7*(6), 91–107.

Ellsworth, P. C., & Gross, S. R. (2012). False convictions. In E. Shafir (Ed.), *The behavioral foundations of public policy* (pp. 163–180). Princeton University Press.

Fassler, J., & Brown, C. (2017, December 27). Prison food is making U.S. inmates disproportionately sick. *The Atlantic.* https://www.theatlantic.com/health/archive/2017/12/prison-food-sicknessamerica/549179/.

Fattah, E. A. (1989). Victims and victimology: The facts and the rhetoric. *International Review of Victimology, 1*(1), 43–66. https://doi.org/10.1177/026975808900100104.

Fessinger, M. B., Bornstein, B. H., Neuschatz, J. S., DeLoach, D., Hillgartner, M. A., Wetmore, S. A., & Douglass, A. B. (2020). Informants v. innocents: Informant testimony and its contribution to wrongful convictions. *Capital University Law Review, 48*(2), 149–188.

Fitzgerald, R., Price, H. L., Oriet, C., & Charman, S. (2013). The effect of suspect-filler similarity on eyewitness identification decisions: A meta-analysis. *Psychology, Public Policy, and Law, 19*(2), 1–14. https://doi.org/10.1037/a0030618.

Fowler, S., Blackburn, A., Marquart, J., & Mullings, J. (2010). Would they officially report an in-prison sexual assault? An examination of inmate perceptions. *The Prison Journal, 90*(2), 220–243. https://doi.org/10.1177/0032885510363387.

Frenda, S. J., Berkowitz, S. R., Loftus, E. F., & Fenn, K. M. (2016). Sleep deprivation and false confessions. *Proceedings of the National Academy of Sciences, 113*(8), 2047–2050. https://doi.org/10.1073/pnas.1521518113.

Gershowitz, A. M. (2009). Prosecutorial shaming: Naming attorneys to reduce prosecutorial misconduct. *UC Davis Law Review, 42*(4), 1059–1105.

Giannelli, P. C. (2007). Wrongful convictions and forensic science: The need to regulate crime labs. *North Carolina Law Review, 86*, 163–235.

Godsey, M. (2017). *Blind injustice: A former prosecutor exposes the psychology and politics of wrongful convictions.* University of California Press.

Goffman, E. (1961). *Asylums: Essays on the social situation of mental patients and other inmates.* Anchor Books.

Grier, K. (2006). Prosecuting injustice: Consequences of misconduct. *American Journal of Criminal Law, 33*(2), 191–222.

Haney, C. (2006). The wages of prison overcrowding: Harmful psychological consequences and dysfunctional correctional reactions. *Washington University Journal of Law & Policy, 22*, 265–293.

Hanson, R. F., Sawyer, G. K., Begle, A. M., & Hubel, G. S. (2010). The impact of crime victimization on quality of life. *Journal of Traumatic Stress, 23*(2), 189–197. https://doi.org/10.1002/jts.20508.

Harris, A. (2019, May 30). The Central Park Five: "We were just baby boys." *The New York Times.* https://www.nytimes.com/2019/05/30/arts/television/when-they-see-us.html.

Haselton, M. G., Nettle, D., & Andrews, P. W. (2015). The evolution of cognitive bias. In D. M. Buss (Ed.), *The handbook of evolutionary psychology* (pp. 724–746). John Wiley & Sons.

Hattery, A. J., & Smith, E. (2010). *Prisoner reentry and social capital: The long journey to reintegration.* Lexington Books.

Hauber, D., & Zank, S. (2021). WWII trauma impacts physical and mental health in the oldest old: Results from a German population-based study. *Aging & Mental Health, 8,* 1–8. https://doi.org/10.1080/13607863.2021.1876637.

Hays, S. (1996). *The cultural contradictions of motherhood.* Yale University Press.

Hensley, C., & Tewksbury, R. (2005). Wardens' perceptions of prison sex. *The Prison Journal, 85(2),* 186–197. https://doi.org/10.1177/0032885505276996.

Hochstetler, A., & DeLisi, M. (2005). Importation, deprivation, and varieties of serving time: An integrated-lifestyle-exposure model of prison offending. *Journal of Criminal Justice, 33(3),* 257–266. https://doi.org/10.1016/j.jcrimjus.2005.02.005.

Hochstetler, A., Murphy, D. S., & Simons, R. L. (2004). Damaged goods: Exploring predictors of distress in prison inmates. *Prison Journal, 50,* 436–457. https://doi.org/10.1177/0011128703257198.

Innocence Project. (2016). Justice at last: San Antonio Four are declared innocent. https://innocenceproject.org/san-antonio-four-declared-innocent/#:~:text=In%202013%2C%20Mike%20Ware%20and,the%20integrity%20of%20their%20convictions.

Innocence Project. (2021, July 15). Illinois becomes the first state to ban police from lying to juveniles during interrogations. https://innocenceproject.org/illinois-first-state-to-ban-police-lying/.

Jackson, R. H. (1940). The federal prosecutor. *Journal of the American Judicature Society, 24,* 18–20.

Jochnowitz, L. D., & Kendall, T. (2021). Analyzing wrongful convictions beyond the traditional canonical list of errors, for enduring structural and sociological attributes, (juveniles, racism, adversary system, policing policies). *Touro Law Review, 37(2),* 579–663.

Johnson, G., & Engstrom, D. W. (2021). Judge Learned Hand's haunting: The psychological consequences of wrongful conviction. *Social Justice, 47(1–2),* 195–251.

Kassin, S. M., & Kiechel, K. L. (1996). The social psychology of false confessions: Compliance, internalization, and confabulation. *Psychological Science, 7(3),* 125–128. https://doi.org/10.1111/j.1467-9280.1996.tb00344.x.

Kilpatrick, D. G. (2000). The mental health impact of rape. www.musc.edu/vawprevention/research/mentalimpact.shtml.

Klaus, P. A. (1994). Costs of crime to victims. Bureau of Justice Statistics. https://bjs.ojp.gov/content/pub/pdf/ccv.pdf.

Landau, S. F., & Freeman-Long, R. E. (1990). Classifying victims: A proposed multidimensional victimological typology. *International Review of Victimology 1(3),* 267–286. https://doi.org/10.1177/026975809000100304.

LaPorte, G. M. (2017). Wrongful convictions and DNA exonerations: Understanding the role of forensic science. *NIJ Journal, 279,* 1–16.

Magid, L. (2001). Deceptive police interrogation practices: How far is too far? *Michigan Law Review, 99 (5),* 1168–1210.

Manikis, M. (2019). Contrasting the emergence of the victims' movements in the United States and England and Wales. *Societies, 9(2),* 35–53. https://doi.org/10.3390/soc9020035.

McGrath, S. A., Marcum, C. D., & Copes, H. (2012). The effects of experienced, vicarious, and anticipated strain on violence and drug use among inmates. *American Journal of Criminal Justice, 37(1),* 60–75. https://doi.org/10.1007/s12103-011-9127-1.

Meade, B., & Steiner, B. (2013). The effects of exposure to violence on inmate maladjustment. *Criminal Justice and Behavior, 40(11),* 1228–1249. https://doi.org/10.1177/0093854813495392.

Miller, M. K., & Bornstein, B. H. (2016). *Advances in psychology and law* (Vol. 1). Springer.

Miller, T. R., Cohen, M. A., & Rossman, S. B. (1993). Victim costs of violent crime and resulting injuries. *Health Affairs, 12(4),* 186–197. doi:10.1377/hlthaff.12.4.186.

*Miranda v. Arizona,* 384 U.S. 436 (1966).

Moreno, J. A., & Holmgren, B. (2013). The Supreme Court screws up the science: There is no abusive head trauma/shaken baby syndrome "scientific" controversy. *Utah Law Review, 5,* 1357–1435.

Morgan, R. E., & Truman, J. L. (2020). Criminal victimization, 2019. Bureau of Justice Statistics. https://www.bjs.gov/content/pub/pdf/cv19.pdf.

Murray, J., & Farrington, D. P. (2005). Parental imprisonment: Effects on boys' antisocial behaviour and delinquency through the life-course. *Journal of Child Psychology and Psychiatry, 46(12),* 1269–1278. https://doi.org/10.1111/j.1469-7610.2005.01433.x.

*Napue v. Illinois*, 360 U.S. 264, 79 S. Ct. 1173, 3 L. Ed. 2d 1217 (1959).

O'Brien, B., & Findley, K. (2014). Psychological perspectives: Cognition and decision making. In A. D. Redlich, J. R. Acker, R. J. Norris, & C. L. Bonventre (Eds.), *Examining wrongful convictions: stepping back, moving forward* (pp. 35–54). Carolina Academic Press.

Office for Victims of Crime. (2004). The crime victims fund: Two decades of making a difference. https://www.ncjrs.gov/ovc_archives/ncvrw/2004/pg4c.html.

Office of the United States Attorneys. (2016). Crime Victims' Rights Act 2004, 18 U.S.C. § 3771. https://www.justice.gov/usao/resources/crime-victims-rights-ombudsman/victims-rights-act.

Oppel, R. A., Taylor, D. B., & Bogel-Burroughs, N. (2021, April 26). What to know about Breonna Taylor's death. *New York Times.* https://www.nytimes.com/article/breonna-taylor-police.html.

Paul, D. (2019, June 29). "When They See Us" tells the important story of the Central Park Five: Here's what it leaves out. *The Washington Post.* https://www.washingtonpost.com/history/2019/06/29/when-they-see-us-tells-important-story-central-park-five-heres-what-it-leaves-out/.

Pérez, D. M., Gover, A. R., Tennyson, K. M., & Santos, S. D. (2010). Individual and institutional characteristics related to inmate victimization. *International Journal of Offender Therapy and Comparative Criminology, 54*(3), 378–394. https://doi.org/10.1177/0306624X09335244.

Petersilia, J. (2003). *When prisoners come home: Parole and prison reentry.* Oxford University Press.

Petherick, W. (2017). Victim precipitation: Why we need to expand upon the theory. *Forensic Research & Criminology International Journal, 5*(2), 262–264. https://doi.org/10.15406/frcij.2017.05.00148.

Possley, M. (2019). Steven Avery. National Registry of Exonerations. https://www.law.umich.edu/special/exoneration/Pages/casedetail.aspx?caseid=3003.

Public Broadcasting Service. (2020). The Central Park Five: Conviction and exoneration. https://www.pbs.org/kenburns/the-central-park-five/conviction-and-exoneration.

Reisman, N. (2021, June 18). Cuomo signs bill creating prosecutor conduct panel. Spectrum Local News. https://spectrumlocalnews.com/nys/central-ny/ny-state-of-politics/2021/06/18/cuomo-signs-bill-creating-prosecutor-conduct-panel?cid=share_clip.

Resnick, H. S., Kilpatrick, D. G., Dansky, B. S., Saunders, B. E., & Best, C. L. (1993). Prevalence of civilian trauma and PTSD in a representative national sample of women. *Journal of Clinical and Consulting Psychology, 61*(6), 984–991. doi:10.1037/0022-006X.61.6.984.

Ricciardi, L., & Demos, M. (Writers & Directors). (2015, December 18). Eighteen years lost (Season 1, Episode 1) [Netflix series]. In L. Ricciardi, M. Demos, L. Nishimura, & A. Del Deo (Executive Producers), *Making a murderer.* Synthesis Films.

Rodriguez, D. N., & Berry, M. A. (2013). Eyewitness science and the call for double-blind lineup administration. *Journal of Criminology, 2013,* 1–10. https://doi.org/10.1155/2013/530523.

Saum, C., Surratt, H., Inciardi, J., & Bennet, R. (1995). Sex in prison: Exploring the myths and realities. *The Prison Journal, 75,* 413–430. https://doi.org/10.1177/0032855595075004002.

Schneider, T., Sauerland, M., Grady, L., Leistra, A., van Lier, S., & Merckelbach, H. (2021). Feeling guilty: Little effect on false confession rate. *Psychology, Crime & Law, 27*(3), 265–281. https://doi.org/10.1080/1068316X.2020.1798427.

Shaw, J. (2011). Exoneration and the road to compensation: The Tim Cole Act and comprehensive compensation for persons wrongfully imprisoned. *Texas Wesleyan Law Review, 17,* 593–601.

Siennick, S. E., Mears, D. P., & Bales, W. D. (2013). Here and gone: Anticipation and separation effects of prison visits on inmate infractions. *Journal of Research in Crime and Delinquency 50*(3), 417–444. https://doi.org/10.1177/0022427812449470.

Simon, J. (2007). *Governing through crime: How the war on crime transformed American democracy and created a culture of fear.* Oxford University Press.

Sims, B., Yost, B., & Abbott, C. (2006). The efficacy of victim service programs: Alleviating the psychological suffering of crime victims? *Criminal Justice Policy, 17*(4), 387–406.

Sluzki, C. E. (1993). Toward a model of family and political victimization: Implications for treatment and recovery. *Psychiatry, 56*(2), 178–187. https://doi.org/10.1080/00332747.1993.11024632.

Struckman-Johnson, C., & Struckman-Johnson, D. (2000). Sexual coercion rates in seven Midwestern prison facilities for men. *The Prison Journal, 80,* 379–390.

Sudnow, D. (1965). Normal crimes: Sociological features of the penal code in a public defender office. *Social Problems, 12*(3), 255–276.

Swavola, E., Riley, K., & Subramanian, R. (2016). Overlooked: Women and jails in an era of reform. The Vera Institute of Justice. https://www.vera.org/publications/overlooked-women-and-jails-report.

Sweet, P. L. (2019). The sociology of gaslighting. *American Sociological Review, 84*(5), 851–875. https://doi.org/10.1177/0003122419874843.

Tankebe, J., & Liebling, A. (2013). Legitimacy and criminal justice: An introduction. In J. Tankebe & A. Liebling (Eds.), *Legitimacy and criminal justice: An international exploration* (pp. 1–6). Oxford University Press.

Tierney, K. (1982). The battered women movement and the creation of the wife beating problem. *Social Problems, 29*(3), 207–220. https://doi.org/10.2307/800155.

Timmer, D. A., & Norman, W. H. (1984). The ideology of victim precipitation. *Criminal Justice Review, 9*(2), 63–68. https://doi.org/10.1177/073401688400900209.

Tobolowsky, P. (2010). *Crime victim rights and remedies* (2nd ed.). Carolina Academic Press.

United Nations. (1985). Declaration of basic principles of justice for victims of crime and abuse of power. https://www.ohchr.org/en/professionalinterest/pages/victimsofcrimeandabuseofpower.aspx.

United States Department of Justice. (2021, June 16). Fair housing act. https://www.justice.gov/crt/fair-housing-act-1.

Warden, R. (2004). The snitch system. Center on Wrongful Convictions. https://deathpenaltyinfo.org/documents/SnitchSystemBooklet.pdf.

Wasserman, E., & Ellis, C. A. (2010). Impact of crime on victims. SILO. https://silo.tips/download/chapter-6-impact-of-crime-on-victims.

Watson, C., Weiss, K. J., & Pouncey, C. (2010). False confessions, expert testimony, and admissibility. *Journal of the American Academy of Psychiatry and the Law, 38*(2), 174–186.

Weber, M. (1968). *Economy and society: An outline of interpretive sociology* (G. Roth & C. Wittich, Eds.). Bedminster. (Original work published 1922)

Wells, G. L. (1988). *Eyewitness identification: A system handbook.* Carswell Legal Publications.

Wemmers, J. (2010). A short history of victimology. In O. Hagemann, P. Schäfer, & S. Schmidt (Eds.), *Victimology, victim assistance and criminal justice: Perspectives shared by international experts at the Inter-University Centre of Dubrovnik* (pp. 33–42). Niederrhein University of Applied Sciences.

Williamson, E. J., Stricker, J. M., Irazola, S. P., & Niedzwiecki, E. (2016). Wrongful convictions: Understanding the experiences of the original crime victims. *Violence and Victims, 31*(1), 155–166. https://doi.org/10.1891/0886-6708.VV-D-13-00152.

Zeman, L. D. (2004). Etiology of loss among parents falsely accused of abuse or neglect. *Journal of Loss and Trauma, 10*(1), 19–31. https://doi.org/10.1080/15325020490890624.

Zimmerman, D. M., Austin, J. L., & Kovera, M. B. (2012). Suggestive eyewitness identification procedures. In B. L. Cutler (Ed.), *Conviction of the innocent: Lessons from psychological research* (pp. 125–148). American Psychological Association. https://doi.org/10.1037/13085-006.

# INDEX

Page numbers in *italics* denote figures, those in **bold** denote tables.

acquittals, wrongful 5
African Americans *see* Black men; Black people;
    Black women
After Innocence 100
age: at false arrest of study exonerees 6, 7; and
    victimization risk 12, 13, 14
Aldape Guerra, Ricardo 29–30
Alexander, M. 36
Alexander-Bloch, B. 131
Alford plea 81
Allen, Dennis 54n2
ambiguous loss, family members 88–89
American Civil Liberties Union (ACLU) 106
Amir, M. 13
Anderson, C. 35, 36, 52
anger: children of wrongly convicted 91; crime
    victims 18, 19, 104, 109; family members 88,
    89, 91
Angola, Louisiana 36
antisocial personality traits 129
anxiety: children of wrongly convicted 91; crime
    victims 18, 104; family members 89, 91; female
    exonerees 81; and incarceration 66, 131;
    post-release 129, 130, 131
apologies, public xvi, 69, 122, 123n5
arrest 29, 59, 104
Avery, Steven 108
awareness-raising, women exonerees 80–81

bail 43, 44, 45–46, 53
Balfour, G. 72
Bard, M. 19
Barnes, Steven 32
battered women 70, 74
Baum, D. 39
Beatrice Six 121

Beerntsen, Penny 103, 108, 109
Beetham, D. 116
Belinsky, Kimberly 3–4
Berger v. United States (1935) 30, 60
Bilge, S. 38
Black Codes (Black Laws) 36, 37
Black feminist theory 38
Black men: and criminal legal/justice system 9,
    35–36, 38–39, 40–46, 51–52, 104, 139; death
    penalty cases 47, 49; exonerations 35, 47,
    48–49, 50, 51, 52, 53, 54; incarceration of 35,
    39, 44, 45–46, 47, 50, 51, 53, 83; lynching of
    16, 51, 52; murder/homicide convictions 47,
    48–49, 50–52; and police practices *see* policing
    and Black people; and rape/murder of white
    women 47, 48–49, 50–52; stereotyping of 51;
    and war on drugs 39; wrongful convictions 35,
    47–49; see also Central Park jogger case; Hunt,
    Darryl Black people 9, 16; Black Codes and
    36, 37; and criminal legal/justice system 9, 16,
    21, 35–36, 38–39, 40–46, 51–52, 104, 139;
    enslaved 36, 38; exonerations 21, 47, 54; as
    ideal victims 21; incarceration of 36–37, 39,
    44–46, 54, 67, 83; intersectional framework
    and experiences of 37, 38; oppression of 36,
    38; and police practices *see* policing and Black
    people; racist stereotypes of 21, 51; as victims
    of violent crime 49; violent crime between 49;
    and war on drugs 39, 52; *see also* Black men;
    Black women
Black women: crime types of exonerees 74;
    incarceration numbers 83; number of
    exonerees 83; *see also* Bland, Sandra; Taylor,
    Breonna
Blackness, criminalization of 36, 52
blaming: family 90; victim 12, 13–14

Bland, Sandra 43, 45–46
Boss, P. 88
Brady v. Maryland (1963) 30, 60
*Brady* violation 4, 10n, 30, 60–61, 135
Brandon, Christopher 33
Brewer, Kennedy 33
Brooks, Levon 33
Browder, Kalief 45–46, 53
Brown, Mike 41, 44
Bruckert, C. 72
Buckley, James 28
Bunch, Kristine 59
Buser, M. E. 44, 45, 53

Caldero, M. A. 29
Campbell, K. M. 24, 79
capable guardians 14, 15, 22
capitalism 36, 38
carceral state 37, 38–39
Carmichael, J. T. 120
Carrasco Flores, Roberto 29–30
Cassell, P. 24
Castelle, G. 26
Castile, Philando 42, 43
Center for Wrongful Conviction, Northwestern
   University 54, 59, 72
Central Park jogger case 27, 49–50, 51, 54n3, 104
Centurion Ministries 47, 100
Chamberlain, A. 130
Chesney–Lind, M. 72
child death 89; forensic evidence and 82–83
child sexual abuse cases 53, 90; exonerations *48*,
   107; exonerations by race *48*; stigma of, family
   members 90; women and 73, 74
children, harms against: women's wrongful
   conviction and 73, 74, 75, 82–83, 85; *see also*
   child death; child sexual abuse cases; shaken
   baby syndrome
children of wrongly incarcerated 61, 133;
   caretaking challenges of family members
   94–95; post-release reconnection with 97;
   prison visits 94; psychological effects on 90–91;
   risk of delinquency 91; and stigma of
   incarceration 91
Christian, J. 95
Christie, N. 21
Chunn, D. 84
Cicchini, M. D. 61
Civil Action for Deprivation of Rights (Civil
   Rights Act of 1871, 2006) 135
Civil Rights Movement 15, 16–17
class 84, 141
class domination 38
classism 68, 141
Clinton, Bill 38–39
Clow, K. A. 122
coerced confessions 59, 60
Cohen, L. 14
Coleman, Christopher 54
Comack, E. 72

commission, crimes of 117, 118
compensation: civil lawsuits 135, 136; female
   exonerees 80, 81; funding of 121; and
   legitimacy 118–120; private bills 135; public
   perceptions about appropriateness of 122;
   statutes 53, 135–136; victim 15, 16, 17, 112;
   wrongly convicted 19–20, 53, 54, 69, 80, 81,
   99, 118, 119–120, 121, 122, 125, 135–136
confessions, false *see* false confessions
control: and criminal justice system 70; and
   perpetrators of domestic violence 70
convict leasing system 37
conviction integrity units 140
Cook, K. J. 57, 68, 102n3, 103, 107, 114, 118
Cooper, Amy 52
Cooper, Christian 52
Correa, Angela xiv
corruption 116; noble cause 29
Cory, P. 118, 119
Cotton, Ronald 103, 108
Council of Economic Advisors 42
counseling: exonerees and their families 100;
   original crime victims 110, 112
crime: fear of 15; war on 15
"Crime Bill" 39
crime control legitimacy 116
Crime Victims Fund 16
Crime Victims' Rights Act (2004) 16–17, 106, 141
crimes of commission and omission 117, 118
criminal investigations: failures in 59; original
   crime victims and 104–105
criminal justice system 5, 10, 12, 15, 18, 20, 24, 29,
   46, 69, 118, 138; Black people and 9, 16, 21,
   35–36, 38–39, 40–46, 51–52, 104, 139; control
   of vulnerable populations 70; family members
   and 88, 99, 120; fear of 130, 132–133; legitimacy
   of 115, 116, 117, 120, 122–123, 140; as offender
   22; original crime victims and 104–106;
   personnel training 114; power of actors in 21, 29,
   30, 60, 69, 84; procedural fairness 116; sexual
   assault/domestic violence victims and 16; trust/
   loss of trust in 67, 99, 130, 132–133; and
   victimization process 57–61; white people and
   38, 104; women in 71–74, 84, 139
criminology, feminist 71–72, 84
critical race theory 37–38
Cunningham, Steven xiv

Daly, K. 72
Daniel, K. 72, 73
Daubert v. Merrill Dow Pharmaceuticals, Inc.
   (1993) 32
death: of wrongly convicted 89, 134; *see also* child
   death
death penalty cases 5, 24, 47, 49, 57, 68
Delgado, R. 37
delinquency, parental incarceration as risk factor
   for 91
demographics: of study exonerees 6, 7; and
   victimization risk 13, 14

denial, victim 19, 110
Denov, M. 79
dental health 66, 134–135
depression: children of wrongly convicted 91;
    family members 89, 91; female exonerees 81;
    and incarceration 66, 131; post-release 130,
    131; and victimization 18, 19
Deskovic, J. M. xii–xv, 121
dignity, loss of 62
direct victims 17, 18, 61–62; *see also* original crime
    victims
DNA evidence xiii, 31, 32, 50, 110, 111, 112,
    122; exonerations and 23, 24, 25, 31, 72, 80,
    81, 106–107, 107–108, 120–121; faulty 22;
    and identification of true perpetrator 109, 121;
    women's cases and 72, 139
Doka, K. J. 97
domestic violence 13, 14, 15, 16, 70, 74;
    perpetrators control of victims 70;
    psychological effects of 70
domination, matrix of 38
Donald, Willie T. 3–4, 139
Dror, I. 59
drug cases: Black women exonerees 74;
    exonerations 74, 107
drug use 18, 130
drugs, war on 38–39, 40, 52
due process 5, 30, 51, 61, 106, 135
due process legitimacy 116
Duncan, Jimmy 33

economic/financial victimization 17
Edmonds, Tyler 33
education, and victimization 14
electronic monitoring (e-carceration) 39
emotional/psychological victimization 17
employment 100, 125–126, 140
empowerment 12, 96, 106
Epp, C. R. 42, 43, 45
Equal Justice Initiative 141
Erlichman, John 39
estimator variables, and eyewitness identification 26
evidence: biasing snowball effect 59; exculpatory
    *see* exculpatory evidence; fabrication of 29;
    forensic *see* DNA evidence; forensic evidence
exculpatory evidence 60–61; ignoring/
    withholding 29, 30–31, 54n2, 59, 135; *see also*
    *Brady* violation
exoneration(s): Black people 21, 35, 47, 48–49,
    50, 51, 52, 53, 54; child sexual abuse *48*, 107;
    and DNA evidence 23, 24, 25, 31, 72, 80, 81,
    106–107, 107–108, 120–121; drug crimes 74,
    107; interracial crime 47, 48–49; murder 24,
    47, 48, 49, 50, 51, 107; NRE definition of 5,
    81, 86n6; numbers 5, 20, 23, 35, 54, 106;
    original crime victims and *see* original crime
    victims and
exonerations; racialization of 36, 38, 39, 47–49,
    51; robbery 107; sexual assault/rape 24, 47, *48*,
    48–49, 50, 51, 75, 107, 109

exoneree(s): number of 5; post-release adjustment
    *see* post-release adjustment/challenges; study
    participants 5–6, *7, 8*; as a term 5; *see also*
    female exonerees; men/male exonerees
expert testimony 9, 23, 31, 32–33, 139
exploitation 36, 38
eyewitness identification: in court 105; estimator/
    system variables and 26; memory and 25, 26;
    police lineups and 26; unconscious transference
    and 26
eyewitness misidentification 9, 22, 23, 25–26, 32,
    50, 82, 99, 105, 117, 135, 139

factual innocence 4, 5, 20, 39, 86n6, 111, 115,
    136, 140
fairness 141; procedural 116
false accusations 82, 83
false confessions 9, 22, 23, 26–28, 29, 69, 117,
    131, 135, 139; coerced 59; coerced compliant
    60, 68; coerced internalized 60; police
    interrogation methods and 26–27, 59–60,
    69, 117; susceptibility to 27–28, 59–60, 69;
    voluntary 60; women and wrongful
    conviction 83
familial relationships, changes in/fracturing of 97,
    99–100, 133–134
families of wrongly convicted xiv, 9, 20, 63,
    87–102, 103, 138, 139–140, 141; belief in
    innocence of exoneree 95–96; child care
    challenges 94–95; coping mechanisms 95; and
    criminal justice system 88, 99, 120; family life
    outside prison 94; financial strain 92; grief and
    ambiguous loss 88–89; prison visits *see* prison
    visits; psychological consequences for 87–90;
    sense of injustice 89; stigma 89–90, 91; trauma
    experienced by 88, 100
families of wrongly convicted, post-release
    adjustment 96–99; continued involvement
    with the system 99; compensation and 99;
    counseling and 100; emotional connection 97;
    familial relationships 97, 99–100; physical
    restrictions 98–99; reentry planning and 100;
    support for exoneree 98; support groups and
    organizations 100; understanding the "new"
    person 97
Fanon, F. 38
Fatah, E. A. 13
fear: of crime 15; of criminal justice system 130,
    132–133; original crime victims 104, 108–109
Federal Bureau of Investigation, Uniform Crime
    Reports 15
felony conviction 24, 52, 53
Felson, M. 14
female exonerees xiii, 9, 139; awareness-raising
    efforts 80–81; compensation 80, 81; crime
    types 73, 74, *75*, 75, 82; employment status
    125–126, *126*; incarceration, experience of
    77–79, 81; mental health issues 78, 79, 80, 81;
    post-release adjustment/ challenges 79–81,
    125–126; prevalence in US 73–74; racial

disparities in crime types among 74; racial distribution 74, 83; sentence lengths 76; time served 76

female wrongful convictions 71, 72–73; child victim cases 73, 74, 75, 82–83; contributing factors 82–83; DNA evidence and exonerations 72, 139; domestic crime cases 74; "good" mother assumptions and 72, 74, 82, 84; intersectional approach to study of 84; intimate partner cases 70, 74; misleading forensic evidence and 82–83; murder/homicide cases 73, 75, 82; "no-crime" cases 58, 72–73, 74, 81–82, 83, 139; sexual assault cases 75; victimization and 84–85

feminist criminology 71–72, 84

Feminist Movement 15–16

feminist theory 71, 72, 84; Black 38

fictitious crimes see "no-crime" cases

financial costs of wrongful convictions 121–122, 140; see also compensation

financial hardship/insecurity: families of wrongly incarcerated 92; original crime victims postexoneration 110; post-release 125–127, 140

financial reparation see compensation

financial/economic victimization 17

Fine, A. D. 67

Fisher, K. A. 129

Fisher, Larry 121

"fishing expeditions" 9, 35, 36, 42–43, 45, 47, 53

Floyd, George 43, 45

Floyd, Philonise 45

food, prison 65

forensic evidence: biological 32; and child death 82–83; core disciplines 32; physical scientific 32; women and wrongful convictions 82–83; see also DNA evidence

forensic science: national standards for 140–141; problematic 9, 23, 31–33, 82–83, 139

Frye v. United States (1923) 32

functional responsibility theory 13

Garner, Eric 43

Garrett, B. L. 47

gender 72, 82, 83, 84, 141; inequality 15, 84; and race, intersection of 74; of study exonerees 6, 7; and victimization risk 12, 13, 14

general victimology 13, 17

Goffman, E. 62

Gorski, T. T. 128, 129, 130

grand jury proceedings 105

grief, family members 88–89

Gross, A. 29–30

Gross, S. R. 25, 29, 30, 31, 34n5, 36, 39, 47, 140

Grounds, A. T. 88, 130

Gudjonsson, G. H. 28

guilt: exonerees' feelings of 68, 130, 131–132; original crime victims feelings of 108; secondary victims feelings of 19; survivor 131–132

guilty pleas 44, 45, 53, 105

guilty victim typology 12

guilty victim/guilty offender typology 12

Haney, C. 66

Hany, M. 129

Harrold, Keyon, Jr. 52

Hattery, A. J. 9, 36, 47, 48, 49, 51

Hayes, C. 42

Hayne, Steven 33

Healing Justice 103, 113–114

health see mental health; physical health

health care see medical care

Henry, J. S. 72, 73, 81, 82

Henry v. Hulett (2020) 63

Herman, J. L. 104

Hill Collins, P. 38, 84

Hindelang, M. J. 14

Hispanic Americans 6, 7, 48

homicide see murder/homicide

homogamy 14

hooks, b. 38

housing, post-release 100, 125, 127–128, 140

Howard, Eddie Lee 51

human rights victimology 13, 17

Hunt, Darryl 50, 51, 52, 53, 54

ICF International 107

ideal victim theory 21

imaginary victims 12

impact stage of victimization 19

imprisonment see incarceration

incarceration 61; Black people 35, 36–37, 39, 44–46, 47, 50, 51, 53, 54, 67, 83; effects of unique to innocent inmates 20, 66–68; experience of violence during 20, 64; financial costs of 122, 140; mass 39, 44, 122, 140; physical consequences of 62–66, 134–135; pretrial 9, 35, 36, 44–46, 105, 139; psychological consequences of see psychological consequences of incarceration; race and experience of 67; racial divide in 83; rates of 61, 83; of women 77–79, 81, 84–85; years of, study exonerees 6, 8, 76; see also prison(s)

incentivized witnesses 9, 23, 28, 135, 139

income: and race 46; and victimization risk 14

indirect victims see secondary (indirect) victims

inequality 38; gender 15, 84; racial 38, 84; social 84; structural 84

informants, jailhouse 22, 23, 28, 32, 82, 117, 140

injustice: confronting 141; family members sense of 89

innocence: factual 4, 5, 20, 39, 86n6, 111, 115, 136, 140; presumption of 106; proof of 136, 140

Innocence Project 23, 25, 26, 28, 30–31, 32, 33, 39, 47, 48, 71, 100, 120

innocent inmates: effects of incarceration unique to 20, 66–68; wrongly convicted as 20

innocent victims 12

institutional victimization 9, 17, 20

institutionalized personality traits 128–129
interactionist (penal) victimology 13, 17
*International Review of Victimology* 13
interracial crime: exonerations 47, 48–49; *see also*
Black men, and rape/murder of white women
interrogations: misconduct in 29; *see also* police
interrogation methods
intersectionality 37, 38, 74, 84
intimate partner cases 70, 74
Irazola, S. 103, 107, 108, 109, 110, 112,
113, 114
isolation 19, 109; of prison inmates *see* solitary
confinement

Jackson, K. 25
Jackson, N. A. 20, 46–47, 62, 134
Jackson, Richard E. 54n2
Jackson, Robert H. 60
jailhouse informants 22, 23, 28, 32, 82, 117, 140
Jenkins, C. 112
Jenkins, S. 87, 88, 89, 92, 93, 94, 95, 97
Jimenez, Bernard 3
Johnson, Lyndon B. 15
Jolliff, Rose 28
*Journal of Victimology and Victim Justice* 13
judges 58, 61, 118, 139; tunnel vision 59
justice: access to 116; confronting injustice in
order to advance 141; obstruction of 106, 113;
procedural 116, 120; racial 116; *see also*
injustice; restorative justice
Justice for All Act (2004) 16, 141

Kaiser, H. A. 119
Kassin, S. M. 26–27, 60
Kauzlarich, D. 68
Kemp, Georgia 51
Kendrick, Jaythan 25–26
Kent, J. 37
Kent, S. L. 120
Kerner Commission 41
Khumo Tire Company Ltd v. Patrick Carmichael
(1999) 33
Konvisser, Z. D. 81
Kopf, D. 93
Kunst, M. 128, 130

La Vigne, N. G. 91
Lacombe, D. 84
Latina women 83
Lauritson, J. L. 14
law: as site of struggle 84; women and 84
Law Enforcement Assistance Administration
(LEAA) 15
Law, T. 72
legal counsel: access to, original crime victims
113; *Miranda* right to 29
legitimacy: compensation and 118–120; crime
control 116; of criminal justice system 115,
116, 117, 120, 122–123, 140; due process 116;
and procedural justice 116; revictimization and

120–121; state 115–116, 118–119; and
wrongful conviction 117
Leo, R. 25, 60, 68
Levey, D. S. 107
Lewis, A. 73
Liem, M. 128, 130
lifestyle exposure theory 14
lineups *see* police lineups
Loeffler, C. 24
Loftus, E. 26
loss, ambiguous, family members 88–89
lying in court *see* perjury
lynchings 16, 51, 52
Lyner, Mary Ellen 28

MacFarlane, B. 29
marital status, and victimization risk 14
Martin, T. L. 97
Martin, Trayvon 44
mass incarceration 39, 44, 122, 140
matrix of domination 38
Maye, Cory 33
McCray, Antron 27, 50, 51, 52
McKay, T. 92, 99–100
media coverage 90, 99, 108, 109, 112
medical care 66, 100, 134
medical victimization 17
Medill Innocence Project, Northwestern
University 4
Meili, Trisha *see* Central Park jogger case
memory, fallibility of 25, 26
men/male exonerees: employment status 125,
*126*; sexual crimes 75; study numbers 6, *7; see
also* Black men; white men
Mendelsohn, B. 12, 23
*mens rea* 14
mental health **69, 70**; battered women **70**;
children of wrongly convicted 91; and false
confession 26; female exonerees 78, 79, 80, 81;
and incarceration 66, 128–131; post-release 80,
125, 128–134, 140; prisoners of war **69**; *see also*
anxiety; depression
mental health services xiii, xiv
mental status, and victimization risk 12, 13
methodology of study 5–6
Milgaard, David 120–121
Miller, Gail 120–121
Miller, J. 72, 74, 82, 83, 84
Mills, L. 104
*Miranda* right to counsel 29
misconduct *see* official misconduct
Mississippi State Penitentiary 36
Mitchell, M. M. 92
Mooney v. Holohan (1935) 61
Morrison, Patricia xiv
Morton, Michael 30–31
mothering/motherhood 72, 74, 82, 84, 85
motivated offenders 14–15, 22
Mozee, Stanley 54n2
multinational corporations 38

murder/homicide 107, 120; Black men and 47, 48–49, 50–52; and DNA evidence 24; exonerations 24, 47, 48, 49, 50, 51, 107; "no-crime" cases 59, 82; white men and 47; women and 72, 73, 75, 82

Nash, A. Jabir 53
National Advisory Commission on Civil Disorders (Kerner Commission) 41
National Crime Survey 15
National Crime Victimization Survey 15
National Institute of Justice 107
National Registry of Exonerations (NRE) 5, 20, 21, 22, 23, 25, 29, 35, 47, 54n2, 71, 73, 74, 106, 121, 132; definition of exoneration 5, 81, 86n6
negligence law, "but for" test in 119
Nixon, Richard 38, 39, 52
"no-crime" cases 4, 5, 58–59, 123n2; women and 58, 72–73, 74, 81–82, 83, 123n2, 139
noble cause corruption 29
Norris, R. J. 80, 119
Norwood, Mark 31
NRE see National Registry of Exonerations

Obama, Barack 42
obstruction of justice 106, 113
occupation, and victimization risk 14
offender(s): criminal justice system as 22; motivated 14–15, 22; and restorative justice 100–101, 113
Office for Victims of Crime 16
official misconduct 9, 21, 22, 29–31, 54n2, 61, 81–82, 83, 132, 139
omission, crimes of 117, 118
oppression 36, 38, 84
oral health 66, 134–135
original crime victims 9, 10, 103; and criminal investigation process 104–105; and criminal justice system 104–106; revictimization of 9, 88, 103–114, 120, 138, 140; and trial procedures 105–106
original crime victims and exonerations 106–114, 138, 140; anger, feelings of 109; compensation 112; confusion and denial 110; counseling needs 110, 112; and emotional burden of others 110; fear, feelings of 108–109; financial struggles 110; guilt feelings 108; legal counsel, access to 113; media and 108, 109, 112; notification and information needs/processes 107–108, 111; peer support 113; physical struggles 110; privacy 112; restorative justice opportunities 101, 113–114; safety and security planning 112; support needs 111–114
overpolicing 41

Packer, H. 116
paranoia 128
Parchman Farm 36

parental incarceration: prison visits and 94; psychological effects of 90–91
parole 39
parole officer visits 98–99
patriarchy 15, 36, 38, 72, 84
peer support, original crime victims 113
penal victimology 13, 17
Pereira, S. 64
perjury 29, 31, 61, 83, 113, 117
personal victimization 9, 14, 15, 17
personality traits, and false confession 27
phantom crimes see "no-crime" cases
physical consequences: of incarceration 62–66, 134–135; for original crime victims postexoneration 110; shared by battered women and wrongly convicted 70; shared by prisoners of war and wrongly convicted 69
physical health: and incarceration 66; post-release 125, 134–135, 140
physical restrictions, post-release 98–99
physical victimization 17, 18
plantation prisons 36–37
plea bargains 24, 105, 106
police 58, 59–60, 118, 139; exculpatory evidence, withholding of 29, 59, 135; fair treatment by 116; fear of 132–133; misconduct 29–30, 31, 34n5, 132, 140; loss of trust in 67, 132; tunnel vision 29, 59
police interrogation methods: and false confessions 26–27, 59–60, 69, 117; Reid technique 27, 33n2, 59
police interviews, recording of 140
police killings, of unarmed Black people 9, 35, 36, 43–44, 47, 139
police lineups 25–26, 59, 104–105, 140; presentation methods 26; witness instructions 26
policing and Black people 9, 35, 36–37, 40–46, 47, 139; "fishing expeditions" 9, 35, 36, 42–43, 45, 47, 53, 139; killing of unarmed Black people 9, 35, 36, 43–44, 47, 139; overpolicing 41; pretrial detention 9, 35, 36, 44–46, 139; stop and frisk 9, 35, 36, 40–41, 43, 47, 53, 139; traffic stops 41–43
political victimization 17
Pollanen, M. S. 32
Post-Conviction Survivor Resources 110
post-release adjustment/challenges 10, 124–137; employment 100, 125–126, 140; female exonerees 79–81, 125–126; financial insecurity 125–127, 140; financial reparations see compensation; fractured relationships 133–134; housing 100, 125, 127–128, 140; mental health 80, 125, 128–134, 140; physical health 125, 134–135, 140; see also families of wrongly convicted, post-release adjustment
postincarceration syndrome (PICS) 128
post-traumatic stress disorder (PTSD) 69, 70, 79, 80, 81, 128, 129

power 37, 38, 115; criminal justice actors 21, 29, 30, 60, 69, 84; male 15; state 118; victims lack of 21, 69; white community 38
President's Commission on Law Enforcement and Administration of Justice 15
President's Task Force on Crime Victims 16
pretrial detention 9, 35, 36, 44–46, 105, 139
primary (direct) victims 17, 18, 61–62; *see also* original crime victims
Prison Industrial Complex 36
Prison Policy Initiative 83, 85, 93
prison visits 63, 92–94, 97, 133; barriers to 63, 93; and children 94; emotional challenges of 93–94; policies 93; positive effects of 63, 92
prisoners of war 68–69
prison(s): adapting to life in 62; cell temperatures 65; deprivations 20, 62–63; food quality and portions 65; forced slavery 64–65; and health 66; overcrowding 62, 66; plantation 36–37; population 61–62, 83; race and experience of 67; recreational activities 63; solitary confinement 64, 130; strip searches 62–63; violence 20, 64; *see also* incarceration
privacy: loss of while in prison 62–63; original crime victims 112
privilege 37, 38
probation 39
procedural fairness 116
procedural justice 116, 120
prosecutors 58, 60–61, 118, 139; and crime victims relationship 105; exculpatory evidence, withholding of 30–31, 54n2, 135; fair treatment by 116; improper closing arguments 61; misconduct 29, 30–31, 34n5, 54n2, 61, 132; tunnel vision 29, 59
psychological consequences: families of wrongly convicted 87–90; shared among battered women and wrongly convicted **70**; shared among prisoners of war and wrongly convicted **69**; of victimization 18, 19; *see also* mental health
psychological consequences of incarceration 66; children of wrongly convicted 89, 90–91; mental health issues 66, 128–131; post–release 128–134, 140; unique to innocent inmates 66–68
psychological victimization 17
public apologies xvi, 69, 122, 123n5
public perceptions about wrongful convictions 122

Rabil, M. 50, 54n3
Rabuy, B. 93
race/ethnicity 84, 141; and eyewitness identification 26; and gender, intersection of 74; and income 46; and prison experience 67; of study exonerees 6, 7; and victimization risk 13, 24; of victims, interaction with race of exonerees 48; and women exonerees 74, 83

racial divide: among wrongly convicted 83; in prison population 83
racial domination 38
racial inequality 38, 84
racial justice 116
racial profiling 41–43
racial wealth gap 46
racialization of wrongful convictions and exonerations 36, 38, 39, 46–49, 51
racialized organizations 37–38
racism 16, 37, 68, 141; and police practices *see* policing and Black people; systemic 83
racist stereotypes, Black people 21, 51
rape 72, 75; Black men and white women 47, 48–49, 50–52; exonerations 47, 48–49, 50, 51
rape victims 14, 47, 48, 107
Ray, V. 37–38
Reagan, Ronald 16, 38
Reasonover, Ellen 28
recoil stage of victimization 29
recreation, prison 63
Redden, M. 73
reentry challenges *see* post–release adjustment/ challenges
reentry services 80, 100, 140, 141
Reid interrogation technique 27, 33n2, 59
relationality 38
religion 79, 95
religious victimization 17
reorganization stage of victimization 19
restorative justice 100–101, 102n3; exoneree and original crime victims 101, 113–114; victim—offender 100–101, 113
revictimization 13; and legitimacy 120–121; of original crime victims 9, 88, 103–114, 120, 138, 140
Reyes, Matias 27, 50
Rice, Tamir 44
Richardson, Kevin 27, 50, 51, 52
rights of victims 16–17, 106; *see also* Victims' Rights Movement
Rikers Island jail 44, 45
robbery 74, 107
Roberson, C. 18
Rodriquez, Hector 44
role expectations 14
routine activity theory 14–15, 21, 22
Royal, J. 72, 73

Salaam, Yusef 27, 50, 51, 52
Sangrey, D. 19
Santana, Raymond 27, 50, 51, 52
*Say Her Name* (documentary) 45
SBS *see* shaken baby syndrome
Schafer, S. 13
Schand, Mark 100
secondary (indirect) victims 17, 18, 19, 20, 87, 141; *see also* families of wrongly convicted
Selby, D. 25–26, 72, 82–83
self-stigma 130, 131

sentence lengths, women exonerees 76
sexism 68, 139, 141
sexual assault 75, 120, 123n2; DNA evidence and 24; exonerations 24, *48*, 75, 107, 109; in prisons 64; victims 13–14, 15, 16; women charged with 75; *see also* child sexual abuse; rape
sexual victimization 17
shaken baby syndrome (SBS) 5, 33, 59, 73, 75, 82, 83, 85–86n4
Simon, Kimberly 32
slave patrols 36
slavery 36, 38, 64–65
sleep/sleeping disorders 18, 19, 110; children of wrongly convicted 91; post-release 129, 134
Smart, C. 71, 72, 84
Smith, E. 9, 36, 47, 48, 49, 51
Smith, Susan 52
social context 38
social harms 118
social inequality 84
social justice 38
social—sensory deprivation syndrome 128, 129–130
social—temporal alienation 128, 130
societal victimization xv, 9–10, 115–123, 138, 140
socioeconomic status 6
solitary confinement 64, 130
Sommervold, S. 73
Sophonow, Thomas 118, 119
Sotomayor, Justice Sonia 40–41, 53, 54
state: legitimacy 115–116, 118–119; power 118
state crime, wrongful convictions as 117–118, 123
state crime victims 57, 68–69
Stefancic, J. 37
stereotypes: of Black men 51; of Black people 21; of women 72, 73, 84, 85, 139
Sterling, Alton 43
Stevenson, Bryan 141
Stevenson, M. 44–45, 53
stigma xiii, 10, 67–68; family members 89–90, 91; self- 130, 131
Stoel, R. D. 59
stop and frisk policing 9, 35, 36, 40–41, 43, 47, 53, 139
Stratton, G. 117–118
strip searches 62–63
structural constraints 14
structural inequality 84
substance abuse 130
survivor guilt 131–132
survivors 12
Sutherland, Justice George 30
Sykes, Deborah 50
Sykes, G. M. 63
system variables, and eyewitness identification 26
systemic racism 83

Taylor, Breonna 43
Thompson, C. 109
Thompson, Jennifer 103, 108, 109, 113–114

time served, study exonerees 6, *8*, 76
tort law 119
torture 69
traffic stops 41–43; "fishing expeditions" 42–43; legitimate 42
trauma, experience of: family members 88, 100; *see also* post-traumatic stress disorder
trial misconduct 29
trial procedures, original crime victims and 105–106
"true" perpetrators 9, 29, 103, 109, 112, 120–121, 140
Trump, Donald 50
trust/loss of trust, in criminal justice system 67, 99, 130, 132–133
tunnel vision 29, 59, 74, 85
Tyler, T. 59, 116

Utah v. Strieff (2016) 40–41, 53, 54

Vera Institute 85
victim blaming 12, 13–1
victim precipitation theory 13–14, 21–22
victim theories 13–15, 21–22
victimization 11–22, 141–142; and age 12, 13, 14; consequences of 18–19; economic/financial 17; and education 14; emotional/ psychological 17; and gender 12, 13, 14; impact stage of 19; and income 14; institutional 9, 17, 20; medical 17; and mental status 12, 13; and occupation 14; personal 9, 14, 15, 17; physical 17, 18; political 17; process 57, 58–61, 70, 138, 139; psychological consequences 18, 19; race/ ethnicity and risk of 13, 14; recoil stage of 19; religious 17; reorganization stage of 19; sexual 17; surveys 15; tangible vs. intangible costs 18–19; types and forms of 17; victims role in own 12, 13–14, 21–22; of wrongly convicted 10, 19, 20,57, 58–61, 70, 138, 139, 141
victimology 9, 139–140; general 13, 17; history of 11–13; human rights 13, 17; penal (interactionist) 13, 17; primary areas of study 12
*Victimology: An International Journal* 13
victim(s): guilty 12; ideal 21; imaginary 12; innocent 12; with minor guilt 12; more guilty than the offender 12; primary (direct) *see* primary (direct) victims; role in own victimization 12, 13–14, 21–22; secondary (indirect) *see* secondary (indirect) victims; state crime 68–69; as a term 11, 12; typologies of 12; wrongly convicted as 19–20, 22, 57, 70, 84–85
Victims of Crimes Act (VOCA, 1984) 16, 17
Victims' Rights Movement 9, 15–17, 18, 106
Victims' Rights and Restitution Act (1990) 106
violence: prison 20, 64; *see also* domestic violence; violent crime
violent crime 16, 24, 48, 72, 104, 107, 120; Black people as victims of 49; *see also* murder/ homicide; rape; robbery; sexual assault
Violent Crime Control and Law Enforcement Act (1994) 39

Von Hentig, H. 12, 13

Walker, L. E. 70
Wallace, H. 18
war on crime 15
war on drugs 38–39, 40, 52
wealth gap, racial 46
weapon presence, and eyewitness identification 26
Webster, E. 72, 74, 82, 83, 84
West, Dr. Michael 51
Westervelt, S. D. 57, 68, 102n3, 118
white men: homicide convictions 47; incarceration numbers 83
white people/community: and criminal justice system 38, 104; see also white men; white women
white privilege 38
white supremacy 36, 37, 52
white women: Black men convicted of rape/murder of 47, 48–49, 49–52; crime types of exonerees 74; incarceration numbers 83; number of exonerees 74, 83
Williams, Rhonda 3–4
Wilson, Darren 43–44
Wise, Korey 27, 50, 51, 52
witnesses: confidence 25, 26; incentivized 9, 23, 28, 135, 139; tampering with 29; see also eyewitness identification; eyewitness misidentification
Wolgang, M. 13
women 15–16; battered 70, 74; caretaking roles 73, 74, 85; in criminal justice system 71–74, 84, 139; incarceration of 77–79, 81, 84–85; and law 84; and mothering, tropes about 72, 74, 82, 84, 85; murder/homicide by 72, 73, 75, 82; and patriarchal society 15; stereotypes about 72, 73, 84, 85, 139; see also Black women; female exonerees; female wrongful convictions; white women
Women's Movement see Feminist Movement
Wrightsman, L. S. 60
"wrong-person" cases 4, 5, 25, 123n2
wrongful conviction(s): challenges in establishing accurate numbers 5, 9, 24; definition of 3–4; extent or incidence of 9, 23–24; families as victims of see families of wrongly convicted; female see female wrongful convictions; and legitimacy 117; main contributing factors 9, 23, 25–33, 139; "no-crime" cases 4, 5, 58, 58–59, 72–73, 74, 81–82, 83, 123n2; original crime victims and see original crime victims; post-release challenges of see post-release adjustment/challenges; racialization of 36, 38, 39, 46–49, 51; society as victim of xv, 9–10, 115–123, 138, 140; as state crime 117–118, 123; "wrong-person" cases 4, 5, 25, 123n2; years lost through 5
wrongly convicted: and battered women, similarity of experiences 70; compensation 19–20, 53, 54, 69, 80, 81, 99, 118, 119–120, 121, 122, 125, 135–136; as ideal victim 21; "innocent inmate" conceptualization of 20; psychological consequences of incarceration unique to 66–68; racial divide among 83; and state crime victims, similarity of experiences 68–69; victim theory applications for 21–22; victimization of 10, 19, 20, 57, 58–61, 70, 138, 139; as victims 19–20, 22, 57, 70, 84–85

Zack, E. 114
Zalman, M. 24, 115
Zannella, L. 128
Zimmerman, George 44